BATTLEGROUNDS

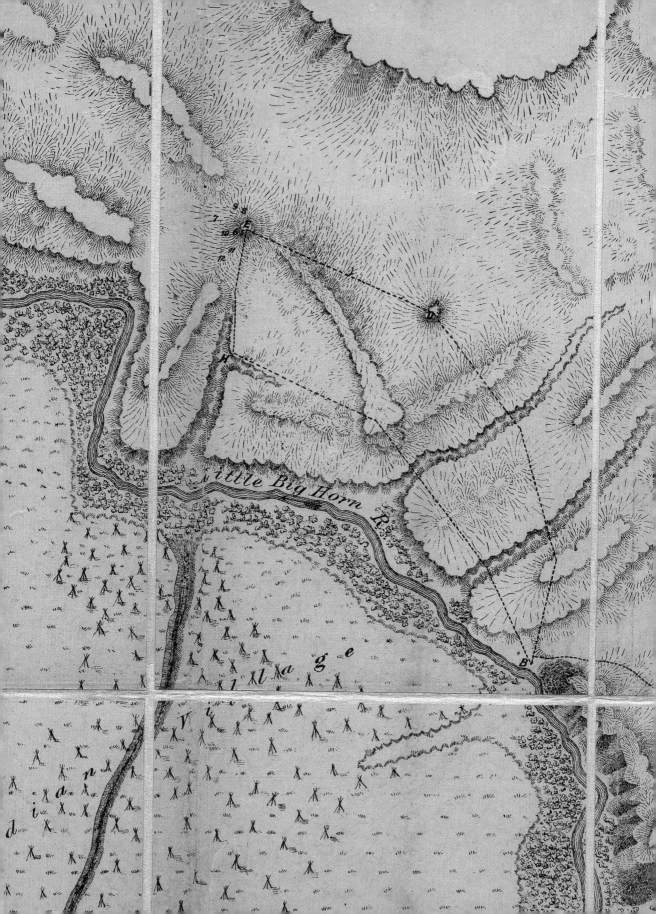

9 8
7 *E*
10 6
11
12

Y

D

H

Little Big Horn R.

B

Village

Indian

BATTLEGROUNDS

Geography and the History of Warfare

Edited by Michael Stephenson
Introduction by Robert Cowley

NATIONAL GEOGRAPHIC
WASHINGTON, D.C.

CONTENTS

Introduction

ROBERT COWLEY

I'm surprised, but hardly shocked, that a book with such a fundamental premise, the influence of terrain on combat, has been so rarely attempted. I can think of an exceptional chapter on the subject in John Keegan's *A History of Warfare* and (for students of the First World War) Douglas W. Johnson's 1921 book, *Battlefields of the World War*. It sometimes appalls me to contemplate the number of military historians who have clearly never visited the places they are writing about. The very obviousness of geography may explain why it is continually overlooked. It shouldn't be. To grasp the special qualities of terrain can be, for a general, a key to conducting a battle—and later, for a historian, to understanding it. The way men have coped with natural obstacles is at the heart of the long chronicle of war.

This book examines close to 40 battles, all of which are defined by their topographical features—peculiarities is probably too strong a word. *Battlegrounds* has deliberately bypassed some of the too-familiar military high points such as Waterloo, the Marne, and D Day—or has chosen to dwell on moments often overlooked but truly decisive. The Union victory at Gettysburg, for example, may have been assured not by the famous turning back of Pickett's Charge on day three but by the holding of Little Round Top the previous afternoon. Had the Confederates succeeded in occupying that rocky outcrop, their artillery could have enfiladed the entire Union line on Cemetery Ridge and compelled a retreat to less favorable ground. There would have been no need for Pickett's Charge.

Most often, struggles for high points like Little Round Top, Bloody Ridge at Peleliu, or Monte Cassino in Italy, where the Germans held out for three months early in 1944, work to the disadvantage of the attacker. ("Mountains are greater obstacles than rivers," Napoleon said. "One can always cross a river, but never a mountain." Whenever possible, he added, it was better to strike the enemy "by way of the plains.") But high ground can also be a trap for the defender, as George Armstrong Custer found to his eternal sorrow at Little Big Horn. There, the very featurelessness of an open hillside became its salient feature. Recent archaeological evidence indicates that, far from the heroic brawl of barroom art, the Sioux and Cheyenne warriors, firing their rifles from protected ravine positions a safe distance away, simply picked off the troopers of the Seventh Cavalry. Custer's men had no place to hide.

The battle sites just mentioned may never witness mass killing again. But certain other areas, as this book points out, are combat-intensive. Armies have always followed the routes of topographical least resistance, whether they are the Bosporus, northern Italy, what is now Israel, the passes from Afghanistan into the northwest Indian plain, or the North Sea dune belt and the lowlands of Flanders (the so-called "cockpit of Europe"). The Duke of Marlborough campaigned around Vimy Ridge early in the 18th century; so did armies in the two World Wars. Douglas W. Johnson, a professor of geography at Columbia University, who served as an intelligence officer with the AEF in World War I, noted about Vimy: "To make an advance of but a few hundred yards the Allied commanders...sacrificed their men literally by the tens of thousands." But the gain, he reasoned, was "to be measured not in linear yards of advance, but in the increased depth and breadth of observation behind the enemy's lines." Today we might question whether the view was worth the price—but Johnson, remember, belonged to the generation that gave us Joffre and Ludendorff and Haig.

Still, the greater part of the Earth has never been touched by war. As Keegan writes, "Almost 70 per cent of the world's 60,000,000 square miles of dry land is either too high, too cold, or too waterless for the conduct of military activities." True desert warfare, for instance, is rare—though, thanks to the increased sophistication of military technology, it is becoming less so. The two Gulf Wars are evidence of that. Even as early as Omdurman in 1898, it was the railroads that followed Lord Kitchener's advance, as well as gunboats and Gatling guns, that provided the British with the massacring edge of victory over the forces of the mahdi. But most of the so-called "desert war" in North Africa during World War II was fought, as *Battlegrounds* makes clear, over arid plains within a hundred miles of the Mediterranean coast (or, as Bryan Perrett elegantly calls it, without too much hair-splitting, "negotiable desert").

"Negotiable water" is a concept we might also consider. Most sea battles have been fought close to land, if only because until relatively recent times navies have depended on easily reachable ports and friendly shores to feed and rest their men, refuel, or to escape to. Battles in the open ocean, such as the Glorious First of June, 1794—"Glorious," that is, to the British victors— Midway, or the convoy encounters of the North Atlantic, are the exception rather than the rule, and they rightly do not belong in this book. Coastlines, as this book notes, have become an intimate part of most naval battle plans. In a sense, Salamis, which took place in the equalizing confines of a narrow channel, was as much an action fought in a pass as Thermopylae.

Though maps did not figure in the victory of Themistocles, he obviously had a sure feel for topography and its relation to the water where he chose to make his stand. Nor did a lack of maps impede Alexander in his march to the borders of the known world. A measure of his greatness as a commander is that he was constantly forced to operate on poor geographical information. Military maps were not introduced until the 16th century. Yet another two centuries passed before generals came to depend routinely on topographical engineers. Napoleon maintained an extensive topographical bureau. Before embarking on a campaign, he would send out officers in civilian dress to survey the *ensemble de pays*—the lay of the land—through which he intended to pass. A copperplate press for maps always accompanied his Grande Armée. Among the reasons advanced for Napoleon's calamity in Russia was the inferior quality of the maps he had to rely on in the planning stages. (He also failed to take into account the happenstances of geography such as the mud months, or *rasputitsa* (roadless period), of the fall that hindered his retreat from Moscow and the inevitable fierceness of the early Russian winter that almost froze his columns in their tracks before their escape across the Berezina.)

There is an old saying that a general is only as good as his maps. One of the cautionary examples of *Battlegrounds* is the misfortune of Ian Hamilton. Rarely has a general been so undone by the unknowns of geography. When the British War Office dispatched him to lead the invasion of Gallipoli in 1915, it provided him with little more than a tourist map of the Turkish peninsula, and not a particularly accurate one at that. No wonder his divisions floundered through unexpected ravines or clung to hillsides that were surprisingly steep, gazing upward at a tenacious enemy who was not supposed to be anywhere near.

But it should be added that good maps do not necessarily make good generals, especially when they rely on maps alone and not on personal observation, as the Western Front commanders of World War I tended to do. War by map led to some of the most sanguinary excesses of that war, the first manmade creation in history of what this book appropriately describes as "The Geography of Hell." Map coordinates and contour lines did not always square with conditions on the ground. Landscapes could not sustain the preplanned torrents of fire unleashed on them: Again and again, the muddy crater fields of places like Passchendaele made forward movement all but impossible. But it was also true that certain topographies resisted even the most furious shellstorms. As Johnson writes of the German attacks at Verdun: "It was hoped that the suddenness and overwhelming power of the assault would offset the natural difficulties of the terrain...The permanent fortresses were less to be feared than the barriers of Nature, against which the strongest explosives were impotent...[N]o masonry fort could withstand for long the crushing weight of fire developed by heavy siege artillery; but against plateau scarps, massive limestone ridges, and deep natural moats no impression could be made. Only in case the defenders of the terrain could be destroyed or demoralized by the fury of the bombardment, and the plateau then overrun by resistless waves of men, could victory be achieved."

It wasn't, of course. The message of *Battlegrounds* is simple and compelling. Men may ordain but nature always determines.

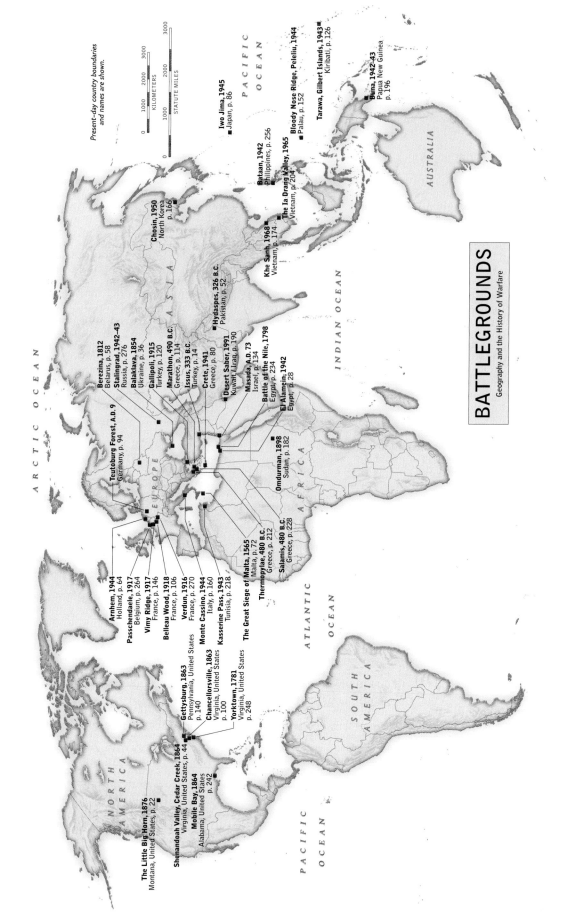

BATTLEGROUNDS
Geography and the History of Warfare

Present-day country boundaries and names are shown.

KILOMETERS

STATUTE MILES

ARCTIC OCEAN

PACIFIC OCEAN

ATLANTIC OCEAN

INDIAN OCEAN

PACIFIC OCEAN

EUROPE

ASIA

AFRICA

AUSTRALIA

NORTH AMERICA

SOUTH AMERICA

The Little Big Horn, 1876
Montana, United States, p. 22

Shenandoah Valley, Cedar Creek, 1864
Virginia, United States, p. 44

Mobile Bay, 1864
Alabama, United States
p. 242

Gettysburg, 1863
Pennsylvania, United States
p. 140

Chancellorsville, 1863
Virginia, United States
p. 100

Yorktown, 1781
Virginia, United States
p. 248

Arnhem, 1944
Holland, p. 64

Passchendaele, 1917
Belgium, p. 264

Vimy Ridge, 1917
France, p. 146

Belleau Wood, 1918
France, p. 106

Verdun, 1916
France, p. 270

Monte Cassino, 1944
Italy, p. 160

Kasserine Pass, 1943
Tunisia, p. 218

The Great Siege of Malta, 1565
Malta, p. 72

Thermopylae, 480 B.C.
Greece, p. 212

Salamis, 480 B.C.
Greece, p. 228

Teutoburg Forest, A.D. 9
Germany, p. 94

Berezina, 1812
Belarus, p. 58

Stalingrad, 1942–43
Russia, p. 276

Balaklava, 1854
Ukraine, p. 36

Gallipoli, 1915
Turkey, p. 120

Marathon, 490 B.C.
Greece, p. 114

Issus, 333 B.C.
Turkey, p. 14

Crete, 1941
Greece, p. 80

Desert Saber, 1991
Kuwait / Iraq, p. 190

Hydaspes, 326 B.C.
Pakistan, p. 52

Masada, A.D. 73
Israel, p. 134

Battle of the Nile, 1798
Egypt, p. 234

El Alamein, 1942
Egypt, p. 28

Omdurman, 1898
Sudan, p. 182

Chosin, 1950
North Korea
p. 166

Khe Sanh, 1968
Vietnam, p. 174

The Ia Drang Valley, 1965
Vietnam, p. 204

Bataan, 1942
Philippines, p. 256

Iwo Jima, 1945
Japan, p. 86

Bloody Nose Ridge, Peleliu, 1944
Palau, p. 152

Tarawa, Gilbert Islands, 1943
Kiribati, p. 126

Buna, 1942–43
Papua New Guinea
p. 196

"Every day I feel more and more in need of an atlas, as the knowledge of geography in its minute details is essential to a true military education."

—GENERAL WILLIAM TECUMSEH SHERMAN

Editor's Note

MICHAEL STEPHENSON

In military terms "geography" has two dimensions. The first could be called strategic: the grand sweep of economic, social, and political factors in the shaping of world history.

The second dimension concerns the micro-geography (what General Sherman referred to as the "minute details") of individual battlefields. This is the main focus of *Battlegrounds*: the terrains on which some of the greatest battles of world history have been fought and the topographical characteristics that played such a large part in their outcomes.

Warfare without geography is, of course, an absurdity. Every battle takes place somewhere, and to a large extent is defined by its local topography. The nature of the battleground determines the kind of fighting that can be undertaken. But not exclusively. Other factors also play their part in the complicated dynamic of warfare. The quality of the troops, the superiority of their training and equipment, the skill and will of their commanders, even—or perhaps especially—the weather (as both Napoleon and Hitler discovered when confronted by "the best general the Russians ever had—winter!") can counterbalance the favorable or unfavorable lay of the land.

If all land battles are about geography, on what principles did I make the choice? It would have been easy enough to simply select the old warhorses—a variation on *Fifteen Decisive Battles of the World*—and look at the geography of those battles. However, a much more interesting approach was to select battles that have been defined by a salient geographic feature that significantly impacted the nature and outcome of the fighting.

For example, many First World War battles are named after rivers—the Marne, Somme, Meuse, Ypres—but it was not the rivers themselves that defined the battle action; they were simply place-tags. On the other hand, Alexander the Great's audacious attack across the Hydaspes in 326 B.C., or Napoleon's desperate effort to get his defeated Grande Armée across the frozen Berezina River in November 1812, had everything to do with a river as the "geographical imperative."

No single battle in history can be held up as the ultimate example of its type. When we think of a coastal assault as a very specific challenge to a commander, do we pick Caesar's landing on Britain's southern coast in 54 B.C. or U.S. Marines at Tarawa 2,000 years later? The solution to the same problem—How do we storm that beach?—will find very different answers at different times, in different places, under different circumstances, and in different military cultures (Alexander facing the Persian host on the Mediterranean coastal plain at Issus in 333 B.C. is quite unlike Montgomery facing Rommel on a Mediterranean plain at El Alamein in October 1942). By selecting battles over a broad span of history I have attempted to show various solutions to similar problems.

Inevitably there are omissions. *Battlegrounds* could not be, nor was designed to be, encyclopedic. The introductions to each chapter mention other notable battles that could well have been included if there had been unlimited space.

A note on naval and air battles: Throughout most of its history, naval warfare has been conducted close to land for obvious logistical reasons, including the need to resupply and refuel vessels, and even in modern sea warfare deep-ocean battles have been rare. Our coverage of sea battles reflects the historical truth that naval operations have been closely tied to land operations, and the book includes some notable ones in which terrestrial factors played a significant part.

Although the air is featureless, for our purposes at least, we can look at air warfare as it has been impacted by geography: for example, the use of the helicopter in Vietnam as a means of fighting in the jungle, and the use of air power in Desert Storm as a way to deal with the demands of a war fought over a vast expanse of desert plain.

PLAINS

In warfare the plain—a relatively large, open, and uninterrupted battleground—is like a giant chessboard. With room to maneuver, opposing commanders may have many options. They must weigh up strengths and weaknesses—their own as well as the enemy's. Flanking, probing, enveloping, it is a game in which numbers and maneuverability are often critical. As in chess, the battle often involves the constriction and isolation of key elements of the opposing force. But like all geographic features, the picture is not quite as two dimensional as the word "plain" might suggest. We are not talking about beautifully smooth playing fields, but individual sites with their own unique characteristics. For example, the first battle in this chapter, Issus, was fought on a coastal plain in what is now Turkey where movement was constricted on both flanks: one by the sea, the other by inland foothills. As it happened, these geographic "bookends" worked in Alexander's favor, as they boxed in the larger number of his Persian foe and to some extent neutralized the numerical discrepancy. Some 2,000 years later General George Custer was to learn a different lesson about numbers and maneuverability on the plains of Montana. In open spaces, movement and superior numbers are king. Brought to bay on his lonely, isolated knoll, outgunned and overrun, there could be only one, grisly, outcome. He was also to learn that plains have their own wrinkles and folds. At Little Big Horn the numerous ravines (coulees) were capable of hiding significant numbers of his enemy. El Alamein, 1942, was also a battle of numbers. On this Mediterranean seaboard plain, victory would go to whichever side could drive its tanks farther and outgun the opponent. Rommel, desperately short of supplies of all kinds and operating at the end of a long supply chain, had, literally and metaphorically, run out of gas.

Alexander at Issus, 333 B.C.

The narrow coastal plain wedged between the Amanus Mountains and the Gulf of Issus confined Darius to a space in which he could not effectively deploy his numerous troops. Alexander's subsequent victory here led him to continue conquering other parts of the Persian Empire.

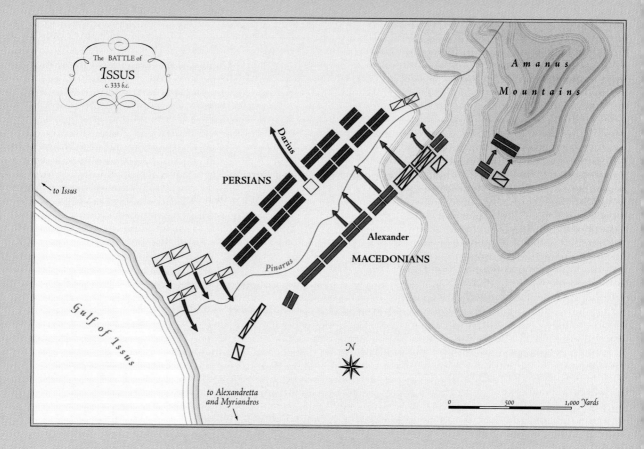

Alexander at Issus
Turkey, 333 B.C.

MATTHEW BENNETT

Alexander II of Macedon's conquest of the vast Persian Empire within just a few years is one of the most remarkable achievements of military history. It was a triumph over geography and the associated logistical obstacles that has not been matched. With an army never numbering much more than about 40,000 men, Alexander marched from the Hellespont to Egypt, and the furthest borders of the empire, into territories now called Iraq, Iran, Afghanistan, and Pakistan. He fought few major battles, but all have been intensively studied as masterpieces of the military art. On the coastal plain at Issus, he showed exceptional skill to fight in difficult terrain and rout the army of Darius III, the Persian Great King.

This was Alexander's second battle against the Persians. He had invaded their empire the previous year (334 B.C.), and had been confronted at the Granicus River (near the Bosporus) by equal numbers of Persian cavalry and Greek mercenary infantry. Despite the river obstacle, Alexander defeated them by a brilliant right-flanking maneuver, crossing the turbulent stream at the head of his heavy cavalry. After the battle he pressed on down the western coast, "liberating" the Greek cities along his way, and so denying the Persian fleet bases for any counterattack on the Greek mainland. He did not venture deeper into the interior until the autumn rains came.

In 333, Alexander did not immediately advance farther south, although he must have been aware that Darius was mustering his forces near his capital, Babylon. When the Macedonians finally set out, probably in July, they had to endure the burning heat of the Anatolian Plateau before forcing the Cilician Gates, which led onto the plain of Tarsus. Here, Alexander first secured the city and the coastline before marching eastward to Issus (near modern Iskenderun, on the Mediterranean coast of southwest Turkey), where he left his sick before moving around the top of the Gulf of Issus (modern Gulf of Iskenderun) and southward down the gulf's eastern shore.

Darius was still south of the Amanus Mountains at Sochoi (exact location unknown, but probably in the vicinity of modern Aleppo, ancient Antioch). At this point Alexander fell ill, and the subsequent delay in the Macedonian advance seems to have convinced Darius and his advisers that Alexander was fearful of a pitched battle. So the Persian forces engaged on a long, strategic flanking march that took them northward, east of the Amanus range and across one or both passes with westward access into the Cilician Plain. In the meantime, Alexander had recovered and pressed on southward to the Beilan Pass (which crosses the Amanus to give access to Antioch).

In early November, Alexander received news that the Persians were now at his rear. Darius had descended on Issus, massacred those Macedonians left there, and cut off Alexander from his line of communication with homeland Greece, forcing him to retrace his steps northward. Darius had achieved strategic superiority and now intended to fight on the line of the River Pinarus (modern Payas), a little to the southeast of Issus.

We are not very well informed of the Persian order of battle because most of the Greek accounts were written very much later and seek to glorify the extent of Alexander's victory. Arrian, who gives by far the most detailed account of the battle, quotes 600,000 Persians (although even he seems somewhat sceptical), an impossible figure on logistical grounds. Even the numbers of the various units of the Persian host have to be taken with a large pinch of salt. Arrian gives the advance guard 30,000 cavalry and 20,000 light infantry, with 30,000 Greek mercenary heavy infantry, and another 60,000 Persian foot in the main battle line. Behind them allegedly lurked an unknowable number of auxiliary infantry from the Persians' many subject nations.

The trouble with figures such as these is that his army could not have fit into the available area. Darius, in his haste to cut off his enemy's line of retreat, had brought his army onto a narrow coastal plain a little over two miles wide from the foothills of the Amanus. So if he was in possession of vastly superior numbers he had no opportunity to deploy them effectively. This meant that, to a certain extent, he had played into Alexander's hands, for it was to Alexander's advantage that the sheer size of the Persian host could be neutralized by the confinement of the coastal plain. The numbers of the Macedonian forces, and their different troop types, are recorded in some detail, which enables us both to interpret the course of the ensuing battle and to estimate the likely size of opposing Persian contingents.

The core of the Macedonian army was its phalanx of pikemen (an innovation of Alexander's father, Philip), each of whom carried an 18-foot pike, twice as long as a normal spear. They also carried smaller shields and, apart from the front rank, were more lightly armored than the traditional Greek hoplite. However, they were exceptionally well drilled, and divided into six 1,500-strong units. They could be deployed up to 16 ranks deep, but more usually fought in 8. Another 3,000 phalangites, known as *hypaspists* (literally, "shield-bearers"), may have been more lightly equipped, and carried handier spears. Their role was to prevent attackers breaking into the vulnerable flanks of the phalanx. The rest of the heavy infantry was made up of allied Greeks, some 7,000 strong, carrying the large round shields (*hoplon*, hence hoplites). Alexander had some 5,000 cavalry, mostly heavy, and personally led the 1,500 Companions: the famed mounted shock troops in his battles. There were also 10,000 light troops: archers, slingers, javelin-men and spear-wielding *peltasts* (named for their light shield, the *pelta*), who could, in a pinch, fight hand to hand.

On the approach march to the Persian position, the phalanx advanced at first 32 deep, covering the rest of the infantry, and with the cavalry in the rear. Then, as the plain widened, the phalanx extended its front and the cavalry rode out to cover the flanks. The Persian advance guard was sent out to harass the enemy, but seems to have had little effect and mostly withdrew across the River Pinarus, although some light troops lurked beneath the foothills on the Macedonians' right, inland flank. Alexander detailed the Agrianian javelin-

men, archers, and supporting cavalry to drive them off. The Persian skirmishers retreated up the slopes, where a mere 300 cavalry contained them for the
rest of the battle.

The topography of the Pinarus River determined the dispositions of the
main battle line. For about 500 yards inland from the sea, the stream is stony
but with shallow banks, allowing the passage of cavalry. For the next 1,000
yards or so, although the stream is only 5 to 15 yards wide, the banks are much
steeper, impassable to cavalry but accessible to infantry. Almost all of the next
mile upstream has steep banks, impassable to horse or foot. Then there is a
narrow ford some 30 yards wide, after which the banks become veritable cliffs
leading up to the mountains. Since this is the area where, according to Arrian,
Alexander was supposed to have led a hell-for-leather charge, it is obvious that
the generally accepted accounts of the battle need correcting.

It seems that Darius had deployed his cavalry on both flanks, seeking to
envelop the Macedonians but, perhaps realizing that his left, inland flank was
unsuitable terrain, he shifted the bulk of his horse to the coastal side. This may
even have been a deliberate tactical move to create a preponderance of his
best troops. For Alexander's deployment did pose an opportunity to his enemy.
From the coast inward, there was first a flank guard, but only about 600 Greek
allied cavalry and some infantry skirmishers (the whole Macedonian left wing
was commanded by the veteran general Parmenio), opposing what turned out
to be the main Persian cavalry, many thousands strong, of which some units
were *cataphracts* (both men and horses were armored), which them made doubly dangerous. Next in the Macedonian line came the main body of the phalanx, with allied Greeks in reserve, and the hypaspists on the right. The phalanx
pikemen opposed the Persians' Greek mercenaries, suggesting that this force
too was about 12,000 strong.

Further inland, where the banks of the stream became inaccessible, stood
the Persian *kardakes*, allegedly 20,000 strong. What these troops looked like
is uncertain. They may have been armed in imitation of the Greek hoplite, with
large round shields and spears, or they could have been more lightly equipped,
like peltasts, yet retaining that traditional Persian weapon, the bow. The latter
would at least have enabled them to play a part in the ensuing encounter,

although it does seem that, whatever their armament, they were not being trusted to oppose Macedonian or Greek in hand-to-hand combat. Alexander had deployed the bulk of the cavalry on his right flank, supported by light troops. Against them, across the ford, stood the depleted left-wing Persian cavalry and some skirmishers.

It is difficult to say who made the first move, but it may have been the Persian right-flank cavalry, seeing such a tiny force opposing them. Led by Nabarzanes, they began to cross the stream and to drive back Alexander's left. At this moment or a little before, the Macedonian phalanx had begun its attack across the stream on the opposing Greek mercenaries. This was a fierce encounter, with the Greek mercenaries, despite their shorter spears, benefiting from standing on the river bank (and possibly protected by a defensive palisade). Alexander, seeing that his phalanx was in danger of being outflanked, despatched 1,800 Thessalian cavalry to his left. Screened by the phalanx, they were able to move undetected and fall on the flank of the advancing Persian cavalry, producing a fierce melee. Meanwhile, Alexander's cavalry wing rode down to cross the Pinarus by the ford, his light troops driving off the Persian skirmishers and allowing the horsemen to re-form on the far side. Once in position, he led his Companions and heavy cavalry against the remaining Persian left-wing cavalry and routed them.

This was the decisive moment of the battle. Most cavalry would have rushed off in pursuit of a defeated foe, but Alexander was able to regroup his squadrons and begin rolling up the Persian left flank. Of the kardakes nothing is heard, but when the Companions and the other heavy cavalry fell on the left rear of the Greek mercenaries, the Macedonian phalanx was at last able to make a decisive breakthrough in the center. Darius had already fled the battlefield at this point, first in his commander's chariot and then, when the ground became too broken, on horseback. When the Persian right-wing cavalry became aware of what was happening, they too began to flee, fearful of being surrounded with their backs to the sea. Even so, they, and the Persian left-wing infantry, were ruthlessly hunted down by Parmenio's lighter cavalry and the rout turned into a catastrophe.

Despite the overwhelming success of Macedonian arms, the battle was hard-fought. Their casualties included Ptolemy, the son of Seleucus, another of Alexander's veteran generals fighting with the phalanx, as well as about 150 cavalry and 300 infantry (Alexander, always a commander who relished being in the thick of the fighting, was himself wounded in the leg). It was normal for the wounded to outnumber the killed by about three to four times (although not as many as the 4,500 that one classical author provides). The Persian losses, as described by some ancient sources, move into the range of fantasy: 10,000 cavalry and 100,000 infantry (although one source concedes 40,000 of these were prisoners). Although it is true that in ancient battles most casualties were incurred by the side that broke and ran, and that no quarter was common (Alexander had a particularly ruthless reputation as far as after-battle slaughter was concerned), it is unlikely that they totaled more than a few thousand. The Greeks always mocked that the lightly equipped Persians were made for a quick getaway. Unless the Persian foot soldiers had found themselves trapped in a killing zone it is probable that they were able to melt into the hills, whereas the cavalry had the advantage of speed to help them.

Issus was a crucial battle, because after it Alexander was able to seize Egypt and the richest parts of the Persian Empire (there was to be a final encounter with Darius at Gaugamela, two years later). But it was Alexander's ability to size up difficult terrain and use it to his best advantage that gave him the victory.

A Good Day to Die
The Little Big Horn, Montana, 1876

BRYAN PERRETT

For centuries the nomadic Sioux and Cheyenne nations had roamed the great plains of what became the modern states of South Dakota, Wyoming, and Montana, unfettered by any laws save their own. These huge, deep-rooted grasslands, unbroken by the plow, provided a home for the immense herds of buffalo, and many other animals, that the Indians depended upon for their food, clothing, and shelter. In winter the plains were swept by bitterly cold, snow-laden winds and in the heat of summer grass fires were common. They were drained by the Powder, Tongue, Big Horn, and Rosebud Rivers, which ran from south to north to empty into the larger Yellowstone, which ran eastward to join the Missouri.

The ancestral lands of the Plains Indians had been invaded by whites since the mid-19th century, and the discovery of gold in the Black Hills in 1874 had escalated these incursions. The failure of the U.S. government to either curtail the gold-seekers or to negotiate a treaty the Indians could accept raised the tension to flash point. Washington, thoroughly alarmed by Indian resistance, turned to the Army to enforce a return to the reservations. In March 1876 Brigadier General Crook discovered just how well the Sioux could fight in defense of their lands when, at the battle of the Rosebud, he came as close to defeat as a man could fear: "that while we were lucky not to have been entirely vanquished, we had been most humiliatingly defeated," said one of his officers.

The Little Big Horn, Montana, 1876

This "birdseye view of Custer's last stand hill" was drawn in 1925 by Native American Russell White Bear. The Sioux and Cheyenne Indians used their familiarity with the terrain and proximity to their base—shown here by the tepees on the left—to their advantage, resulting in the annihilation of Custer and his troops.

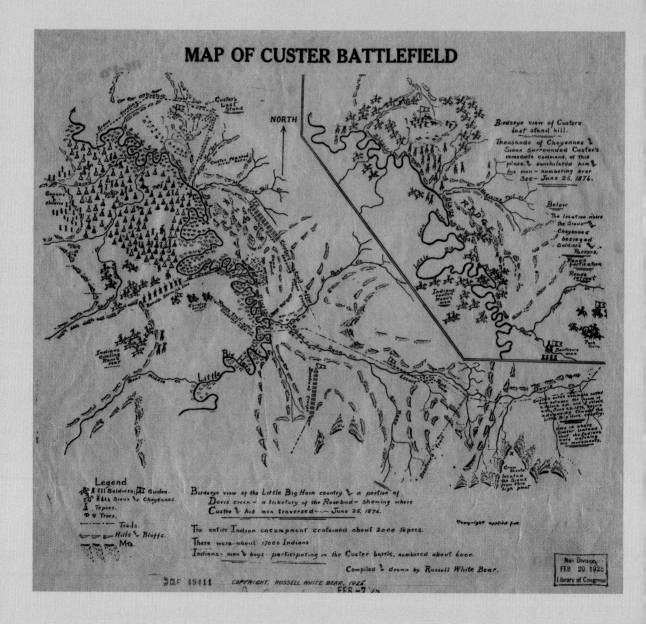

In May it was decided to try again, using larger forces. The hostiles were known to be somewhere in the vast empty area between the Yellowstone River and the Big Horn Mountains. The Indian Bureau estimated that there were approximately 800 braves on the warpath. In fact, there were somewhere between 2,500 and 6,000. The Bureau further suggested that as the Indian custom was to move to fresh hunting grounds every few days, it was unlikely that all the hostiles would be encountered at once. Again, it was wrong, as the tribes, anticipating further action by the Army, were traveling together.

Maj. Gen. Alfred H. Terry, responsible for the operation, accepted the Bureau's faulty intelligence and planned accordingly. Having assembled over 1,300 men from various units on the Yellowstone, he proposed to enter the disputed area from the north while a second force, containing over 1,000 men under Crook, converged from the south. The theory was that, finding themselves trapped by overwhelming numbers between the two, the Indians would submit. In reality, Terry and Crook, separated as they were by hundreds of miles, could neither communicate with nor support each other. They also completely underestimated the enemy's intimate knowledge of, and fighting experience in, their own terrain.

The ensuing drama centered on Lt. Col. George Armstrong Custer's 12 troops of the Seventh Cavalry, part of Terry's command. None would impugn Custer's courage, or his Civil War record, or his achievements as an Indian fighter in the post-Civil War period, or the fact that he had given the Seventh Cavalry an unmatched esprit de corps. He did, however, possess a darker side, being an incorrigible self-publicist who demanded not merely loyalty but also admiration from his officers. Any who failed to give it or were critical in some way were excluded from his favor and treated with hostility; among those were Maj. Marcus A. Reno, the regiment's second-in-command, and Capt. Frederick W. Benteen, its senior captain. Shortly before the campaign began, Custer had dabbled dangerously in politics and had come within an ace of losing command of his regiment. He was now in urgent need of a spectacular success that would restore his reputation.

On June 21 Terry briefed his senior commanders as to the action to be taken. Custer was to take the Seventh up the Rosebud to its headwaters, ignoring an Indian trail that had been discovered on an earlier reconnaissance by Reno, then cross the watershed and drive down the Little Big Horn Valley. Simultaneously, a force under Col. John Gibbon was to proceed up the Big Horn and march into the Little Big Horn valley from the north, thereby providing a blocking force. Trapped between Custer and Gibbon, the Indians would have to fight or surrender.

On June 23 the Seventh, with its pack train, marched 35 miles. The following day it covered another 45, reaching the trail found by Reno. Custer's orders specifically stated that he was to cross it. Disobeying, he turned along it. After a brief halt, he summoned his officers, telling them that the march would continue through the night, that the regiment would rest the following day and attack on the 26th, as Terry had ordered. The night march lasted five hours and covered ten miles. Custer halted in a ravine of the Wolf Mountains, the range dividing the Rosebud from the Little Big Horn, where he permitted his weary men and horses six hours' rest. After climbing to a high point on the ridge, his Crow scouts reported that the valley beyond contained a huge pony herd, many cooking fires, and a far greater number of hostiles than anyone had suspected. One of Custer's scouts, Mitch Brouyer, reported to Custer: "General, we have discovered the camp. ...It is a big one! Too big for you to tackle! Why, there are thousands and thousands of Sioux and Cheyennes down there." Custer, characteristically, retorted, "I shall attack them!" Meanwhile, more Indians had been observed, watching the regiment's progress. However, obsessed as he was with restoring his reputation, Custer feared that he would be blamed for allowing the hostiles to escape from the trap. He would have to rely on what others had called "Custer's Luck." He then committed what many historians have seen as the cardinal military sin of dividing his force in the presence of an enemy whose precise numbers and whereabouts he knew nothing of.

Captain Benteen, with three troops, was given vague orders to carry out a reconnaissance along the bluffs to the south, prevent the Indians from escaping, attack any hostiles he encountered, or return to the regiment's main axis of advance, as he thought fit. Major Reno, with another three troops, was to cross the Little Big Horn and mount a diversionary attack on the southern end of the big Indian village. Simultaneously, Custer, with five troops under his personal command, would launch the main attack on the opposite end of the village, approaching the objective under cover of the hills to the east of the river. The pack train, escorted by the remaining troops, was to follow Benteen.

Having crossed the watershed around noon, the regiment descended a stream known as Benteen's Creek. Benteen's detachment swung away to the south, while the rest of the regiment descended toward the river. Custer's column diverged onto the high ground to the right, while Reno's continued downstream and forded the Little Big Horn. The scene was set for an unnecessary tragedy.

Reno's advance on the village began at about 3:00 p.m. The troops formed into line, but scarcely had Reno ordered the charge to be sounded than hundreds of warriors swarmed out of the village toward him. He formed a dismounted skirmish line, which was quickly outflanked, and fell back to a copse beside the river. Here it became apparent that unless he reached the high ground across the river his men would be annihilated. He led a disorderly retreat back to the ford, found his path blocked by the enemy, and headed for a second and more difficult ford, where he succeeded in crossing. Thus far, 3 officers and 29 troopers and scouts had been killed, 7 were wounded, and a further 15 were missing. The survivors prepared to defend themselves on the summit of what became known as Reno's Hill, suddenly aware that most of the Indians had gone.

Only two men, a sergeant and a trumpeter, survived from the five troops with Custer, because they had been sent back to bring up Benteen and the pack train. Both gave Benteen the impression that everything was going according to plan. Only the Indians knew precisely what happened next.

Although Chief Sitting Bull was acknowledged by the tribes as their spiritual leader, their real tacticians were Chiefs Crazy Horse and Gall. When Custer arrived at what is now the Little Big Horn battlefield he kept three companies (C, I, and L) on the knolls of what is now Calhoun and Custer Ridges. Observing two troops (E and F) approaching the river down a reentrant at the northern end of the ridge, Crazy Horse dispatched a blocking force that was quickly reinforced by Gall, who had carried out the counterattack against Reno.

Crazy Horse, with the rest of the warriors, now swung round the northern end of the ridge to attack the remaining three troops, still strung out in line, from the east. Calhoun's L Company took the brunt of the assault and fell back on Custer Ridge and the whole command dismounted to fight on foot. The Indians, many of whom were armed with modern Henry and Winchester repeating rifles, possessed overwhelming numbers and made short work of the horse-holders, thereby preventing escape. A few of the troopers tried to surrender or run, but no mercy was shown. The rest, according to a Sioux named Crow King, "kept in order and fought like brave warriors as long as there was a man left." Another Sioux, Red Horse, said that "they made five brave stands," which suggests that each troop fought its own battle, its end marked by frenzied hand-to-hand struggles followed by mutilation. From start to finish, the fighting lasted about an hour or, according to one of the Sioux participants, "as long as it takes a hungry man to eat his dinner."

At about the same time Custer's command was being destroyed, Reno was joined on his hill by Benteen and the pack train. Reno wisely decided to remain on the defensive, for although he now had seven troops at his disposal, three of them had been severely mauled and were badly shaken. Insubordinately, Capt. Thomas Weir took his troops off in a mindless attempt to join Custer, and was followed by others. No sooner had they reached Weir's Hill than the Indians swarmed to attack them, forcing them into headlong flight back to Reno's Hill, where the entire command was forced to fight for its life. By the time the sun set, another 18 men had been killed and 43 wounded. The hill remained under virtual siege throughout the night, during which a number of those earlier listed as missing managed to rejoin.

During the morning of June 26, two determined assaults on the summit were repulsed, but during the afternoon the Indians broke their great encampment and, after setting fire to the grass, departed in the direction of the Big Horn Mountains. The following day, Terry and Gibbon entered the Little Big Horn valley from the north, coming upon "a scene of sickening, ghastly horror" when they reached the battlefield. Custer lay dead, as did two of his brothers, Tom and Boston, his nephew Autie Reed, and his brother-in-law, Capt. James Calhoun, as well as 215 officers and men. Edward Godfrey viewed the knoll through his field glasses. "We saw a large number of objects that looked like white boulders...these objects were the [stripped] dead bodies. Captain

Weir exclaimed, 'Oh, how white they look.'" It was a gruesome blurring of topography and death.

Reno observed that "the dead had been scattered in the wildest confusion, in groups of two or three, or piled in an indiscriminate mass of men and horses...." and Pvt. Jacob Adams described how "...men were scalped and horribly mutilated. Some were decapitated. ...As I walked over the field I saw many unfortunate dead who had been propped into a sitting position and used as targets by bowmen. ...Some bodies were set up on their knees and elbows and their hind parts had been shot full of arrows." Custer had not been scalped (as were all the others) but had been stripped of everything but his socks, "He had a gunshot wound in his head," recorded Jacob Adams, "and another in his side...I am sure he did not commit suicide. There were no powder burns on his face and it would have been next to impossible for a man to hold a gun that far away from his face to escape such burns...." Sitting Bull's verdict on Custer was blunt: "He was a fool who rode to his death."

The Indians had not only used the vast spaces available to them to keep the generals guessing as to their whereabouts, but had also taken full advantage of the local terrain, particularly the coulees (ravines), to conceal themselves until they could emerge in overwhelming numbers. They also had the advantage of "interior lines," which is to say proximity to their base with the supplies and reinforcements it provided, and this had enabled them to defeat Crook and Custer in turn.

In the aftermath of the battle the Indians correctly anticipated a massive response from the Army. Some of the war parties sought refuge in Canada, some returned voluntarily to the reservation, and some returned sullenly under compulsion. For Crazy Horse the end came in September 1877 when, attempting escape from the guardhouse at Fort Robinson, he was bayoneted to death. And two months later the Sioux ceded the Black Hills.

El Alamein, Egypt, 1942

The Associated Press released this map during the battle, and it was printed in a Washington, D.C., newspaper, The Sunday Star, on July 12, 1942.

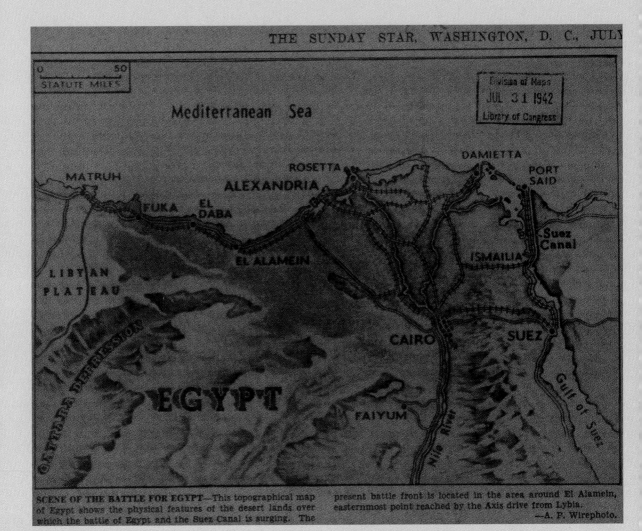

SCENE OF THE BATTLE FOR EGYPT—This topographical map of Egypt shows the physical features of the desert lands over which the battle of Egypt and the Suez Canal is surging. The present battle front is located in the area around El Alamein, easternmost point reached by the Axis drive from Lybia.

—A. P. Wirephoto.

The End of the Beginning
El Alamein, Egypt, 1942

BRYAN PERRETT

The Western Desert of Egypt and Libya presents many faces. It contains areas of hard, level going, but there are many topographical features that can hinder movement, including soft sand-seas, shifting dunes, deep wadis or ravines, salt flats, boulder fields, and ancient sea cliffs that have become escarpments. Rainfall is sparse and confined to a few months of the year, yet monsoon conditions can result in sudden torrential storms, causing flash floods to sweep down the wadis. Water is rarely present in such quantities as to satisfy more than the needs of the few indigenous inhabitants. In high summer, noon temperatures can exceed 130° F. In winter the climate is mild, but after sunset the temperature plummets and before dawn can fall to below zero. Winter, too, is the season of howling dust storms, some of which can block the light of the sun for hours at a time.

The El Alamein battlefield, 60 miles west of Alexandria, is a 35-mile-wide strip of plain comprised of negotiable desert (compacted rocky soil rather than soft sand) bounded on the north by the Mediterranean and on the south by the impassable shifting sands and salt marshes of the Quattara Depression, which lies below sea level. Within the strip are three ridges running roughly from east to west, Meteiriya in the north, Ruweisat some miles to the south, and Alam Halfa to the southeast. None were more than a swelling in the stony desert, but the overview they offered made their possession extremely important. In the north the desert was hard, gray and stony but farther south consisted of loose yellow sand. The only metaled road followed the coastline and was paralleled by a railway. Elsewhere, continuous heavy use had pulverized the desert tracks to a fine dust.

In June 1942 Field Marshal Erwin Rommel had led his German/Italian forces in smashing victories over his British and empire adversaries at Gazala and Tobruk. He had driven them back down the Mediterranean coastal plain, out of Libya and almost to Alexandria in Egypt. At the first battle of El Alamein in July 1942 the British had made a stand and held. Now Rommel was in a strategic straitjacket. He was working off long lines of supply that were particularly vulnerable to air attack, and resupply by sea from Italy was also hazardous, with British submarines and aircraft taking a heavy toll on Axis shipping. Gas, ammunition and food were now critically short, whereas his enemy enjoyed shorter lines of supply and was steadily building its superiority in men, tanks, and all the other necessities of war. He knew the longer he waited the more inexorably the scales would tip in his enemy's favor.

Both armies hunkered down behind extensive minefields stretching from the Mediterranean inland to the Quattara Depression. The land, at a superficial glance, seemed perfect tank country. But even on this desert plain there were hazards for tanks, principally minefields several miles in depth. Through these the fast-moving tank thrust of popular imagination was as impossible as it was for infantry to charge through barbed wire.

Lt. Gen. Bernard Montgomery was appointed commander of the British Eighth Army with a typically emphatic directive from Churchill: Destroy the Axis forces in front of him, totally and finally. Montgomery immediately reimposed the strict orthodoxy that would be necessary for a successful frontal assault on the Axis positions, assisted by the fact that his troops were close to their own supply bases and could be reinforced at a rate the Axis could not hope to match. Painfully aware of this, at the end of August Rommel used his last reserves of fuel in a final attempt to capture Alexandria, and with it the Suez Canal. Having taken longer than expected to break through the southern British minefields, he was decisively repulsed at Alam Halfa when he tried to swing north, and was forced to retire into his own lines. From this point on

he was neither able to renew the attack nor engage in the type of mobile warfare that would become necessary if he withdrew. His only recourse was to
strengthen his minefield defenses, which ultimately reached a depth of between
two and five miles.

Knowing his opponent's predicament, Montgomery planned to fight what
he called a "crumbling" battle by attacking first in one place then another,
thereby forcing the Axis armor to burn up its priceless fuel in movement and
counterattacks. His intention was to strike first in the north, but elaborate deception measures were put in hand to convince the enemy that the blow would
fall in the south. These included a dummy water pipeline complete with pump-
ing stations and storage towers, dummy ammunition and fuel dumps, and constant radio traffic between nonexistent armored formations. It was to be the
most elaborate exercise in deception until the preparations for D Day in 1944.

On the eve of the battle the Eighth Army possessed over 195,000 men
(British, Australians, Indians, New Zealanders, South Africans, French, and
Greek); 1,000 tanks in first-line service, plus 200 more in immediate reserve
and a further 1,000 in workshops; 435 armored cars; 908 field and medium
artillery weapons; and 1,451 antitank guns. The Axis army could field only
100,000 men (roughly equally divided between German and Italian); 520 tanks
plus 32 in workshops; 192 armored cars; 500 field and 18 heavy guns; and 800
antitank guns including 86 dual-purpose 88mm guns. In the air, the Western
Desert Air Force, supplemented by American squadrons, outnumbered its Axis
counterparts by a ratio of five to three.

Montgomery's army contained three corps. In the north was Lt. Gen. Sir
Oliver Leese's XXX Corps, containing five infantry divisions that would have the
support of 23rd Armoured Brigade, a formation possessing 200 tanks, specially
trained in infantry cooperation. Overlaying XXX Corps' rear areas was Lt. Gen.
H. Lumsden's X Corps, consisting of two armored divisions. In the south was Lt.
Gen. B.G. Horrocks's XIII Corps, containing one armored and two infantry divisions, supplemented by one Greek and two Fighting French brigade groups. For
his part, Rommel interposed German units at intervals along the line to provide
a stiffening for the Italian divisions. His four armored divisions were disposed
in two groups, 15th Panzer and the Italian Littorio in the north, and 21st Panzer

and the Italian Ariete in the south, their role being to counterattack promptly before the British armor could deploy properly from the minefield gaps. On September 23 Rommel, tired and ill, left for home on sick leave, handing over command to Gen. Georg Stumme, recently transferred from the Russian Front and not at all as seasoned a desert campaigner as Rommel.

Montgomery needed a night illuminated by a full moon to give his mine-clearing teams the necessary light to do their painstaking work. On October 23 the conditions were prime, and at precisely 9:40 p.m. the British opened up with a bombardment by 592 guns, 456 of which were located in XXX Corps' sector. Under cover of the barrage the mine-clearing parties and the infantry rose from their trenches, followed slowly by their supporting tanks. In the face of determined opposition, progress was slower than expected. On the 24th Stumme died of a heart attack after falling from his staff car during an artillery bombardment and Gen. von Thoma assumed command of the Axis army until Rommel returned the following evening. From the outset, Rommel knew that he was locked into what he described as "a battle without hope." He was shaken by the volume and flexibility of his enemy's "tremendous" artillery fire and depressed by the carefully rehearsed British mine-clearing/infantry/tank tactics that were steadily eating their way through his defenses. "Everything," he later wrote of Montgomery's plan, "went methodically and according to a drill." In fact Montgomery was to succeed at El Alamein because he could afford to be more flexible, shifting attacks from one front to the other, whereas Rommel, hamstrung by shortages, was forced into a more static response.

On October 27, when it appeared that the British 1st Armoured Division might break through in the area of Kidney Ridge, a feature to the northwest of Meteiriya Ridge, Rommel counterattacked with his own armor. He succeeded in containing the threat but lost a disproportionate number of tanks, largely as a result of the epic stand of an outpost named Snipe, where nineteen 6-pounder antitank guns manned by the Second Battalion, The Rifle Brigade, and the 239 Battery, Royal Artillery, destroyed 21 German and 11 Italian tanks, plus five assault guns or tank destroyers, and knocked out a further 15, possibly 20, tanks that the enemy recovered but was unable to repair by the end of the battle.

On the night of October 28-29 Montgomery shifted the emphasis of his attack to the coastal sector, where the Ninth Australian Division began striking northward and all but isolated a heavily defended enemy locality known as Thompson's Post. On October 30 Rommel mounted a major counterattack that was contained with difficulty, and as a result those Axis forces trapped in Thompson's Post were able to escape.

With Rommel's attention now focused firmly on the sensitive coastal sector, Montgomery again shifted his axis of attack to a point just north of Kidney Ridge. On the morning of November 2 the Second New Zealand Division and its supporting armor broke through the last minefield defenses. Passing through, the Ninth Armoured Brigade fought a battle of mutual destruction on the fortified ridge of Aqqaqir. It was an action that showed another side of Montgomery's generalship. He had fought and almost died in the First World War and as a legacy of that experience was averse to high-casualty tactics. But, when necessity demanded, he could be utterly ruthless. When the commanding officer of the Third Hussars, part of the Ninth Armoured Brigade, heard of the plan to attack Aqqaqir, he suggested to Montgomery that it was suicidal. Montgomery replied, "It's got to be done and, if necessary, I am prepared to accept 100 percent casualties in both personnel and tanks." In any event the brigade was to lose 87 of its 94 tanks, the Third Hussars alone losing 21 officers and 98 soldiers killed, wounded, and missing. However, in its wake came the Second and Eighth Armoured Brigades of the First Armoured Division, to engage in a daylong battle with the Axis armor. When it ended, although the British had sustained the heavier loss, the Italian armored divisions had ceased to exist and only 24 tanks remained to the Afrika Korps.

Some scrappy fighting was to follow, but on the night of November 3-4 probes by the 51st Highland and Seventh Armoured Division revealed that the enemy had gone. Encouraged by Kesselring, his superior, to ignore Hitler's order to stand fast, Rommel decided to save what he could from the wreck of his army and embarked on the retreat that would take him across North Africa to Tunisia. Montgomery's pursuit was initially hampered by the demands of too many units, for fuel and torrential rain had rendered the task of the heavily laden supply trucks impossible. And so Rommel skillfully and successfully executed his retreat.

It mattered little, for Montgomery's victory had been as complete as any in history. Total Axis casualties amounted to about 50 percent of their manpower—55,000—with 20,000 killed or wounded and 30,000 taken prisoner, of whom nearly 11,000 were German. Rommel's material losses included 450 tanks, 1,000 guns, and 84 aircraft. His German divisions had been reduced to skeletons and most of his Italian divisions, lacking transport, were destroyed where they stood. The uncompromising rule of desert warfare was that defeat could also mean death by thirst unless surrender followed promptly. The Eighth Army sustained 13,500 casualties, including approximately 4,500 dead, the majority incurred by the infantry divisions. Five hundred tanks had been knocked out, of which all but 150 were repairable, and 110 guns had been destroyed by shellfire. In the air 77 British and 20 American aircraft were lost. Winston Churchill, placing the Second Battle of Alamein in the overall context of World War II, commented that it marked "not the beginning of the end, but certainly the end of the beginning." "Before it," he was later to say, "we never had a victory. After it, we never had a defeat."

VALLEYS

The two battle accounts that follow (the Charge of the Light Brigade during the Battle of Balaklava, 1854, and the crucial Cedar Creek Battle during the second campaign in Virginia's Shenandoah Valley during the Civil War) show two very different faces of the valley in warfare. The Shenandoah is, and was in 1864, richly fertile and productive, and it was just this plenitude that attracted the Confederate Army, always hard-pressed for supplies. Stonewall Jackson had been in the Valley during his whirlwind campaign between March and June 1862, and had brilliantly exploited one of the characteristics of the valley—as conduit and passageway. He rushed his men up and down, in one of the most dazzling strategic exploits of military history. He won at McDowell in the south on May 8, went back to the northern end for victories at Front Royal and Winchester on May 23 and 25 respectively, then traveled back down south for victories at Cross Keys on June 8 and Port Republic the next day. It was breathtaking. He marched his men so furiously fast and far that they became known as "Jackson's Foot Cavalry." As Professor Gallagher shows in his account of the greatest battle in the Valley during the whole Civil War, Gen. Philip Sheridan of the Union Army could also use the geography brilliantly and inspire his men in the most galvanizing way. In the words of a brigade historian: "Such a scene as [Sheridan's] presence produced and emotions it awoke cannot be realized once in a century." Balaklava shows a very different face of the valley battle. This is more like the place of despair invoked in the 23rd Psalm: "the valley of the shadow of death." If this valley was a conduit it went just one way: into the cannon's mouth. Here we have the valley as trap and killing cauldron. In human terms too it shows the darker face. There were no inspirational Jacksons and Sheridans at Balaklava. As Ian Knight recounts, almost all the key players—Lords Raglan and Lucan, the Earl of Cardigan, and that dark figure who bore the enigmatic order to charge, Captain Nolan—seemed to have been consumed by mutual loathing and mistrust—to the fatal end.

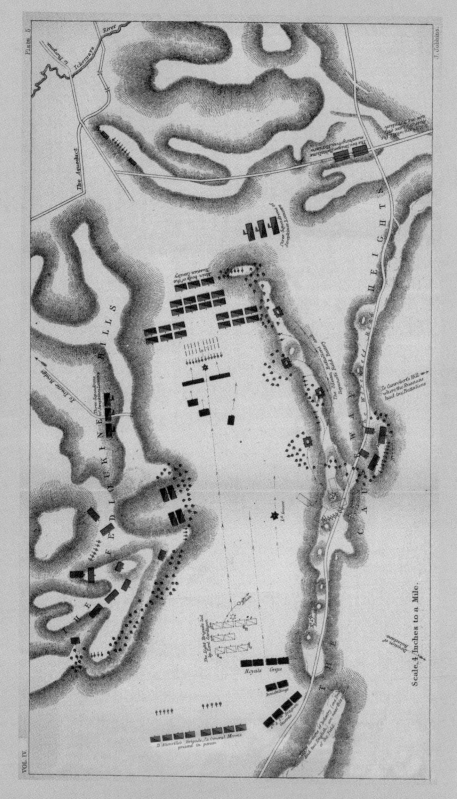

Balaklava, Russia, 1854, from *The Invasion of the Crimea*, by Alexander Kinglake
Anticipating an attack from the British light cavalry, Russian batteries took up new positions in the North Valley and on its surrounding slopes. Arrows traversing the center of the valley indicate the deadly path attempted by Lord Cardigan and the Light Brigade.

Death Ride
Balaklava, Russia, 1854

IAN CASTLE

The Crimean Peninsula juts out as a defiant bastion from the coastline of southeastern Ukraine into the Black Sea. It is a fertile land that has drawn numerous invading armies over the centuries. Greeks, Romans, Goths, Huns, and the Genoese all occupied it before the Turks expanded across the territory in 1475. They retained control until the late 18th century when it became absorbed into the Russian Empire. In 1941 the German Army invaded the Crimea and, having captured the main port of Sevastopol, occupied the region from July 1942 until Soviet forces recaptured it in the spring of 1944.

Yet through thousands of years of history it is a cavalry charge by fewer than 700 British soldiers that brings the Crimea most readily into the spotlight of history. Against the accepted rules of war, a brigade of light cavalry advanced along a hitherto insignificant valley to the east of Sevastopol and attacked frontally a battery of Russian guns at the Battle of Balaklava. The charge was to earn the "noble six hundred" an enduring fame as they rode on a hellish journey to death or glory.

A combined British and French army landed on the west coast of the Crimea on September 14, 1854, brought to these distant shores by Russia's determination to take advantage of the decline of the 300-year-old Turkish Empire. In particular, Constantinople (modern-day Istanbul) attracted Russia's covetous glance. If they could gain the city and the narrow Bosporus, the Black

Sea fleet would have free access to the Mediterranean, causing a shift in the balance of power the allies were determined to oppose.

Pushing aside the Russians at the Alma River the allies circled around Sevastopol, the home port of the Black Sea fleet, and established themselves with their Turkish allies to the south on the Chersonese Uplands. The British captured the tiny port of Balaklava to serve as a base for landing their supplies, but the exposed route from Balaklava to the siege lines overlooking the Russian port caused concern. If the British lost Balaklava, their ability to continue the war would be seriously damaged.

To the north of Balaklava, beyond its flanking rocky heights, the ground opens out into the South Valley, which runs west/east, gradually rising to a low undulating ridge crowned by a series of rounded knolls. The British named the ridge the Causeway Heights, rather a misnomer as it generally runs only 40 yards above the valley floor. Northward from the ridge the ground drops away again into the narrower North Valley, again running on a west/east line before gently descending away to the northeast. Across the valley the ground slowly ascends about 40 yards again to a series of undulating rises known as the Fedioukine Heights. At the western end of both valleys the ground rises dramatically for 160 yards to the Sapoune Ridge, defining the edge of the Chersonese Uplands. The only well-constructed road in the area ran from Sevastopol, down over the Sapoune Ridge, and along the crest of the Causeway Heights. Minor roads ran north toward the Fedioukine Heights and south toward Balaklava from a crossroads on the Heights.

To add strength to Balaklava's weak defenses the British commander, Lord Raglan, ordered the construction of six earthwork redoubts on the knolls along the Causeway Heights. However, when the Russians launched their attack just before first light on the morning of October 25, 1854, only four were complete and manned by Turkish garrisons. Three columns of infantry, totaling about 15,000 men, advanced on the Causeway Heights, followed by a supporting column of 5,000 men detailed to take up a position on the Fedioukine Heights and a strong force of over 2,000 cavalry under Lieutenant General Ryzhov, ready to exploit any opportunity that developed.

The initial attack proved a great success, with the Turkish garrisons driven off all four redoubts, their guns—which had been supplied by their British allies—falling to the Russians. However, the ineffectual cavalry quickly lost the advantages gained by the infantry. The repulse of four squadrons advancing toward Balaklava and the humiliation of the rest of Ryzhov's cavalry at the hands of the outnumbered and disorganized Heavy Cavalry Brigade swung the advantage back to the British. Russian discomfort was complete when British artillery opened on them, forcing a withdrawal along the Causeway Heights into the North Valley, where they re-formed behind a battery of Don Cossack artillery drawn up across the valley floor facing to the west.

From his position high above on the Sapoune Ridge, Lord Raglan could only wonder why the Light Brigade had not attacked the Russian cavalry, turning the retreat into a rout, and his agitation grew as he observed the Russians strengthening their positions on the Causeway and Fedioukine Heights. He had ordered two divisions of infantry forward but they were moving painfully slowly. Frustrated, he sent an order to the cavalry division commander, Lord Lucan, for the cavalry to "advance and take advantage of any opportunity to recover the Heights," adding they would receive infantry support. Lucan moved the Light Brigade, commanded by his despised brother-in-law, the Earl of Cardigan, into the North Valley facing eastward and awaited the promised support. However, he had not understood from the brief order that he was to advance at once in the hope of inducing the Russians to abandon their positions. Looking down, Raglan seethed at the continued inactivity below.

On the Sapoune Ridge Raglan's anger became explosive. A member of his staff reported that the Russians were removing the British artillery pieces captured in the attack on the redoubts. That was too much. To lose your guns to the enemy suggested defeat. Raglan blamed Lucan for this setback and rapidly issued another order. In his haste it was ambiguous and it would destroy the Light Brigade. It read, "Lord Raglan wishes the cavalry to advance rapidly to the front—follow the enemy and try to prevent the enemy carrying away the guns." Captain Nolan, a splendid horseman and expert on cavalry tactics—but a man highly critical of Lucan's handling of the cavalry since they had landed in the Crimea—galloped away to deliver the order. Nolan passed the brief scribbled note to Lucan, who was dumbfounded. It told him the enemy was carrying away the guns, but he could see nothing of this from where he stood. In Raglan's aerie-like position the two valleys and the intervening ridge appeared as gentle folds in the ground, and he failed to consider that the undulations of the Causeway Heights would greatly limit Lucan's view at ground level. Lucan asked Nolan to clarify the orders. Nolan had shared the anguish of the staff on the Sapoune Ridge at the failure of the cavalry to exploit the success of the Heavy Brigade and now the cavalry leader he held in contempt did not comprehend what appeared to him a simple order. Lucan is reported to have demanded, "Attack sir! Attack what? What guns?" To this Nolan contemptuously replied, throwing his arm forward, pointing not at the Causeway Heights but up the North Valley, "There, my Lord, is your enemy, there are your guns!" What he was pointing to was not the Turkish batteries that the Russians had overrun, but the very substantial Russian artillery emplacements both in the North Valley as well as on its commanding slopes. This was a suicidal mission, but the antipathy between the two men prevented Lucan from questioning Nolan further. He had received specific orders from the commander of the army and it was his duty to carry them out.

Lord Lucan rode across to the Light Brigade and issued orders to Cardigan. Such was the strained relationship between these two that little discussion followed. Earlier their mutual hostility had convinced Cardigan against launching the Light Brigade at the retreating Russian cavalry. Cardigan now merely responded by pointing out that a Russian battery lay across the valley with other batteries and infantry on the high ground to left and right. Lucan replied resignedly, "I know it but Lord Raglan will have it. We have no choice but to obey."

The Light Brigade formed in three lines about one and a quarter miles from the Russian battery: the 17th Lancers and 13th Light Dragoons in the first line, the 11th Hussars alone in the second, with the Fourth Light Dragoons and Eighth Hussars in the third. Lucan formed the Heavy Brigade to the rear, as they were to advance in support.

The bugles sounded and the Light Brigade trotted forward. Cardigan rode some distance ahead of his men, and he had not quite covered 200 yards when a Russian battery of ten guns, now established on the Fedioukine Heights, opened fire into the left flank of the brigade. The first casualty of the charge fell within a few feet of Cardigan; it was Nolan, his chest ripped open by shrapnel from an exploding shell. And with him to his grave went the explanation of why he had misdirected Lord Lucan.

A recent study of the charge estimates that the Light Brigade received about 70 rounds as it passed this first battery. Perhaps 40 were of solid iron round-shot, which bounced menacingly across the ground, capable of destroying whole lines of men, and 30 of common shell, which, if fused correctly, would explode above the target and shower it with jagged pieces of shrapnel.

The Light Brigade increased its pace to a canter. Clear of the first battery it then ran into a more devastating field of fire as a battery of eight guns on their right raked it with shot and shell. At the same time the eight guns of the Don Cossack battery drawn up across the valley opened fire, joined by infantry looking down into the shallow valley from the Causeway Heights.

For the men of the Light Brigade it appeared they were riding through hell itself. Survivors' accounts describe the horrors they witnessed as man and horse were literally torn apart before their eyes. Headless corpses continued to ride on for some distance, torsos and limbs flew through the air, blood and gore were everywhere. Desperate to get to the guns to end this torture the Light Brigade increased to a gallop. Lord Lucan, observing the slaughter ahead, reined in the Heavy Brigade, who were falling behind, and withdrew back up the valley. The Light Brigade was alone.

Although devastated by the Russian fire the front line rode on. The indistinct dark mass of horsemen that the Russian gunners had first opened fire at was now frighteningly close. To the Russians they were madmen. Having been exposed to concentrated artillery fire, perhaps 200 rounds in total, from left, right, and front, the Light Brigade passed through the final burst at the charge with a sensation an officer compared to riding into the mouth of a volcano. Then they were among the guns. The charge had reached its target, but to what purpose? Unsupported the disorganized cavalrymen hacked at the Russian gunners or rode at the confused Russian cavalry standing and watching behind the guns. However, there was nothing more that could be achieved against a numerically superior albeit hesitant opponent. The shattered cavalrymen returned back up the valley, picking their way through the human and animal debris of the charge, their passage eased by the efforts of French Fourth Chasseurs d'Afrique who attacked and drove off the Russian guns on the Fedioukine Heights.

The charge lasted no more than seven and a half minutes but the mythology surrounding it leaves us believing massive casualties occurred. Surprisingly, this is not the case. Of the 668 men who took part, 103 were killed; 130 wounded, of whom seven later died; and 58 were taken prisoner by the Russians. These figures suggest over half must have returned relatively unscathed. However, about 360 horses were killed or later shot because of their wounds. A cavalry brigade without horses is no longer effective and, with further losses caused by the approaching cruel Crimean winter, those who survived the charge were unable to contribute further to the war.

There was no clear winner of the Battle of Balaklava; each side could take something from it. The poet laureate Alfred, Lord Tennyson, immortalized the attack in his poem "The Charge of The Light Brigade"—which, even though grandly heroic, even a little hyperventilating in the grand Victorian style, recognizes not only the magnificent bravery but also the futility: "Theirs not to make reply/Theirs not to reason why/Theirs but to do and die," an observation echoed by General Bosquet, a French officer who watched the charge from the Sapoune Ridge. As the Light Brigade advanced toward the Russian guns and became engulfed in the storm of shot and shell he observed, "It is magnificent, but it is not war!"

Jubal Early in the Shenandoah
Cedar Creek, Virginia, 1864

GARY GALLAGHER

Virginia's Shenandoah Valley extends from the Potomac River southward to beyond Lexington. With the Blue Ridge Mountains on the east and the more imposing Alleghenies to the west, it runs southwest to northeast and drops gently in its course to meet the Potomac. Between Strasburg and Harrisonburg, Massanutten Mountain divides the Valley. West of Massanutten, in the Valley proper, flows the North Fork of the Shenandoah River, while to the east the South Fork runs through the Luray Valley on its journey to join the North Fork at Front Royal. The lower Valley, as the northern portion is known, includes the broad expanse between Williamsport on the Potomac and Strasburg.

The greatest battle fought in the Shenandoah Valley during the American Civil War took place on October 19, 1864, at Cedar Creek, just beyond the northern terminus of Massanutten Mountain between Strasburg and Middletown. During the previous two months, Union Maj. Gen. Philip H. Sheridan's Army of the Shenandoah and Confederate Lt. Gen. Jubal A. Early's Army of the Valley had waged a campaign of maneuver and combat, with Sheridan thrashing Early in the battles at Third Winchester on September 19 and Fisher's Hill three days later. By the third week of October, the Federal Army, which numbered approximately 35,000, lay in camps near Cedar Creek, a tributary of the North Fork of the Shenandoah. The geography of the valley was such that Sheridan expected no trouble on his left. Any Confederate advance,

Cedar Creek, Virginia, 1864

Maj. Jedediah Hotchkiss (1828-1899) filled many notebooks with diary entries, topographic drawings, and strategic maps during his time with the Confederate Army. This page details the area around Cedar Creek. A topographical engineer, Hotchkiss also drew detailed battle maps for General Lee and General Jackson to assist in the planning of their campaigns.

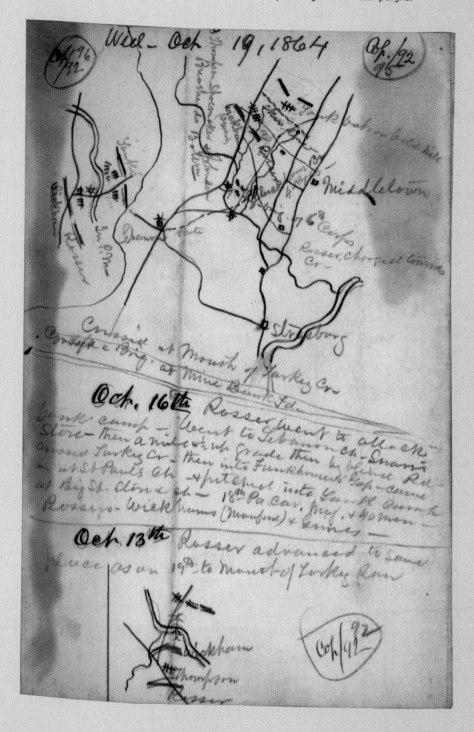

he conjectured, would have to proceed northward from the old battlefield at Fisher's Hill, located just south of Strasburg in the narrow part of the Valley. With his opponent constrained by the North Fork and the rugged shoulders of the Valley, Sheridan believed the Rebels possessed few options and posed little threat. He spent the night of October 18 in Winchester, a dozen miles north of his army's encampments, where he had stopped on his return from a meeting in Washington.

Jubal Early, who commanded fewer than 15,000 men of all arms, hoped to disrupt his opponent's sense of security. Encamped at Fisher's Hill, his force occupied a section of the Valley that, as Sheridan knew from his success on September 22, was too wide for Early to defend effectively yet too narrow to permit the Confederates any useful tactical maneuvering. In effect using this geographical obstacle to his advantage, Early had planned a surprise attack that played upon his opponent's sense of security. He ordered a nighttime flanking march that would take the bulk of his infantry from Fisher's Hill across the North Fork of the Shenandoah, around the hulking nose of Massanutten Mountain, and back across the North Fork to take up positions from which to strike the Federal left flank. Only four miles wide where the North Fork began its curve around the slope of Massanutten, the Valley quickly widened into a rolling landscape where Early believed surprise and audacity might yield tactical success.

Early's soldiers marched toward their assigned positions during the predawn hours of October 19. Shortly before 5:00 a.m., five divisions of infantry and supporting artillery prepared to attack. Gabriel C. Wharton's 1,100 men had reached a point just above Hupp's Hill on the Valley Turnpike. Joseph B. Kershaw's 3,200 lay east of Cedar Creek, near the point where that stream formed a large loop before joining the North Fork. East of Kershaw, Stephen Dodson Ramseur's 2,500 soldiers, John B. Gordon's 1,800, and John Pegram's 1,650, all of whom had crossed the North Fork below its confluence with Cedar Creek, went into line facing northwest. As the hour of attack drew near, Early turned to Samuel J.C. Moore of his staff. "Colonel," confessed the general, "this is the most trying experience of my life; if only I could pray like Stonewall Jackson, what a comfort it would be."

Three Union infantry corps occupied camps north and west of the Confederates. Nearest the Rebels were the two divisions of George Crook's Eighth Corps, with Joseph Thoburn's 1,700 men camped near earthworks on high ground overlooking Kershaw's position and Rutherford B. Hayes's 2,400 east of the Valley Pike to Thoburn's left rear. West of the Pike, William Dwight's and Cuvier Grover's divisions of William H. Emory's 19th Corps, which numbered 2,600 and 6,100 men respectively, occupied works that roughly paralleled Cedar Creek. The three divisions of Horatio G. Wright's Sixth Corps—Frank Wheaton's 2,000 men, George W. Getty's 2,500, and James B. Ricketts's 6,000—spread across undulating ground north of the 19th Corps. The works erected by the Eighth and 19th Corps faced generally south, underscoring the Federals' lack of concern about their left.

The echo of musketry about 5:00 a.m. ended Federal illusions of safety. Kershaw's brigades surged forward, crushing one of Thoburn's brigades and pressing the other toward the Valley Pike. A South Carolinian described pursuing Union soldiers who, "shoeless and hatless, went flying like mad to the rear, some with and some without their guns." Gordon's and Ramseur's troops added their weight to the Confederate assault. They pummeled Hayes's and Kitching's divisions, the bulk of which mounted only feeble resistance before withdrawing toward Emory's position.

Alerted by musketry to the southeast and east, members of the 19th Corps soon saw fugitives from the Eighth Corps stream through their ranks. "[I]t was apparent that our left...was helplessly broken," commented one of Emory's soldiers: "The surprise was complete." As fragments of the Eighth Corps fought a delaying action, Emory reconfigured his lines to meet the impending threat. But momentum and the weight of numbers eventually carried the Confederates across the Pike. Between 6:30 and 7:00 a.m., Early's infantry forced the 19th Corps northward across fields near Belle Grove house.

The Federal Sixth Corps next took up the defense. Some of Wright's soldiers initially had crossed Meadow Brook, a stream that flowed across the battlefield from northwest of Middletown to Cedar Creek. When it became clear that Crook and Emory could not stop the enemy, the bulk of the Sixth Corps formed a line west of Meadow Brook on Red Hill, where they were supported by units from Emory's corps that rallied to anchor the right. Kershaw, Gordon, and Ramseur mounted assaults against Red Hill from the southwest and south. In a brief period of fierce combat, the Union line disintegrated, and the Confederates pushed the defenders to the northwest. The mass of Federals conducted a sometimes chaotic withdrawal from Red Hill to wooded ground northwest of Middletown.

By about 8:00 a.m., after three hours of fighting, Early's little army had swept two divisions of the Sixth Corps and all of the Eighth and 19th Corps from the field, inflicting more than 4,000 casualties and capturing 24 pieces of artillery. The Confederates had become disorganized in the process, however, and one Union division remained intact—Getty's three brigades from the Sixth Corps, which stood in a horseshoe-shaped line on Cemetery Hill west of Middletown. Between 8:00 and 9:00 a.m., Getty's soldiers repulsed attacks by brigades from four of Early's divisions. Union cavalry under Brig. Gens. George A. Custer and Wesley Merritt bolstered Getty's right flank, extending it across the Valley Pike.

Confederate artillery proved decisive in this phase of the contest. More than two dozen guns massed near the Pike south of Middletown pounded Cemetery Hill. Three southern brigades then hit the Federal right, which rested in a piece of woods. "The enemy gave way," wrote a Confederate lieutenant colonel, "and rapidly, in confusion, withdrew from the woods." At 9:30 a.m., Getty's division retreated to the northeast. By 10:00 a.m., the Confederates had moved through Middletown. Soon they formed a line that extended from Middle Marsh Run on the left, across Meadow Brook to the northern edge of Middletown, and eastward to a point well beyond the Valley Pike.

Although many Confederates expected orders for another attack against their badly mauled enemy, Early decided not to renew the offensive. He later explained that his men were too exhausted and scattered to attack again: "I determined, therefore, to try and hold what had been gained, and orders were given for carrying off the captured and abandoned artillery, small arms, and wagons." This decision led to criticism at the time and later, but a number of factors militated against further attacks. Thousands of Union cavalrymen hovered opposite the Confederate right flank east of the Valley Pike. Early's men had marched all night and fought for several hours. The lure of easy plunder caused a significant number of them to leave their units and ransack Federal camps. By the time Early could have gathered his troops for another full-scale attack, it is likely they would have been repulsed.

About 1:00 p.m., Gordon, Kershaw, and Ramseur moved their divisions forward about a half mile to establish the final southern line. Pegram and Wharton remained in their positions at the edge of Middletown, and William H.F. Payne's small cavalry brigade kept watch beyond Wharton's right flank. Between 1:00 and about 3:30 p.m., Early received word of growing Federal strength in front of Gordon's lines. Confederate signalmen on Massanutten Mountain also warned of a northern buildup. As the afternoon hours ticked by, a number of Confederates later testified, a sense of dread replaced feelings of triumph in Early's army.

Sheridan saw to it that the Confederates experienced their worst fears. He learned at 7:00 a.m. that artillery fire was audible from the direction of Middletown. Leaving Winchester about 9:00 a.m., he and his staff moved up the Valley Pike at a trot. They arrived at the battlefield about 10:30 a.m. to find, as Sheridan later described it, a "stricken army—hundreds of slightly wounded men, throngs of others unhurt but utterly demoralized, and baggage wagons by the score, all pressing to the rear in hopeless confusion...." Sheridan's soldiers responded almost instantly to his presence. "Hope and confidence returned at a bound," stated one Federal. "Now we all burned to attack the enemy, to drive him back, to retrieve our honor and sleep in our old camp that night."

Commanding the army in Sheridan's absence, Wright had stabilized the Federal line by the time his chief arrived. Sheridan turned his attention to a counterattack. By 3:30 p.m., he had organized a massive striking force. Wright's corps was on the left, its eastern flank touching the Valley Pike; Emory's two divisions were on the right. Crook's corps was in reserve east of the Valley Pike and slightly behind Wright's left. Custer's and Merritt's divisions of cavalry massed beyond the infantry's right and left flanks respectively. The expansive width of the Valley near Middletown would work against the rebels in the final phase of the battle, affording the more numerous Federals an opportunity to menace both of Early's flanks.

Federal assaults lurched forward at about 4:00 p.m. and quickly precipitated a crisis on Early's left. Outflanked by Custer's cavalry and under severe fire from Federal infantry, Gordon's troops broke, and with their left thus uncovered, Confederates to the right also retreated. Ramseur rallied fragments of his and other commands, creating a pocket of resistance amid general collapse. He soon fell wounded, however, and his makeshift line disintegrated. By 5:00 p.m., Early's army was in full retreat. One northern captain described the Confederates as "a great, rushing, turbulent, retreating army…hurrying and crowding on in mad retreat." The Confederates fled back through Strasburg, south of which the Valley narrowed sharply. The crush of men and animals and vehicles created a scene of great confusion, and the Federals, continuing their pursuit past Fisher's Hill, captured many prisoners, reclaimed their lost artillery, and took two dozen Rebel guns.

The Confederates had lost roughly 1,860 killed and wounded and more than 1,000 captured. Federal losses were 644 killed, 3,430 wounded, and 1,591 missing or captured. Begun as a brilliantly executed surprise attack against a much larger foe, the battle provided an ignominious coda to major Confederate military operations in the Shenandoah Valley. The contours of geography had both shaped Confederate planning that led to the battle and assisted the Federals in their triumphant final offensive sweep.

RIVERS

The three battles in this chapter represent not only divergent historical periods but also very different military problems. However, they are joined in one respect, for in each the river is less a highway and more a barrier. Alexander needed to cross his in order to get at his enemy, Napoleon needed to cross his in order to prevent the remnants of his army being totally destroyed, and Montgomery had planned to take and hold his as a bridgehead. Rivers can be formidable lines of defense, and storming a defended river is one of the most difficult military maneuvers in the book. For example, eight years before Hydaspes Alexander met a Persian army on the Granicus River (in what is now Turkey). Macedonian and Persian cavalry clashed in the river itself, and the Macedonian advance guard suffered heavily from archers posted on the far bank. Alexander was himself in the thick of the fighting and pushed across the Granicus at the head of his elite cavalry force, the Companions. Once across, he folded up the Persian left flank and fell on the center, cutting it down ruthlessly. Jumping to 1944, the problem of frontal assault was no easier. In fact it was made far more deadly due to the increased lethality of the defender's weaponry. The battle of Cassino in Italy (see page 159) was begun and ended with two such attempts. On January 20, 1944, six battalions of the 36th (Texas) Division splashed through heavily mined water meadows to reach the Rapido River. Paradoxically, it is easier to attack across a wide river so that the period of highest vulnerability, the launch, is furthest from the enemy. But where the Texans chose their jumping-off point the Rapido was only 60 feet wide. The two days of slaughter that followed would cost the 36th 1,681 men in the failed attack. The Rapido was finally breached by British and Indian troops on May 11, 1944, and, as an indication of the difficulty, one brigade of the Indian Division lost 35 of its 40 boats. Being an infantryman in a rubber boat on a river within the sights of a well-entrenched enemy on the far bank is not an experience recommended by the actuaries of life insurance companies.

Alexander at Hydaspes, 326 B.C.

Days before fording the River Hydaspes, Alexander used movement bluffs to create a false sense of security among Porus's troops, who were waiting on the other side. The Indians were taken by storm and unprepared to sufficiently guard the muddy riverbank.

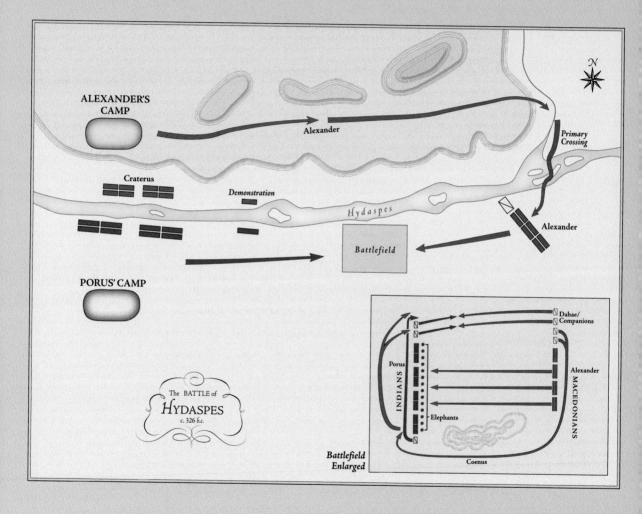

ALEXANDER'S CAMP

Alexander

Primary Crossing

Craterus

Demonstration

Hydaspes

Alexander

Battlefield

PORUS' CAMP

The BATTLE of
HYDASPES
c. 326 b.c.

Battlefield
Enlarged

Dahae/ Companions

Porus

INDIANS

Alexander

MACEDONIANS

Elephants

Coenus

Alexander at the Hydaspes
India, 326 B.C.

MATTHEW BENNETT

In the winter of 327/326 B.C., Alexander the Great was concluding his victorious campaigns in the eastern provinces of the Persian Empire, and his ambitions now turned to the conquest of India. Geography, though, was not an exact science in Alexander's day, and his Greek geographers gave such a misleading impression of the extent of what is actually a subcontinent that Alexander believed India to be much smaller. He led a veteran army, confident in its leader and capable of overcoming any geographical obstacle as demonstrated by the crossing of the Indus using a bridge of boats, constructed in advance of the army's arrival. The army entered the Punjab—the land of five rivers—in the spring of 326.

Alexander first made an alliance with Omphis, king of Taxila (Takshaçila, modern Rawalpindi), who requested support against the rival kingdom of Paurava, ruled by Porus (the Greek rendering of the throne-name Puru), which lay between the rivers Hydaspes (modern Jhelum) and Hydraotis (modern Ravi). So Alexander advanced to the Hydaspes in May 326 B.C., despite the fact that the monsoon season had begun and swollen the river, making it all but impassable. It seemed that all Porus needed to do to keep Alexander at bay was to guard the river crossings. There were no bridges, and he ordered all available vessels gathered in to prevent the Macedonian army from crossing. But Alexander was also prepared. Earlier he had had the boats he had used to navigate the Indus (small ships in reality, for some were as large as 30-oared galleys) dismantled and carried by wagon overland with the army.

It is far from clear where Alexander arrived at the Hydaspes. It used to be thought that he established a base at modern Jhelum, but nowadays it is believed that he chose the ford opposite Haranpur (now bridged) as the site for his camp. He led about 40,000 men, including 5,000 Indian troops from Taxila, but his reconstructed flotilla could carry only a fraction of that number at a time. So, in preparation for a possible river crossing, he instructed his men to make flotation bags from sewn leather stuffed with straw. Both armies were clearly visible to each other across the wide expanse of the Hydaspes, and Alexander kept the enemy guessing by moving detachments of troops along the bank, instructing groups of cavalry to ride up and down, and shouting and blowing trumpets, as if about to make a crossing. At first, Porus reacted by moving troops, as well as his war elephants, to block his side of the fords but, after days of inactivity, was lulled into a false sense of security.

This is what Alexander had been waiting for. All the while he had been reconnoitering upstream to find a likely crossing point, and he settled on a site 18 miles further upriver from his main encampment. Here his troop movements could be shielded by the lush vegetation that grew along the bank. He then chose his best troops to make the crossing. They comprised 4,000 heavy cavalry and 1,000 Dahae (Scythian) horse-archers, the infantry hypaspists (guard-troops, 3,000 strong), two units of the pike-armed phalanx (1,500 each), the Agrianian javelin-men (1,000), and archers (1,000). Leaving Craterus with about 5,000 men at the original encampment, Alexander set out under cover of darkness on a night of torrential rain, which also helped to conceal the troops' movements.

The next morning at dawn, as the storm abated, the men began to cross. Alexander went in the first 30-oared galley with half the Companion cavalry, followed by other vessels and men swimming on the float bags. The transport was so limited that the troops had to cross in three waves, and as they began to disembark, it became apparent that they had landed not on the far bank as they had intended, but on an island midstream. The Indian scouts had spotted the movements and rode off to warn Porus. There remained only a narrow channel to cross, but it had been deepened by the overnight rains, and the men had to wade in fast-flowing water almost up to their necks. It is unknown how long it took to get the landing over, but not all the troops arrived, and the infantry numbers were reduced to some 6,000 men. At this point Alexander was executing a maneuver of extreme difficulty and danger but, undeterred (and luckily unmolested), he deployed his troops and advanced against Porus's main army downstream. The horse-archers led the way, followed by the heavy cavalry in two bodies, then the archers, with the phalanx supported by the Agrianian javelin-men on its flanks.

When Porus heard of the crossing, he dispatched his son with 120 chariots and 2,000 cavalry to conduct a delaying action. It was too small a force and was easily routed, the chariots proving particularly ineffectual, as they could not maneuver on the muddy ground. Some 400 Indians were killed, including Porus's son. Meanwhile, Porus had to make a decision about how to react to Alexander's bold outflanking movement. If he stayed where he was, then he risked being caught between Alexander and Craterus's troops across the ford. So he decided to move the bulk of his army to oppose Alexander, leaving just a few troops to guard the crossing, including some war elephants to dissuade any cavalry (war elephants were not entirely new to the Macedonians. Darius had some at the battle of Gaugamela five years earlier but had not deployed them aggressively. But horses unused to elephants became terrified by them).

Porus's force, comprising approximately 30,000 infantry, 2,000 to 3,000 cavalry, 300 chariots, and up to 200 elephants, advanced over ground soggy from the monsoon rains until it found a spot that was sandy and firm, suitable for the use of cavalry and chariots. Then the mounted troops were deployed on both wings, while the elephants stood in the center, about 100 feet apart, with the infantry massed behind and between them (historians at the time referred to it as a "fortress," the elephants being the towers, the infantry the in-filling wall). Alexander, aware that he could not charge into the elephant line, massed his cavalry on his right wing with his phalanx in the center, supported by the light troops. His horse-archers led the attack, shooting down the horses and men of the chariots (there could be as many as six men in a war chariot) and utterly destroying them.

Seeing their left wing outnumbered, the Indian right-wing cavalry streamed across the front to give support. At this point Coenus's squadrons, riding behind and concealed from the Indians by the Macedonian phalanx, swung out of hiding and fell on the rear of the right-wing Indian cavalry. This, combined with a charge of Macedonian heavy cavalry, drove the entire body of Indian mounted troops back upon their elephants. The Macedonian cavalry, terrified by the huge animals, could not pursue, and so allowed the enemy a brief breathing space.

Now it was down to the phalanx to attack the Indian center. Initially, the Macedonian pikemen suffered heavily from the elephant charges (with tusks tipped with bronze and trained to trample opposing infantry, war elephants could be very formidable indeed). The phalanx was thrown into disorder until the Agrianians and other light troops came to its aid. With their javelins and arrows they were able to wound the beasts and pick off the mahouts who guided them. As a result, some of the elephants began to stampede back into their own infantry, causing more damage than the Macedonians could. Indeed, since the Indian foot soldiers are not described as taking part in the battle at all, neither by shooting their powerful long bows, nor wielding their two-handed swords, it may be that they could not get in a blow because of the confused scrum created by their own cavalry and elephants.

The Indian cavalry did manage to re-form and charge again, but once more they were driven back by a better equipped, better trained, and more maneuverable enemy. Also, the Macedonian foot soldiers began to get the upper hand, driving the elephants back into the massed Indian infantry. In Arrian's evocative phrase, the elephants began to retreat "like ships backing water," still trumpeting but posing no further threat. At this point Alexander seized the advantage. He commanded the phalanx to "lock shields" for close-order combat, while his cavalry began to work around the flanks of the panicking mass of enemy horses, elephants, and infantry. So surrounded, the Indians were massacred where they stood, except for some on the right wing who managed to find a gap and escape.

Alexander's men were too exhausted to chase them, but Craterus, seeing the Macedonian triumph, pushed his men across the ford and sent them in pursuit of the fleeing Indians. Porus himself, a giant of a man, was captured, having received so many wounds that he fell fainting from his command elephant. Indian losses were claimed to be up to 20,000 infantry and 3,000 cavalry, along with all the chariots. It is probable that about half these numbers represent those taken prisoner, due to being surrounded, along with 85 elephants that fell into Alexander's hands as booty. Macedonian casualties are recorded as 700 infantry (many killed in the initial elephant attack) and 280 cavalry, and although these seem trifling in comparison with the slaughter inflicted on their opponents, it was the greatest number of casualties ever recorded in an Alexandrian victory. (After Alexander's death at Babylon three years later, the generals who ruled his empire as the Successors took care to include elephants in their armies as a powerful weapon.)

But this was to be in the future. No one could have predicted Alexander's death at the early age of 32. Few could have guessed that his army would mutiny soon after the great victory at the Hydaspes, and refuse to follow him farther east. His loyal Macedonians, many of whom had followed him devotedly for almost ten years in his search for world empire, feared that not only was India a vast area, greater than that they had already conquered, but that it was full of kings with elephant armies much larger than that possessed by Porus. This is not to downplay Alexander's achievement in overrunning the Punjab in such a short time. His initiative, careful planning, and sheer daring enabled him to triumph over geography and weather in a way that most commanders would not even have attempted. His self-confidence and trust in his troops, which led him to cross a river in flood, placing himself without support or route for escape, in the face of odds of at least three to one, has never been matched in military history.

According to Arrian, Alexander also left his mark on the geography of the country by founding two cities near the point where he crossed the Hydaspes. One, Nicaea (after Nike, the Greek goddess of victory), to commemorate the battle; the other, Bucephala, in memory of Alexander's favorite horse, Bucephalus (Ox head), which died during the Indian campaign at the age of some 30 years, not of wounds, "but of old age and exhaustion." Many a cavalry horse that gave Alexander his victories, and indeed many a Macedonian soldier, must have felt the same way!

1812 map of the Russian campaign

Napoleon's campaign began at the Polish-Russian border in June, advancing to Moscow by September, where Napoleon and his men stayed until winter and supply shortages forced them to retreat. The bandwidth on the bottom chart chronicles the dwindling numbers of Napoleon's troops during the campaign, starting with 422,000 men at the initial invasion and diminishing to 100,000 by the time the troops reached Moscow. The dark lower band depicts Napoleon's retreat through the winter, and across the Berezina River, after which only 10,000 men remained.

Crossing the Berezina
Russia, 1812

PHILIP HAYTHORNTHWAITE

Rivers and river crossings provided strategic objectives in many campaigns, but only rarely did the crossing of a river represent the difference between salvation and death. Such was the passage of the Berezina in November 1812, which involved, in the words of Sir Robert Wilson, a British military observer attached to the Russian army, "a pandemonium of horrors...madness and indescribable woe."

Napoleon initiated his great invasion of Russia by crossing the River Niemen on June 24, 1812. His appropriately named Grande Armée was a host of unprecedented size, drawn from France and all its allies and satellite states. It numbered about 450,000 men with some 225,000 in reserve. He advanced deep into Russia, whose defenders withdrew before him, declining the decisive battle he desired, every step lengthening his lines of communication.

Napoleon's progress compelled the tsar to recall the veteran general Mikhail Kutuzov, who halted the retreat and prepared his army to face Napoleon at Borodino on September 7, 1812. With great slaughter on both sides the battle was inconclusive, and the Russian retreat resumed. Moscow was abandoned to the invaders, though much of it was burned as the French marched in. There Napoleon remained as the winter drew on, until chronic shortages of provisions forced him to retrace his steps, a retreat that has become synonymous with military disaster. Starved, frozen, exhausted, and constantly harassed by Cossack and Russian cavalry the Grande Armée was whittled down remorselessly.

The pursuing Russians were not content to let winter, exhaustion, and malnutrition do their work. They devised a plan of annihilation. Midway between the city of Smolensk and the relative safety of the Niemen lies the river Berezina, rising in the marshes of Borisov and flowing south and east for some 350 miles. It lay squarely in the path of Napoleon's retreat.

Of the 95,000 men who had left Moscow, perhaps no more than 25,000 were in any kind of fighting shape, and to complicate matters they were encumbered with a horde of fugitives and camp followers. Following them was Kutuzov with probably fewer than 80,000 men. From the north a Russian army about 30,000 strong under Gen. Ludwig Wittgenstein, and from the south 34,000 under Adm. Pavel Tchitchagov, prepared to execute a pincer movement designed to deny Napoleon the Berezina crossing. If Napoleon could be trapped on the eastern bank, Kutuzov would be able to finish him off.

The army with Napoleon, however, was not the only force at his disposal. Two corps d'armée had been left behind to secure his line of march: IX Corps, led by Marshal Claude Victor, and II Corps under Marshal Nicolas-Charles Oudinot, a fearless soldier who had been wounded more times than almost anyone else in the army (Napoleon once saw him giving coins to his soldiers and quipped, "Oudinot, why is it you give away the silver but always keep the lead?"). Another, the Bavarian VI Corps, was well to the north of the Berezina crossing and took little part in the operation that followed.

As Napoleon's army struggled westward, Tchitchagov captured Minsk, a depot key to the French. Even more significant, it put Tchitchagov west of the line of the Berezina, cutting off Napoleon's retreat into Poland and safety. Now the emperor faced the daunting prospect of having to fight his way across a defended river while also being harassed from the north and rear. In response, he ordered Oudinot to oppose Tchitchagov, while Victor was directed north to hold off Wittgenstein's arm of the pincer. In addition, Gen. Jean Dombrowski's 17th Division of V Corps was sent to hold the Berezina crossing point at Borisov. To increase his speed Napoleon ordered much of the army's transport to be burned or abandoned near Orsha although, inexplicably, he allowed a vast concourse of privately owned vehicles to remain with the army, choking its route of march.

The bridge at Borisov, which carried the main Smolensk-Minsk road, was believed to be the only crossing over the Berezina, which thereafter widened, with impassable marshy ground on both banks. It was a catastrophe for Napoleon, therefore, when Tchitchagov drove Dombrowski from the bridge on November 21. However, the ever dependable Oudinot counterattacked and ejected the Russians. But a terrible blow had been struck. The Russians had burned the bridge. Napoleon was trapped.

By chance, a brigade of Oudinot's cavalry, commanded by Gen. Jean-Baptiste Corbineau, had a Polish-speaking regiment, and they were able to find out from local inhabitants the existence of a ford eight miles north of Borisov, near the village of Studianka. Corbineau reconnoitered it and passed on his vital intelligence to Oudinot. Here was the lifeline Napoleon so desperately needed.

Napoleon ordered Oudinot to make a feint some miles to the south in the hope that the Russians would be duped into thinking that was to be the crossing point. The ruse worked, and Tchitchagov concentrated his force there, leaving Studianka virtually unguarded. By this time, however, the Berezina had been swollen by floodwaters until it was almost 200 yards wide at places and far too deep to be crossed on foot. A bridge was needed, but in the panic of retreat the pontoons had been destroyed. Luckily for Napoleon, Gen. Jean-Baptiste Eblé, the commander of the pontoon-train and more foresighted than his emperor, had managed to preserve two field forges, some wagonloads of charcoal to fire the forges, and some metal fittings, as well as his men's tools and equipment. It was the stuff of salvation.

Napoleon met Oudinot on the morning of November 26 and declared, "You shall be my locksmith and open the passage for me." Oudinot drove off the few Russians remaining at the ford and Eblé went to work on what was to be one of the most heroic feats of battlefield engineering in the annals of military history. Using his own materials and wood from the houses of Studianka, Eblé began constructing two bridges about 130 yards apart: one for the infantry and one, more robust, for the heavy artillery and wagons. The supports had to be driven into the riverbed, which meant engineers were forced to wade chest high in the frigid water. Some died of hypothermia as they stood, but the work progressed.

By the afternoon of November 26 the bridges were complete, and all through the next day the army trudged across, the *pontonniers* repeatedly plunging back into the freezing river to make the lifesaving repairs. Thanks to their Herculean efforts only Victor's corps, and a horde of stragglers, remained on the east bank on the evening of the 27th.

From early on the 27th Tchitchagov, realizing his error, moved back northward and began to attack Oudinot, who, together with part of Marshal Ney's III Corps, held him off. Ney took command when Oudinot was wounded yet again. Now Wittgenstein's corps descended on Victor, standing guard on the east bank. However, by noon on the 27th Napoleon and the Imperial Headquarters and the Imperial Guard had safely crossed to the west bank.

In addition to keeping the bridges in repair Eblé's *pontonniers* and engineers guarded the bridgeheads and tried to keep order. Capt. Eugène Labaume described the scenes: "The crowd was so great that the passage was completely choked up, and it was absolutely impossible to move...the dead bodies of men and horses so choked every avenue that it was necessary to climb over mountains of dead bodies to arrive at the river. Some, buried in these horrible heaps, still breathed and, struggling with the agonies of death, caught hold of those who mounted over them; but they kicked them with violence to disengage themselves and, without remorse, trod them underfoot."

Gen. Philippe de Ségur also recorded the wild panic as the Russian artillery began to fire into the heaving mass of stragglers and camp followers, how the vehicles, "driving against each other and getting violently overturned, killed in their fall those who surrounded them." Like Labaume, Ségur was horrified by the cruelty sheer panic induced, where "the strongest threw into the river those who were weaker.... Many hundreds were crushed to death [while] others, hoping to save themselves by swimming were frozen in the middle of the river."

The scenes on the line of battle were scarcely less dreadful. At one point the center of Victor's line seemed about to give way, until his small cavalry contingent—the Baden Hussars and Hessian Chevaux-légers—put in a sacrificial charge. This so-called Charge of Death stabilized Victor's position but both cavalry regiments were all but annihilated. As the Russian pressure slackened, Victor's decimated command withdrew to the bridges, and on the night of November 28-29 were the last combatant elements of the once glorious Grande Armée to cross the Berezina.

Even though there still remained a huge body of stragglers on the east bank, Eblé was instructed to destroy the bridges. He waited as long as he dared, but at 8:30 a.m. he set the pontoons alight, which triggered yet another stampede. Sir Robert Wilson watched as some "sprang forth on the fiery platform, and were engulfed or consumed; some dashed into the river and [were] crushed by massive blocks of ice. All those who remained on the east bank fell into the hands of the Russians." To be captured, especially by the Cossacks, was a fate almost as chilling as the frigid waters of the Berezina. Most of the stragglers (an estimated 10,000) were to die of hunger and exhaustion. The overall French losses have been estimated at 55,000, combatants and noncombatants combined.

Thanks to the crossing of the Berezina, Napoleon's retreat was able to continue and the remnant of his army escaped to fight another day. The whole Russian campaign had cost about 400,000 French and allied and 150,000 Russian lives. The myth of Napoleon's invincibility had been shattered and his former allies were about to turn on him, destroying his empire. Although there were undoubtedly many incidences of panic and *sauve qui peut*, it is also important to realize how difficult a military operation the French were undertaking. It has to say something about their discipline and skill that they were able to do it at all in the circumstances. For the loss of about 25,000 battle casualties and perhaps 30,000 noncombatants, the Grande Armée inflicted perhaps 20,000 losses on the Russians. Only 25 guns had been lost, in itself an incredible testament. The crossing also saw many acts of individual bravery and self-sacrifice. Above all, no praise was too high for the *pontonniers*, especially Eblé. But he was to have little opportunity to enjoy his reputation as the savior of the army. Worn out, he died at Königsberg one month later.

Dutch resistance map of Arnhem, Holland, 1944

This map of Arnhem appears in *The Battle of Arnhem,* by Lt. Col. Theodore A. Boeree of the
Dutch resistance. In his preface Boeree reflects on the unfortunate miscalculations that led to
an allied defeat: "An officer in command, who has to make a decision, will try to calculate all
circumstances, all factors, which may affect it. But it will remain a vague estimate, so all operations will include a maximum of risk...Of course, there have been mistakes, but little by
little I got an untempered admiration for the men who fought (at Arnhem) and gave such brilliant proofs of bravery and discipline."

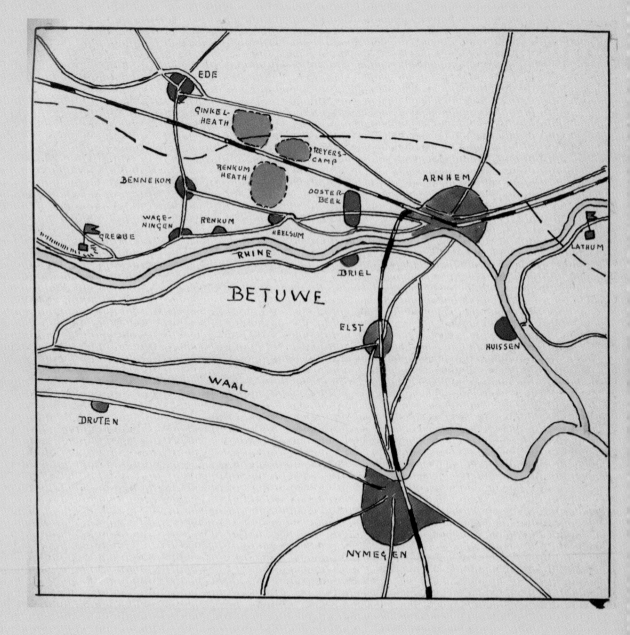

"A Drop Too Many"
Arnhem, Holland, 1944

PETER A. HUCHTHAUSEN

In September 1944, just three months after landing in Normandy, the Allies were in an exuberant mood pursuing the battered remnants of von Rundstedt's German Army Group West. In the north, German general van Zangen's 15th Army was in chaotic retreat chased through Belgium and into Holland by Field Marshal Bernard Montgomery's 21st Army Group. His Canadian First and British Second Armies had dashed more than 250 miles after their breakout from the Normandy beaches and were a mere 60 miles from the Rhine. To the south, Gen. Omar Bradley's 12th Army Group had raced across Belgium and Luxembourg, crossed the Moselle River, and was 40 miles from the Rhine. The new U.S. Ninth Army in Brittany was approaching Brest, and the Sixth Army Group fighting northward from southern France was joining up with General Patton's Third Army to complete a contiguous front stretching from Antwerp to Switzerland. Morale was high and there was an air of optimism among the Allies that the Germans were close to defeat. The majestic Rhine soon became a symbol of victory to the advancing Allies, and units all along the front raced to be first to cross that grand river, enter Germany, and seize Eisenhower's primary goal: the Ruhr, industrial heartland of the Reich.

While the Allied commanders were preoccupied with being first across the Rhine, three factors were to influence their advance to the east: first, the delicate logistics line, especially fuel, which had been calculated to support a methodical advance but was now stretched dangerously thin because of the rapid dash on all fronts; second, the growing need to secure and open the re-supply port of Antwerp, still infested with die-hard German units along the 60-mile Schelde River estuary; and third, intense pressure from the War Department in Washington, mainly from chief of staff Gen. George C. Marshall and Air Force chief of staff Gen. Henry H. Arnold, to use the newly created First Allied Airborne Army made up of battle-tested troops, restlessly biding their time in England. By early September as the Allies approached the Rhine, 18 different airborne operations had already been planned and canceled, three of which had proceeded to the launch stage only to be aborted at the last moment.

Flushed with success, Montgomery was poised to send his army group through Holland on an end run, crossing the Rhine north of the Ruhr, but was faced with three major river barriers, the Maas, the Waal (the main downstream branch of the Rhine), and the Neder Rijn or lower Rhine, plus myriad smaller canals. Montgomery devised a plan for a massive airborne assault to breach the water barriers and a powerful armored thrust along the narrow corridor using the bridges seized by paratroopers. After crossing the lower Rhine at Arnhem, he would dash into Germany.

Eisenhower approved the twofold plan, called Market Garden. Operation Market would lay a carpet of three divisions of airborne troops along the 80-mile corridor from Eindhoven to Arnhem, deep in the enemy's rear. Operation Garden would consist of the British Second Army attacking across the Lek River, sending its XXXth Armoured Corps ahead and up the narrow 64-mile corridor to Arnhem, linking with the air-dropped parachute infantry on the way. The primary objective was to cross the Rhine. The follow-on objectives were to cut off troops of the German 15th Army remaining in Holland, outflank the German Siegfried Wall, and take up position for a subsequent drive south to the Ruhr.

On September 17 at 2:00 p.m. the three airborne divisions began their drop from the largest armada of troop-carrying aircraft ever to assemble for a single operation, while half an hour later the XXXth Armoured Corps attacked north toward Eindhoven. The U.S. 101st Airborne Division quickly captured three bridges north of Eindhoven, at Son, St. Oedenrode, and Veghet, while, after three days of vicious combat, the 82nd Airborne Division captured the key bridges at Grave, Waal, and Nijmegen. Gen. Urquhart's British First Airborne Division was dropped accurately on its drop zone four miles northwest of the Arnhem bridge with the mission of taking and holding the bridge until relieved by the advancing tanks of XXXth Corps. However, as luck would have it they landed practically on top of the Ninth Waffen SS Panzer Division, which, with the Tenth Waffen SS Panzer Division, was refitting north of Arnhem. British intelligence had been warned by the Dutch underground that there were tanks in the area, but they had ignored it because over the years they had grown to distrust Dutch underground reports. As a result, in the harsh fighting that followed, the British paratroopers were able to capture only the northern approach to the Arnhem bridge, and were then subjected to numerous devastating counterattacks.

German General Student's First Parachute Army and General Model at his headquarters in Oosterbeck, which was nearly overrun by the British, reacted quickly and immediately moved reinforcements against the British in Arnhem and the Americans at Nijmegen. By September 21 Lt. Col. John Frost's Second Battalion, First Parachute Brigade, holding the northern approach to the Arnhem bridge, was separated from the rest of its division, which was still fighting overwhelming odds northwest of the town, by a German counterattack. During the next week of fighting at the bridge Frost and his men, who had fought their way to the bridge in brutal house-to-house combat, took up positions covering the northern end of the Arnhem bridge and awaited the German counterattacks from the south over the bridge as well as from the exposed northern and eastern edges of the town. Although outgunned and outnumbered, and possessing few antitank weapons, the British paratroopers nestled in basements of the buildings surrounding the square overlooking the bridge and repelled repeated assaults across the bridge by German mechanized and armored units. The British sniper fire was so accurate it picked off the exposed drivers of the German vehicles as they wove their way across the bridge, which was littered with wrecked and burning hulks of half-tracks, armored cars, and tanks. The drivers were unable to navigate among the wrecked vehicles without exposing themselves; thus the sharp-shooting British held the bridgehead for more than a week. Although German artillery and tank fire from across the river methodically destroyed the buildings around the British, they continued fighting from the collapsed and burning houses surrounding the square. Unable to evacuate their wounded, the British fought on while Dutch citizens and members of the Dutch Resistance collected wounded and attempted to evacuate them to makeshift dressing-stations located in homes around the town.

Bad weather since the airdrop had severely curtailed Allied close air support and on the 21st, after suffering extremely heavy losses, the British paratroopers trapped north of Arnhem were forced to surrender, leaving Frost and his men virtually isolated at the bridge. The XXXth Corps was seriously behind schedule at the Lek River and unable to cross after having been attacked repeatedly as they fought to advance along the narrow causeway to relieve the 101st and then the 82nd Airborne Divisions.

Much of the First Polish Airbourne Brigade was decimated on September 20 when trying to reinforce the British by jumping almost on top of the Tenth Waffen SS Panzer Division southeast of Arnhem. The Polish paratroopers were shot out of the sky like birds, sustaining more than 75 percent casualties during the drop, which rendered the brigade nearly useless, and unable to fight their way to the south side of the Arnhem bridge to relieve Frost's weary and battered Red Devils. Frost's Second Battalion stubbornly held the Arnhem bridge approach against increasing odds and repeated counterattacks until September 25, when, after fighting for an incredible eight days, they were forced to retreat across the river.

Urquhart and Frost organized a stealthy and disciplined withdrawal reminiscent of the brilliant disengagement of Anzac forces from the Gallipoli beaches in 1916. Frost's men kept the enemy pinned down with sporadic but deadly accurate sniper fire and, gradually depleting their forces a handful at a time, sent them down to the river and into boats crossing to the south bank under the very guns of the Germans perched above the riverbanks. The British counted on the Germans to believe the increase in cross river traffic was reinforcing rather than withdrawing the men. Thus, during this daring maneuver, they succeeded in safely withdrawing more than 2,000 paratroopers across the Neder Rijn, leaving the town of Arnhem in German hands.

The two American airborne divisions continued to fight on until finally relieved by the advancing XXXth Armoured Corps on November 6. The continued poor weather, the slow advance of the British Second Army, and the inability to reinforce Arnhem adequately, coupled with the swift German reaction by well-trained, veteran troops, had doomed Market Garden.

The battle for the Arnhem bridge was certainly a gallant fight but it was also the final objective of the Allies' flawed Market Garden plan. Like the battles in Gallipoli in World War I, the stunning courage of those troops in the forefront tended to obscure the greater facts that both operations were extremely complex and called for the utmost in timing and coordination, and ultimately failed. Nevertheless, as John Frost wrote afterward, "The fundamental mistake of dropping airborne troops on the far side of a long water obstacle when you actually require them on both sides appears altogether obvious now. The whole idea of parachutists was that they should land behind the enemy and not be forced to cross rivers in the face of intense fire...." Thus the scourge of the Arnhem battle was the river obstacles, for it was they, in the long run, that had caused the delay of the main thrust of the British XXXth Armoured Corps.

"We would have made more headway, if we had used the civilians' local knowledge to a greater extent, and if we had taken more advantage of Dutch liaison officers attached to the division," wrote Gen. Urquhart. "I doubt however, in view of the opposition and the time taken by XXX Corps, whether anything less than the whole division, plus the Polish Brigade, would have been able to hold the bridge area until the arrival of the 2nd Army." It is ironic that after Market Garden, Dutch military officers commented that a plan to capture Arnhem had been a standard war-game problem given to young field-grade officers in their Army war college. The school recognized two options for capturing the objective: (1) to advance along the exposed high road causeways from the southeast, crossing the string of river obstacles, the last of which spanned the Neder Rijn at Arnhem, or (2) to approach on the flanks in maneuver actions, keeping vulnerable forces off the exposed high road. Dutch students choosing the first option automatically failed the exam!

The Allies suffered more casualties—17,000 killed, wounded, and missing—during the nine days of Market Garden than in the first 24 hours of the invasion of Normandy, when 10,000 to 12,000 were estimated lost. Gen. James Gavin, commander of the 82nd Airborne Division, said after the battle, "There is a quality of adversity that summons the noblest in British valor but so often obscures defeat that a heroic legend is remembered long after defeat is forgotten. Arnhem followed in that British tradition. Monty had been turned back short of his goal but so valorous was the defeat that the strategic rebuff passed unnoticed."

ISLANDS

The purpose of the three contributions to this chapter (the Great Siege of Malta in 1565; Crete, 1941; and Iwo Jima, 1945) is to illustrate some of the similarities and differences of military tactics when faced with the same problem: capturing what is essentially a sea-girt fortress. Of course, the history of war is itself a veritable archipelago of island battles, and a whole book could be devoted to the subject in its own right: from the Mycenaean conquest of Minoan Crete in circa 1450 B.C., to the British ouster of the Argentines on the Falklands in 1982 and the American invasion of Grenada in 1983. Some islands have been particular military focal points. Sicily alone could fill books, and has. The revolving door of invasions and occupations by Greeks, Romans, Carthaginians, Franks, Normans, Saracens, Spaniards, French, and, finally, British and Americans during World War II, makes the island seem as crowded with comings and goings as the concourse of Grand Central Station. The three island battles in this chapter include one that was successfully defended (Malta), and two that fell to attackers. Iwo Jima almost defines the Pacific island warfare of World War II: the murderous beach assault followed by the bloody winkling-out of a fanatically determined defender. Crete is a very different model. Here, for the first time, paratroopers literally circumvented the seaborne assault phase by using new technology and the tactical innovation it made possible. Ironically, as Will Fowler points out, the casualty cost of the airborne assault was so high that it put paid to any further use of paratroops by the Germans. Kurt Student, the father of the Fallschirmjäger, the Reich's paratroop arm, had great plans to use it to take Malta, among other places. But Hitler—strangely prone to paralyzing bouts of anxiety—thought it too risky, declaring, after Crete, that "...the day of the paratrooper is over"—words the U.S. 101st and 82nd Airborne Divisions would make him eat in Normandy in 1944.

Malta, published by the Palombis in 1565, reissued by Gaspare Alberti in 1566
This map, drawn in 1565, illustrates the final stage of the siege of Malta, resulting from the arrival of the Christian relief force from the west on September 6, 1565. The three ships to the southwest of the island bear crosses and are discharging firearms to celebrate the Turkish defeat.

Crusaders' Last Stand
The Great Siege of Malta, 1565

BRYAN PERRETT

The island of Malta, lying some 60 miles south of Sicily, measures only 17 miles by 8, lacks natural rivers, and is covered in shallow, rock-strewn soil in which vegetation is burned brown in the furnace heat of summer. It does, however, contain several excellent harbors that give the island enormous strategic significance. Any naval power possessing Malta has the capacity to interdict traffic between the eastern and western basins of the Mediterranean, attack the North African coast, or carry out raids on southern Europe. In 1565 it was to be the scene of one of the greatest sieges in history.

In 1530 the Order of the Knights of St. John of Jerusalem established itself on the north coast of the island, where the rocky peninsula of Mount Scibberas divided the harbor of Marsamuscetto, to the east, from what became known as Grand Harbour, to the west. At the tip of the peninsula the Knights built a star-shaped fortification with outworks, Fort St. Elmo, to protect the entrances of both harbors. Two parallel peninsulas, Birgu to the north and Senglea to the south, reached out into Grand Harbour from its western shore. Both contained towns, the sea and land approaches to which were fortified by the Knights, who also built the Castle of St. Angelo on the tip of Birgu and Fort St. Michael in Senglea. Between the two lay Dockyard Creek, where the Order's galleys were berthed. The only other major fortified position on the island was its ancient capital, Mdina, lying approximately in its center. None of these fortifications possessed the grandeur they would later present, but they were nonetheless formidable.

The Knights of St. John was among the most ancient of the crusading orders, having originally been founded to care for the health of pilgrims on their way to the Holy Land, for which reason its members were also known as Hospitallers. This mission was progressively extended to the protection of pilgrims between the coast and Jerusalem itself, and finally to a full military role, in which it acquired unparalleled expertise in the field of fortification. Like other military monastic orders, its hierarchy was led by a grand master and his immediate administrative officers, and consisted of knights, who became full brothers on taking their monastic vows, confrère knights who served for short periods, sergeants, men-at-arms, and auxiliaries. Internally, the order was divided into eight "Langues" (Tongues) reflecting the origins of its members from Auvergne, Aragon, England, France, Germany, Italy, Provence, and Spain.

When Acre, the last Crusader stronghold in Palestine, fell in 1291, the Knights of St. John moved first to Cyprus, then to the island of Rhodes, off the southern coast of Asia Minor. Here they became a sea power possessing a small but extremely efficient and highly motivated navy that harried Muslim shipping throughout the eastern Mediterranean. Naturally, the sultans of Egypt and the Ottoman Empire reacted violently. Rhodes was unsuccessfully besieged three times, but in 1522 Sultan Süleyman the Magnificent decided to rid himself of this menace on his own doorstep and invaded the island with a huge army. After a long and costly siege the point was reached at which the knights faced the stark choices of extermination or surrender. Süleyman, greatly impressed by their tenacious defense, permitted them to leave the island with the honors of war, which they did with a great and lasting sense of sadness. It was an act of generosity that Süleyman would come to bitterly regret. The Hospitallers remained without a permanent home until the Emperor Charles V offered them the Maltese archipelago, which suited their purpose admirably, for by now the entire Mediterranean had virtually become a Muslim lake in which corsairs from North Africa ravaged commercial traffic and even raided the Spanish and Italian mainlands.

No sooner had the knights settled into their new home than their galleys put to sea, disrupting Muslim commerce and successfully attacking corsairs and even the sultan's warships. The last straw for the aging Süleyman came in 1564, when the knights captured a large ship carrying an extremely valuable cargo belonging to members of his court. Regretting his earlier generosity to the order, he decided that its base on Malta must be destroyed forever, and dispatched a force in excess of 30,000 men, carried in over 200 ships. In joint command were an elderly general, Mustafa Pasha, who had performed badly during the 1522 siege of Rhodes and wanted his revenge, and a younger admiral, Piali Pasha. On May 18, 1565, the Turkish fleet dropped anchor in Marsaxlokk Bay, on Malta's west coast.

Commanding the island's garrison was Grand Master Jean Parisot de la Valette, another veteran of the last siege of Rhodes who, though now in his 70s, was still a vigorous leader. At his disposal were 540 of the order's knights and men-at-arms, 1,000 Spanish troops, and over 3,000 Maltese militia, supplemented by Maltese civilians who, though they might not care for their new masters, feared the Turks a great deal more. These he divided between Fort St. Elmo, Birgu, Senglea, and Mdina. La Valette had already sent an urgent request for reinforcements to Philip II of Spain, but for the moment he was on his own. The problem was that the crusading ideal had faded with the passing of time, and the order itself had suffered because of the Reformation; the Langue of England, for example, was now represented by a single knight, Sir Oliver Starkey, although he would be joined by two more countrymen as the siege progressed.

The siege began with a dispute between Mustafa and Piali. The latter wanted to anchor his ships in Marsamuscetto harbor, which was less open to the weather than Marsaxlokk, whereas Mustafa would have preferred to direct his efforts at Birgu and Senglea. In the end he gave way and was forced to embark on the capture of Fort St. Elmo. The fort proved to be an incredibly tough nut to crack. Because of the rocky nature of Mount Scibberas, soil for gun positions and trenches had to be carried from the Turkish camp at La Marsa, at the head of Grand Harbour. Even when the guns were in position and subjecting the walls to constant battering, every assault was thrown back with fearful loss. After each assault the garrison worked feverishly to repair breaches in the defenses.

Every night la Valette sent boats across Grand Harbour with reinforcements and brought out the wounded. At one point the grand master received a delegation of the garrison's senior knights who told him that the position was no longer defensible. He agreed, but knowing that the longer St. Elmo held out the greater would be the chance of relief from mainland Europe, he shamed them into returning by offering to defend the fort personally. However, the arrival of the noted corsair Dragut (much more than a mere pirate, he was an experienced commander, had the confidence of Süleyman, and exercised effective overall command on his arrival) put fresh heart into the besiegers. He introduced Turkish boats into Grand Harbour, thus severing the fort's lifeline, and sited fresh batteries so that St. Elmo was under continuous fire from many directions. Apart from the defenders' own fire, two heavy guns on the highest point of St. Angelo harassed the Turks by firing across the harbor, killing Mustafa's master gunner and the commander of the elite Janissaries as well as mortally wounding Dragut. Finally, June 23, St. Elmo, now little more than a ruin, was subjected to a heavy bombardment by land and sea before being assaulted yet again by the best troops in Mustafa's army. By now, only 100 men were left alive in the fort, almost all of them wounded, and their crippled commanders, Colonel Eguaras and Captain Miranda, had themselves carried to the breach in chairs so that they could meet the attackers. The garrison of St. Elmo died fighting, its last act being to light the beacon that would tell la Vallette the fort had fallen.

It had taken Mustafa almost five weeks and no fewer than 8,000 casualties to capture a small fort that should have been overwhelmed in days. As he stared from the ruins across Grand Harbour to the towering Castle of St. Angelo he is said to have remarked, "Allah, if this small son cost so much, what do we pay for his father?" He then had the bodies of the knights beheaded, nailed to wooded crosses, and thrown into the sea. When four drifted onto the opposite shore, la Valette's response was predictable: if Mustafa wished to play the game that way, so be it. All the Turkish prisoners were decapitated and their heads were fired into the enemy camp. No wars are as cruel as those of religion.

During the misty night of July 3, while the Turks were hauling their siege train round Grand Harbour to bombard Birgu and Senglea, 700 reinforcements led by 42 knights entered the defenses, having been guided from their landing place along little-known tracks by Maltese peasants. At this point Mustafa offered the same generous terms that his master had offered at Rhodes, only to have them contemptuously rejected. Several Turkish galleys were dragged over Mount Sciberras into Grand Harbour and fire was opened on the two peninsulas from every direction.

On July 15 a combined land and sea assault was launched against Senglea. Having foreseen the latter, la Valette had constructed an underwater palisade of stakes beyond the point at which the enemy could disembark. As the crews of the impaled boats tried to fight their way through the obstacle, not only were they raked by arquebus fire but the survivors were intercepted by Maltese swimmers armed with knives, who quickly dispatched them. Simultaneously, a diversionary attack by janissaries in ten large boats unexpectedly came under fire from a concealed battery at the base of St. Angelo, nine of the boats being sunk. A land attack was also repulsed.

It was now high summer and the Turkish Army became ravaged by dysentery and cholera. Preceded by a long and heavy bombardment that could be heard as far away as Sicily, a major assault was mounted on Birgu and Senglea on August 2. It failed, with serious loss. On August 7 the Turks stormed through a breach in the walls of Birgu only to find that a new wall had been constructed beyond. After being shot down in their hundreds by crossfire, they fled. Simultaneously, at Senglea, they had come within an ace of capturing Fort St. Michael. La Valette himself, running to join the fighting after hastily donning a helmet, believed that the fort was lost, but suddenly the enemy's trumpeters sounded the recall. At first Mustafa thought that a relief force had landed behind him, but the reality was that a small force of cavalry in Mdina, anxious to help their comrades, had fallen on the Turkish camp at La Marsa, killed everyone within it, and burned the tents.

Thus it went on for the rest of August, with continuous bombardment punctuated by suicidal assaults, sometimes after the explosion of a mine beneath the defenses. The collapsing, gap-toothed walls were manned by a declining number of defenders, despite the hospital being combed for every man who could still walk. At one point la Valette pointedly rejected a suggestion by his council that the survivors should be concentrated in St. Angelo, arguing that he would never desert the brave Maltese who had played so notable a part in the defense.

On September 6 the Christian relief force, numbering only 8,000 men, landed at Mellieha Bay in the northeast corner of the island. Mustafa, doubting whether he could obtain sufficient supplies to prosecute the siege throughout the winter, and Piali, anxious for the safety of his ships in the autumn gales, decided to withdraw rather than incur further loss. Wisely, they sent a fast galley ahead to warn the sultan of their defeat, and so saved their heads. Süleyman raged that he would personally return to Malta the following year and slaughter every inhabitant, but died before he could realize his ambition. Of those who had originally set out to conquer Malta, only 10,000 returned home.

As for la Valette's garrison, only 600 fighting men remained on their feet to greet the relief force. Two hundred fifty of the knights had died, together with 2,500 soldiers and 7,000 Maltese men, women, and children. La Valette received every honor possible and was to live almost three years more, long enough to see the foundations of the city that would bear his name being laid on Mount Sciberras.

The siege emphasized the vital strategic position of Malta and its fine harbors. If Süleyman had taken Malta, southern Europe would instantly have become vulnerable to further Ottoman expansion. Even the Protestant Queen Elizabeth I of England gave instructions for prayers to be said for the success of the defense. The Turkish defeat at Malta had removed the immediate threat to the western basin of the Mediterranean, and six years later Don John of Austria was to emphatically end Ottoman maritime supremacy in the Mediterranean at the Battle of Lepanto.

Out of the Blue
Crete, Greece, 1941

WILL FOWLER

Crete is the largest island in Greece and separates the Aegean from the Libyan Sea and so marks the Mediterranean boundary between Europe and Africa. The island is 173 miles long and between 5 and 30 miles wide. There is a coastal plain to the north with the Levka, Psiloritis, and Dikti Mountains in the center that drop steeply away on the south coast. Plateaus are split by deep gorges and end up in fertile valleys. The scenery can be harsh and barren, yet in other areas wooded and gentle.

At the western end of the island is the large natural harbor of Suda Bay, to the east the old capital Canea with its port. In the west it is covered with lush evergreens, while at the east it is more arid and even hosts palm groves at Vai. Roughly in the center is the port of Retimo with the commercial capital Herakleion to the east. In 1941 they were linked by rough unsurfaced roads. To the west of Canea at the mouth of the River Tavronitis at Maleme is a level area where an airstrip had been constructed.

In May 1941 Crete was held by 28,000 British, Australian, and New Zealand troops. Greek battalions and Cretan irregulars contributed to a total strength of 42,500. Although the Allied forces under Maj. Gen. Bernard Freyberg VC were very poorly equipped, Freyberg had a unique asset in ULTRA and so had a complete breakdown of the German plans for an airborne attack. Nevertheless, Freyberg was curiously complacent about this threat. On May

Map of Crete created by the OSS (Office of Strategic Services)

This image of Crete was produced in the Office of Strategic Services, America's first intelligence agency, in 1943. Operation Mercury, the German mission to capture Crete, divided the island into four "drop zones" running from east to west to better organize its air campaign.

CRETE

5 he reported to Churchill: "Cannot understand nervousness; am not in the least anxious about airborne attack." Churchill was not as sanguine, urging that more tanks be sent to beef up the mere half dozen that were there.

Freyberg knew where the proposed German drop zones (DZs) were to be located but was under orders not to compromise his ULTRA intelligence by exactly second-guessing the German moves, and so as a cover also positioned troops on the coast. He was aware that seaborne reinforcements were part of the German plan, but though concerned to reinforce the Maleme area, he was overruled.

For Operation Mercury—*Unternehmen Merkur,* the capture of Crete—the Germans committed 13,000 paratroops of the Seventh Air Division under *Generallieutenant* Kurt Student and 9,000 men of the Fifth *Gebirgsjäger* (Mountain) Division under *Generalmajor* Julius Ringel, with *Generaloberst* Alexander Lohr in overall command. They were supported by 500 fighters and bombers, 500 transports, and 80 gliders. The first air attacks on the island began on May 15. In light of the Luftwaffe's overwhelming superiority, four days later Freyberg ordered the remaining RAF aircraft to fly to Egypt. He assured the Theater HQ in Cairo that the airfields on the island would then be rendered unusable.

Mercury divided the island into four DZs, from west to east: Maleme, Canea, Retimo, and Herakleion. For lack of sufficient transport aircraft the island was attacked in two waves in the morning and the afternoon of May 20. Some 500 tough, reliable Ju-52 transport aircraft were available in the XI Air Corps commanded by *Generalmajor* Conrad. The Corps consisted of *Geschwader* 1, 2, and 3 making up ten transport groups. They would fly from airfields at Tanagra, Topolis, Dadion, Megara, Corinth, Phaleron and Elevsis. The first wave, Group West under *Generalmajor* Eugen Meindl, would land in the Maleme/Canea zone, spearheaded by troops carried in DFS230 gliders who would land to the west of Maleme airfield and around Suda Bay to neutralize any AA guns that had survived the air attacks. This would prepare the way for the paratroops. In the afternoon Group Center under *Generalmajor* Wilhelm Süssmann would land at Retimo and Canea/Suda and Group East under Ringel would seize the airfield at Herakleion. This would allow the bulk of the Fifth *Gebirgsjäger* Division to be flown in by Ju-52s.

Just before 6:00 a.m. on May 20, the day of *Unternehmen Merkur*, the daily Luftwaffe air attacks, known to the soldiers on the island as the "Morning Hate," reached a crescendo when they concentrated on the AA gun sites as well as any identified infantry positions. At Maleme all but one of the AA guns was silenced. "This went on firing for some time," recalled a survivor, "till a host of Stukas and Me-109s fastened on it and shot and blasted it out of existence."

Bad luck dogged the German airborne operations from the outset of the attack. The glider carrying Süssmann crashed on an island off the Greek mainland and Meindl was critically wounded shortly after landing. The Germans had also underestimated the physical difficulties of fighting in Crete and the size and determination of the garrison. The olive groves provided excellent camouflage for the defenders and the terraced hillsides reduced much of the effect of bombing. The German airborne attack philosophy was to jump directly onto the objective—even though this ran the risk of incurring heavy casualties. In fact, Gen. Student, commander in chief of the German operation, remembered that "much of the loss was due to bad landings—there were few suitable spots in Crete, and the prevailing wind blew from the interior toward the sea. For fear of dropping the troops in the sea, the pilots tended to drop them too far inland—some of them actually in the British lines. The weapon-containers often fell wide of the troops, which was another handicap that contributed to our excessive casualties." When they jumped the men were lightly armed and had to collect heavier weapons from containers that were parachuted with them. But in the short time that men were in the air on their parachutes they were easy targets for riflemen below. On the ground the British and Anzac troops quickly established that the most effective technique was to aim at the paratrooper's feet as he descended. One defender described it as being "like the opening of the duck shooting season in New Zealand." The gliders came in so low and slow that the defenders could fire right into them, killing many of the occupants before they had even hit the ground. Even those that landed with the soldiers alive hit rocky, terraced terrain and broke up, killing or injuring the occupants.

In the afternoon the second wave flew into disaster. In just one hour a force of 1,500 *Fallschirmjäger* was reduced to 1,000 men in small scattered groups being hunted and trapped. At Retimo Group Center in the second wave was trapped in an olive factory besieged by the British and Australian forces. Dust now shrouded the airfields in Greece, and in the chaos the Luftwaffe released aircraft that arrived at Herakleion in relays that offered easy targets for the well-camouflaged defenders.

On the morning of May 21 Piper Macpherson of the Black Watch climbed out of his slit trench at Herakleion and sounded reveille—the British and Anzac troops with their Greek allies were confident, almost cocky. By the end of the day 40 percent of Student's assault force was either dead, wounded, or taken prisoner. "Today has been a hard one," Freyberg cabled Wavell in Egypt. "We have been hard pressed. So far, I believe, we hold aerodromes at Herakleion and Maleme.... Margin by which we hold them is a bare one, and it would be wrong of me to paint an optimistic picture. Fighting has been heavy and we have killed large numbers of Germans. Communications are most difficult." Only at the western end of Maleme airfield did the paratroops manage to find cover and set up a viable base in the dried-up riverbed of the Tavronitis.

The key feature that dominated the airfield was the 350-foot-high Kavza-kia Hill, known on plans as Point 107. It was held by the New Zealand 22nd Battalion commanded by Lt. Col. Les Andrew. Under heavy air attack and enemy probes he sent runners to his commanding officer, Brig. James Hargest, requesting assistance. Hargest promised a counterattack against the Germans in the Tavronitis but his men were pinned down by air attacks. Andrew attempted an attack with a tiny force of 40 men and two Matilda tanks—it failed, only 3 men returning unwounded. A brave and experienced soldier, Andrew (who had won the Victoria Cross in World War I) was under intense pressure and without reliable communications. His battalion appeared to be in danger of being cut off, so Andrew pulled back A Company on Point 107 and this gave the Germans their opening.

With an airfield in their possession, albeit under spasmodic artillery fire, the Germans poured in reinforcements. On that first day aircraft landed 650 Mountain Troops, as well as 550 more paratroops. The Germans now prepared to "roll up" the island, pushing eastward from their secure base at Maleme.

In Athens, Student took the tough but tactically sound decision to abandon the operations at Retimo and Herakleion. On May 20, 1,500 and 2,000 men had been committed to these locations, a day later only 120 men landed at Herakleion, while at the Maleme/Galatas/Suda Bay area 1,880 were parachuted in. On May 22 this figure jumped to 1,950, and on the 23rd the Luftwaffe landed 3,650 men. On May 25 a haggard Student landed at Maleme; the airfield was littered with smashed Ju-52s.

On May 22 Freyberg decided that he would have to pull his forces back on Suda to secure the naval base. In five days of hard fighting the paratroops had reached the outskirts of Canea and Freyberg had to face the fact that the battle of Crete was lost. He signaled Cairo: "From a military point of view our position is hopeless," and on May 27 London gave permission to withdraw. He organized an evacuation initially from the better appointed port of Herakleion on the north coast, but was eventually forced to use the tiny south coast port of Sphakia. To cover these operations two commandos commanded by Brig. Robert Laycock and designated Layforce were landed at Suda Bay on the nights of May 23-24 and 26-27.

"The Navy has never let the Army down," signaled Adm. Sir Andrew Cunningham. "No enemy forces must reach Crete by sea." On the night of May 21-22 a Royal Navy force commanded by Rear Adm. Irvine Glennie, acting on ULTRA intelligence, intercepted a convoy of 25 commandeered caiques (Greek fishing boats) escorted by the Italian destroyer *Lupo*. The Royal Navy sank several caiques and turned others back. They were carrying elements of the Fifth *Gebirgsjäger* Division.

These attacks came at a cost; on May 21 the Royal Navy had suffered its first casualties when at dawn German aircraft sank the destroyer HMS *Juno* and damaged the cruiser HMS *Ajax*. A day later they mounted as the cruisers HMS *Gloucester* and *Fiji* sank along with the destroyer HMS *Greyhound*. *Gloucester* and *Greyhound* had been patrolling the Kithira Channel to the northwest of the island on the lookout for troop convoys. On May 23 the destroyers HMS *Kelly* and *Kashmir* were lost, the former captained by Lord Mountbatten. On May 29 the destroyers HMS *Imperial* and *Hereward* were sunk off the north coast.

For the men making the fighting withdrawal to the south coast it was a grim slog across the mountain spine of the Levka (White) Mountains to Sphakia. The men at Retimo never received the order to withdraw, and when German forces finally arrived in the area they found that 500 paratroops were virtual prisoners in the olive oil factory surrounded by 1,500 Australian and Greek troops. In the olive groves and fields lay the bodies of over 700 *Fallschirmjäger*.

At Retimo and Herakleion Australian and British forces had quickly learned how to confuse the Luftwaffe transports and bombers. They laid out captured swastika flags on their positions, stopped shooting when aircraft appeared, and when the Germans fired green recognition flares, fired similar signals. On a number of occasions laying out captured recognition panels produced the prompt delivery of weapons, ammunition, rations, and medical stores. The evacuation of the garrison by the Royal Navy had been costly, but when it ended on June 1 16,500 men had been saved. Cunningham was an inspirational leader for his crews: "It takes the Navy three years to build a ship. It would take 300 years to rebuild a tradition." The Royal Navy lost well over 2,000 dead in the operations around Crete. The British and Commonwealth losses were 1,742 killed and missing and 2,225 wounded, with 11,370 captured. The Germans reported taking 5,255 Greek prisoners, but casualties are hard to determine. German casualties were around 4,000 killed and missing, and about 2,600 wounded.

Shocked by the casualties, Hitler declared to Student that "the day of the paratrooper is over. The parachute arm is a surprise weapon and without the element of surprise there can be no future for airborne forces." And with these words he condemned this superb force to a ground role.

U.S. Army target map, Iwo Jima, 1945

Because of the island's strategic location, after the U.S. captured Iwo Jima, the bombing campaign against Japan became much more successful since American bombers were no longer routinely intercepted on their way to Tokyo. Use of the island's airstrips also allowed U.S. fighters to accompany B-29s to Tokyo and back, and provided emergency landings for returning fighters damaged in battle.

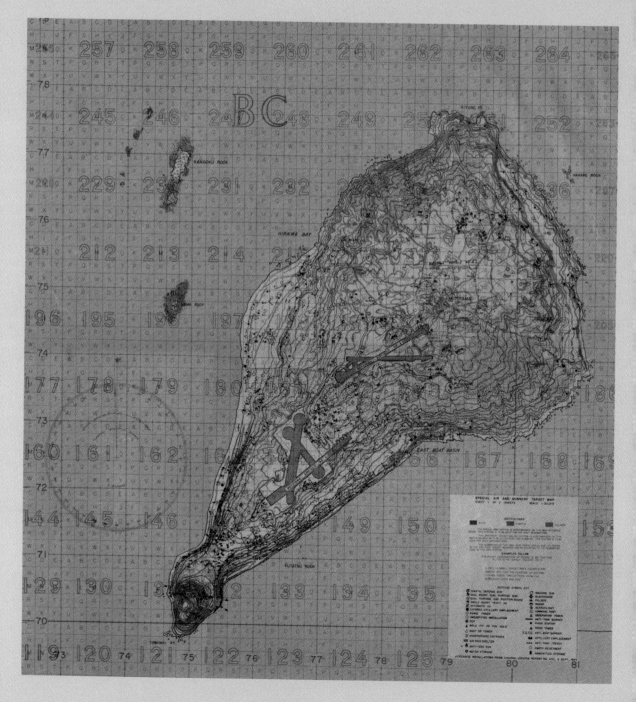

Sulfur Island
Iwo Jima, 1945

COLONEL JOSEPH H. ALEXANDER, USMC (RET.)

As 1945 began, the United States intensified its advance toward Japan, attacking along parallel axes across the Central Pacific and through the Philippines. In February the tides of war reached Iwo Jima, a small, barren rock in the Volcano Islands, located within fighter range of Tokyo. Iwo Jima lay halfway between Tokyo and the U.S. B-29 bomber bases in the Marianas. The island's radar site and airfields represented a major thorn in the side of the American strategic bombing campaign because it provided Tokyo with a two-hour warning of approaching B-29 formations, enabling Iwo Jima-based fighters to intercept the giant bombers along their flight path. In addition, crippled B-29s, shot up over Tokyo, lacked an emergency landing field along the 1,200-mile return flight to the Marianas.

Both sides realized Iwo Jima's strategic importance. "The enemy will surely invade this Iwo Jima," predicted Lt. Gen. Tadamichi Kuribayashi, the redoubtable commander of the island's garrison, upon his arrival the previous summer.

Kuribayashi knew that without the Japanese fleet (essentially destroyed in the Battle of Leyte Gulf the previous autumn), the best he could hope for would be to delay the enemy advance by a few months. He came to regard Iwo Jima as more of a strategic liability for the Japanese than an asset. With its inevitable loss, the Americans would gain airfields from which to launch fighters to escort the B-29s to Tokyo and back, thereby increasing the destruction the bombers could inflict on the homeland. At one point Kuribayashi even considered the feasibility of blowing the island in two, thereby depriving the enemy of any future use of the airstrips. When this proved impractical, Kuribayashi set about ensuring his 22,000-man garrison would sell their lives so dearly that it might deter American plans to invade the home islands.

Wresting Iwo Jima from Gen. Kuribayashi's garrison became the mission of the V Amphibious Corps, whose Third, Fourth, and Fifth Marine Divisions would comprise a landing force of more than 70,000 troops, the largest single battle the Marines would fight in the Pacific War. Other services augmented the Marines, including Navy Sea Bees and underwater demolition teams; Army antiaircraft, medical, and occupation units; and U.S. Army Air Force fighter squadrons.

The first enemy the V Amphibious Corps had to overcome on Iwo Jima proved to be the island itself, eight square miles of moonscape, one of the most bizarre combination of topography and hydrography the Americans ever invaded, all compounded by the defensive positions excavated by Kuribayashi's troops. "Iwo Jima was an island ideally constructed by nature for defense," observed *New York Times* military correspondent Hanson W. Baldwin during the battle, "and the Japanese had cunningly contrived and fashioned it…into an underground labyrinth, possibly the most heavily defended spot per acre of ground in the world."

Seizing Iwo Jima would cost the Marines about 700 killed in action for every square mile assailed. Indeed, Iwo Jima would become the only battle of the Pacific War in which the attackers suffered higher casualties than did the defenders. Here, as at Peleliu, the island's distinctive geography favored the defense.

Mount Suribachi, a 556-foot dormant volcano, dominated the southern half of the island, including the landing beaches that stretched for 3,500 yards along the southeastern coastline. The rough ground rose steadily from the volcano's northern base in a series of steppes, which contained the island's airfields. Hilly outcroppings and jagged ridges dominated the approaches to the central highlands. In the far north the terrain deteriorated into twisting gorges and narrow canyons. Within this lunar landscape Gen. Kuribayashi's mining engineers and labor troops built more than 11 miles of tunnels, elaborate command and observation posts, and recessed firing positions for hundreds of pieces of heavy artillery. Suribachi itself contained a complex network of caves and tunnels, the subterranean home for 2,000 Japanese defenders.

Iwo Jima's peculiar geography would impede the Marines' landing operations and their ability to maneuver once ashore. Although the island lacked the barrier reefs that had characterized earlier landings in the Central Pacific, its unprotected beaches were steep and sharply terraced, subject to pounding surf. A coarse, black volcanic sand covered Iwo Jima's beaches, terraces, and steppes, the thick granules hobbling the infantry and proving impassable to wheeled vehicles. "It was like trying to run in a vat of coffee grounds," said Cpl. Edward Hartman, a rifleman in the 24th Marines.

Moreover, the island reeked with the rotten-egg smell of sulfur fumes, the ghostly, yellow-brown mist rising from hidden cracks in the twisted rocks. Iwo Jima's name means "Sulfur Island," yet more than a few disenchanted Marines compared it to Dante's Inferno. Not even the Japanese favored the place, with one Imperial Army officer describing Iwo Jima as "an island of sulfur, no water, no sparrow, and no swallow."

The V Amphibious Corps' mission at Iwo Jima was twofold: to enhance the strategic bombing campaign and facilitate the invasion of Japan. In mid-February the U.S. Fifth Fleet escorted a 500-ship invasion armada to the Volcano Islands. The assault force surrounded Iwo Jima like a gray steel blanket, cutting off the island from resupply or reinforcements and opening a methodical bombardment with ships' guns and carrier-launched dive bombers.

D Day was February 19, 1945, and as the gunships fired their final barrages, scores of troop transports and other amphibious ships advanced closer to the island, preparing to "land the landing force" in accordance with a detailed choreography of preliminary events.

Perhaps the best contemporary description of Iwo Jima as it appeared on the morning of D Day came from the journal of Lt. David H. Susskind, USNR, a 24-year-old New Yorker assigned to the troop transport U.S. *Mellette* (APA 146): "Gradually, out of fast-fading darkness we saw the outlines of the island....The southern end of Iwo was dominated by a sharp mountain—this must be Suribachi, we thought—and the rest of its 2 by 5 mile area was a mass of steep, vertical cliffs rising sharply to a plateau that we could barely discern....Approaching the island from the sea it appears to be no more than a great rock, a freak land formation, too small and ragged to be of any value, not fit for human habitation....Only a geologist could look at it and not be repelled."

The morning of D Day dawned remarkably clear, revealing the massive assault waves of the Fourth and Fifth Marine Divisions approaching the dark island under fire, a spectacle observed by tens of thousands of men on both sides. Naval gunfire and carrier-based aircraft delivered a crescendo of shells and bombs along the surrounding heights as hundreds of tracked amphibian vehicles lurched up the steep beaches. Lt. Col. Justice M. Chambers, USMC, commanding the First Battalion, 25th Marines, observed as he approached the extreme right flank of the landing beaches, "That whole island seemed to be on fire."

Akin to the Normandy landings the previous summer, Iwo Jima represented the pinnacle of amphibious assault against a fortified coastline in the Pacific War, a summation of the lessons learned and technological advances of the preceding four years. Within a matter of minutes the Marines had 8,000 men ashore, closely followed by the first of their tanks and artillery support. An Imperial Navy officer, captured in the subsequent assault on Mount Suribachi, wrote in his journal on D Day, "At nine o'clock in the morning several hundred landing craft with amphibious tanks in the lead rushed ashore like an enormous tidal wave."

Then the wind and surf picked up, wrecking hundreds of small craft and vehicles along the steep beaches. At this point, as momentum slowed and the troops concentrated among the open terraces below the first airfield, Gen. Kuribayashi ordered his gunners to open fire from their hidden positions in the central highlands. Artillery, mortars, rockets, and antiaircraft guns raked the Marines below. Most of the 2,400 American casualties sustained on D Day occurred during this sustained fire.

Michael F. Keleher, a Navy surgeon with the 25th Marines, landed the afternoon of D Day and reported being appalled by "such a sight on that beach!

Wrecked boats, bogged-down jeeps, tractors and tanks; burning vehicles; casualties scattered all over."

The ranks of the two assault divisions contained many veterans, including some making their fourth major landing under fire. These men steadied the rookies, slogged forward through the soft sand, seized the first airfield, and cut the island in two. By dusk there were 30,000 Marines ashore. Already they outnumbered the Japanese garrison.

The battle for Iwo Jima raged relentlessly for 36 days. On the fourth day the 28th Marines reached the top of Mount Suribachi and raised a small flag. "Hot damn—our flag's up!" exclaimed Navy Lt. David Conroy over the fleet radio net as he flew his fighter over the summit at that dramatic moment. Other Marines replaced the original flag with a larger one several hours later, and this was the epic scene captured by AP photographer Joe Rosenthal, whose hurried snapshot won the Pulitzer Prize and became an icon for American teamwork in World War II.

A less dramatic but equally significant turning point occurred on March 4, the 13th day of the battle. The Marines now had all three divisions ashore, attacking northward into the heart of Kuribayashi's defenses in the jumbled highlands above the second airfield. The Marines had already suffered 13,000 casualties, and few of the survivors had ever seen a live Japanese. "The Japanese were not on Iwo Jima," said former Lt. Thomas M. Fields of the 26th Marines, "they were in it." Indeed, the battlefield gave the impression of a single army of Americans, struggling ever northward through the cluttered rock formations against an invisible army of Japanese buried beneath the island's surface.

At that moment, both sides paused to watch with fascination as a crippled B-29 bomber nicknamed "Dinah Mite" swooped low over the island to attempt an emergency landing. The captured field was not yet ready to receive bombers, and the entire strip was under direct enemy fire, but the pilot had no viable alternatives. The big plane shuddered to a halt at the far edge of the runway, and after some frantic tinkering it was able to take off for its home base at Tinian. The Marines cheered. This is what they were fighting for. Their sacrifices were already enhancing the strategic bombing campaign. The Marines' early capture of the island's airfields and radar sites also produced instant improvement in the accuracy and safety of the bomber raids against Honshu.

Gen. Kuribayashi on the same date abandoned his fortified command post in the central highlands for a crude cave in the northernmost gorges. The fighting in these badlands dragged on another three weeks. Here the convoluted terrain proved almost unassailable. The exhausted Marines discovered that "there were too many holes. They would attack one only to be shot at from another one half a dozen feet away....By the time the Marines got close enough to that hole, the Japs had left it and were shooting from another one twenty yards away and higher up in the wall."

Clearing out the last pockets of resistance in "Bloody Gorge" befell the Fifth Marine Division, whose ranks would sustain the lion's share of casualties in the fighting on Iwo Jima. These troops applied tank-mounted flamethrowers, armored bulldozers, demolition charges, and cold steel to root out the Japanese diehards.

General Kuribayashi died with the remnants of his men in a final counterattack the night of March 23-24, and the incessant gunfire fell silent. Very few of the 22,000 Japanese garrison surrendered. The V Amphibious Corps sustained 24,053 combat casualties in seizing the small island. Fleet Adm. Chester W. Nimitz had already provided an enduring benediction for the fallen, proclaiming, "Among the Americans who fought at Iwo Jima, uncommon valor was a common virtue."

Most survivors considered Iwo Jima worth the price. The effectiveness of the strategic bombing campaign against Japan improved exponentially. The capture of the island saved as many lives as the casualties it cost: More than 2,250 B-29s were able to make emergency landings before the war ended, thereby saving the lives of more than 24,000 airmen. Meanwhile, the invasion of Okinawa began a week after Iwo Jima ended. The Americans would soon be in position to execute the largest amphibious landings in world history—the assaults on southern Kyushu scheduled for November 1, 1945—before the atomic bombs rendered them unnecessary.

WOODS AND FOREST

"Scarce an officer or soldier can say they even saw at one time six of the Enemy and the greatest part never saw a single man." So wrote one of the ambush victims of the woodland engagement near the Monongahela River on July 9, 1755. A force of British regulars and American colonial troops (including the young George Washington) under British Maj. Gen. Edward Braddock were on their way to attack Fort Duquesne (now Pittsburgh) during the French and Indian Wars. As the column marched through the woods they were attacked on their flanks by 70 French regulars, a few Canadian irregulars, and 650 Indian allies. It was a classic guerrilla ambush, and within minutes Braddock's force was cut to pieces, hightailing it back through the woods as fast as they could run. Braddock and many of his men paid the ultimate price, but the British had learned a valuable lesson. Light infantry were created with specific skills in woodland warfare, the most famous being Rogers' Rangers, the forerunners of today's special forces. They discarded the red tunic for green-and-brown outfits that blended with their surroundings and they applied woodland skills: If the terrain is your foe, then make it your friend. The three battles in this chapter all illustrate the way in which heavily wooded terrain dissolves the fixed architecture of conventional military maneuver. Roman gen. Varus in the Teutoberg Forest, like Braddock, could not deal with the hit-and-run tactics of his hidden enemy. It was only when the columns of the legions had been chewed ragged that German tribesmen moved in en masse for the kill. Union General Hooker at Chancellorsville also saw his numerical superiority dissolve in the dismal uncertainties of the Wilderness. "This is no place to stop," declared Union Maj. Gen. George Meade. "We ought to get into the open country beyond." He was right. Belleau Wood presented a different military problem. Here the woods had been turned into a camouflaged fortification, hiding machine-gun nests, and dug-in artillery, which the Marines attacked in regular line-abreast order, to be mown down in swaths. Woods and forests may be delightful picnic grounds in peacetime, but in war they are full of the nastiest surprises.

Teutoburg Forest, from *Die Schlacht im Teutoburger Walde,* **Albert Wilms, 1899**
The treacherous and unpredictable terrain of the Teutoburger Wald, a forested ridge extending from the central German Plateau, posed obstacles for Varus and his Roman troops. German leader Aminius lured the invaders into the punishing territory, giving the Germans the
upper hand and allowing them to surround the Roman column.

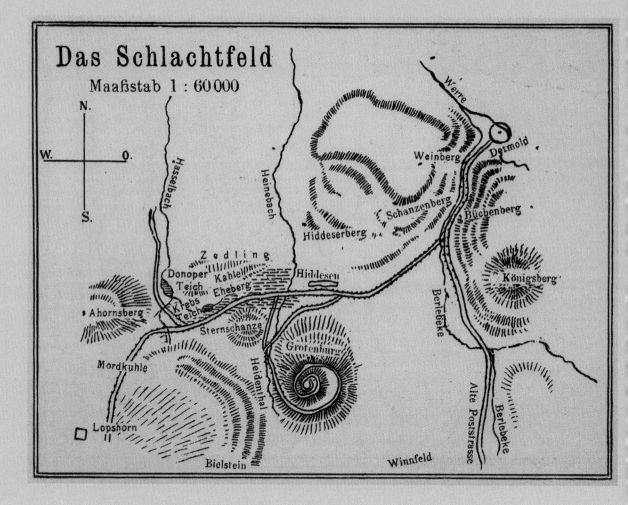

The Massacre of the Legions
Teutoburg Forest, Germany, A.D. 9

BRYAN PERRETT

At the beginning of the first century A.D. much of the North German Plain was covered by forest and marshland. Through this flowed the Rivers Rhine, Lippe, Ems, Weser, and Elbe in their northward course to the North Sea. The tribes inhabiting the area lived in villages around which land had been cleared to provide for their basic agricultural needs, their diet being supplemented by hunting and fishing. From the central German plateau several low ridges reach like fingers northward into the plain in the area between modern Bielefeld and Hannover. Of these, the most westerly is named the Teutoburger Wald. Here, in A.D. 9, the Roman Army sustained one of the most disastrous defeats in its entire history, a defeat that was to affect the course of European history.

The precise site of the battle remains uncertain. In his book *The Fifteen Decisive Battles of the World*, Sir Edward Creasy quotes his contemporary, the German scholar Dr. Plate, who describes an area near Detmold, just to the east of the Teutoburger Wald, as being "a table-land intersected by numerous deep and narrow valleys, which in some places form small plains, surrounded by steep hillsides and rocks, and only accessible by narrow defiles. All the valleys are traversed by narrow streams, shallow in the dry season but subject to sudden swellings in the autumn and winter. The vast forests which cover the summits and slopes of the hills consist chiefly of oak; there is little underbrush and both men and horses could move with ease in the forests if the

ground were not broken by gullies or rendered impracticable by fallen trees."
Dr. Plate goes on to say that a number of place names in the same area, handed
down from one generation to the next, indicate that a great victory followed
by a massacre took place there. The probability is that this was the final act
of struggle lasting days and fought out over several miles of country.

In the years shortly before the birth of Christ, Caesar Augustus decided
that the northern frontier of the Roman Empire should be extended from the
Rhine to the Elbe. By A.D. 5 the emperor's adopted son, Tiberius, had overcome local opposition and imposed the Roman will on the new province. The
following year he was sent to put down a rebellion in Pannonia and was
replaced by a man of very different character, Publius Quintilius Varus, who
had married into the imperial family. Varus, described as mild, mentally slow,
lazy, and self-indulgent, had previously served as governor of Syria, where the
soft living had suited him. His appointment sowed the seeds of disaster and
weakened the operational efficiency of the Roman troops serving in Germany.

Rome ruled its conquered peoples harshly, taxing heavily but paying little or no respect to local laws and customs. A minority of Germans welcomed
the arrival of the Roman way of life, but most of the population detested it.
Prominent among them was Arminius, a young nobleman who had seen active
service with an auxiliary unit of the Roman Army, the strength and weaknesses
of which he had observed firsthand. His hatred of Rome was inflamed even
further when his pro-Roman uncle, Segestes, refused him his daughter's hand
in marriage, a difficulty he solved by carrying off the lady.

In A.D. 9 the garrison of Germany consisted of five legions. The summer
found Varus with three of them, XVII, XVIII, and XIX, a total of approximately
20,000 soldiers, in the area of present-day Minden, where their presence was
intended to overawe the local population. Contrary to their normally strict operational practice, the legions were accompanied by some 10,000 camp followers and a huge train of baggage wagons. Arminius despised Varus, whom he
correctly evaluated as being more of a politician than a soldier, and sensed
that the time was ripe for a general rising of the tribes, which he organized with
great efficiency, keeping the time a closely guarded secret. Word of the plot
reached Segestes, who warned Varus. The latter, however, simply regarded the

accusation as being an extension of the family feud and did nothing. Nor did he heed further warnings from other friendly Germans.

As September turned to October, Varus was preparing to march back to his winter quarters at Aliso on the Lippe when he received word of a minor rising near the Weser. Arminius intended for this to draw him off his route through the difficult country of the Teutoburger Wald, where the main rebel force would attack the Roman column. Varus accepted the bait and, with the stubbornness of the weak man who objects to having his decisions questioned, rejected his officers' advice that the wagons and camp followers should be sent to Aliso by the direct route, which offered easy going. His decision simply confirmed that he had no conception of the terrain through which he intended to pass.

To add to the Romans' difficulties, the weather broke, and torrential rain turned muddy tracks into quagmires. Nevertheless, the first day's march passed without incident, whatever suspicions that may have existed about Arminius and his auxiliaries being lulled by the fact that they formed part of the column. The first hint of trouble came when they deserted during the night. The following day little progress was made as most of the legionaries were engaged in creating a road for the wagons. At this point the Germans attacked, overwhelming the rear guard and slaughtering the camp followers. With difficulty, the Romans built a fortified camp for the night (as was standard practice for any Roman army) on one of the few areas of level ground.

Next morning, Varus marched out, arraying his troops for a conventional battle, insofar as the broken ground permitted. Arminius would have none of it, and his men were busily working on the construction of barricades and ambush sites farther along the forest route. Finding no enemy to fight, Varus ordered all except the legions' baggage wagons to be burned, then resumed his march. Better progress was made for a while, but then the Germans closed in from every direction, hurling spears and shooting arrows into the disordered ranks as they struggled through defiles and over ridges in the heavy rain. In some areas discipline became strained as soldiers left the ranks to recover possessions from the baggage wagons before they, too, were destroyed.

When the column was sufficiently disorganized, Arminius ordered a general attack upon it. The Roman line, lacking its usual tactical depth, was pierced in numerous places, and because of the heavily wooded, broken ground its officers were unable to exercise proper control. Whenever a counterattack was made, those taking part were quickly surrounded and cut to pieces by the enemy's broadswords. Varus gave the order for the legions to retire along their route, but it was too late as his troops were now fighting for their lives in a series of fragmented battles. Two eagles were lost and an attempt by the legionary cavalry to cut their way out failed when the horses, unable to keep their footing, were brought down. Varus, seriously wounded during an attack on his part of the line, retained enough of Roman virtue to acknowledge failure by taking his own life, as did his senior officers.

Fighting may well have continued during the next two days, for the Roman soldier was a professional who did not give up easily. Traces of a bank and ditch were later discovered upon a mound, suggesting that this was where the final stand was made. Those who were taken alive suffered the fate of being nailed to trees, buried alive, or ritually sacrificed to the German gods.

Having completed the massacre, Arminius and the tribes then attacked Aliso. Here, in a fine feat of arms, an officer named Lucius Caedicius not only beat off every assault but also broke out and, despite being encumbered with many women and children, reached Vetera (Wesel), where he was joined by the two legions remaining in Germany.

The disaster in the Teutoburger Wald cast a pall over the remaining years of Augustus's reign. Several punitive expeditions under Tiberius and Germanicus succeeded in inflicting heavy loss on the Germans, but it was realized that in military and economic terms there was no point in occupying northern Germany. Thereafter, the boundary of the Roman Empire remained firmly fixed on the left bank of the Rhine.

The long-term consequences of the battle of the Teutoburger Wald, however, were to be of even greater importance. Both Sir Edward Creasy and Maj. Gen. J.F.C. Fuller, the distinguished soldier and military historian, make the point that the subsequent history of Germany would have been radically altered by prolonged contact with Graeco-Roman influences, and that the Anglo-Saxon migration to Britain would not have taken place. What then would have been the future history of the English-speaking world?

Into the Wilderness
Chancellorsville, Virginia, 1863

GARY GALLAGHER

The Confederate victory at Chancellorsville capped a remarkable 11-month period during which Robert E. Lee built the Army of Northern Virginia into a self-confident and formidable weapon. The sheer odds against Confederate success at Chancellorsville elevated it to a special position among Lee's victories. Union Maj. Gen. Joseph Hooker had rebuilt and reinspired the Army of the Potomac in the wake of its defeat under Ambrose E. Burnside at the Battle of Fredericksburg in December 1862.

Hooker entered the Chancellorsville campaign at the head of a powerful force with ample equipment, strong discipline, and high morale. He pronounced it "the finest army on the planet," and an astute Confederate observer later spoke of "Hooker's great army—the greatest this country had ever seen." Terrain played a critical role in the undoing of Hooker and his imposing army, as Lee and Lt. Gen. Thomas J. "Stonewall" Jackson used the heavily wooded "Wilderness of Spotsylvania" to mask their movements, befuddle their foe, and diminish the numerical odds against them.

During the winter of 1862-63, Lee had dispersed his cavalry to secure sufficient fodder and detached two divisions under James Longstreet to Southside Virginia. These measures left him with approximately 61,000 men to face 133,000 Federals. Hooker thus enjoyed the widest margin of manpower of any Union general who had fought against the Army of Northern

Map of the Battlefield of Chancellorsville, 1863

This 1863 map of Chancellorsville shows troop positions and movements on the heavily forested battlefield. Confederate Generals Lee and Jackson used their knowledge of the wilderness to their advantage, ultimately leading to a morale-boosting Confederate victory—at the cost of Jackson's life.

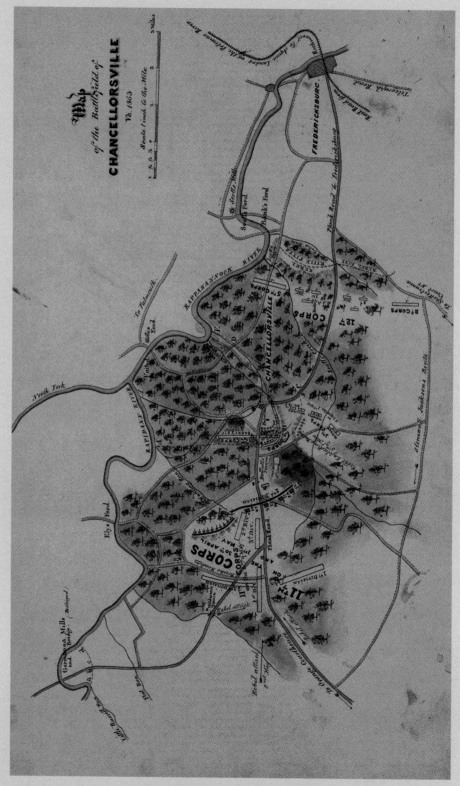

Virginia to that point in the conflict.

Hooker added an impressive strategic blueprint to his material advantages. He envisioned marching the bulk of his army up the Rappahannock River in a wide turning movement around Lee's left. A sizable force under John Sedgwick would remain opposite Lee at Fredericksburg to hold the Confederates in place. As a third element in the plan, Federal cavalry would swing around Lee's left before striking south toward Richmond. If all went well, Lee would be caught between Hooker's powerful turning column to the west and Sedgwick's troops in his front. Confederate options, thought Hooker, would be limited to a retreat toward Richmond or desperate assaults against one or both of the major components of the Army of the Potomac.

The campaign unfolded rapidly after Hooker began his march up the Rappahannock on April 27, 1863. The Federals crossed the Rappahannock and Rapidan Rivers, and by evening on April 30 the advance elements of the flanking force, which eventually would number more than 90,000 in several infantry corps, reached the crossroads at Chancellorsville ten miles in Lee's rear. Hooker brimmed with confidence on the night of April 30, stating that "our enemy must either ingloriously fly, or…give us battle on our own ground, where certain destruction awaits him."

At Chancellorsville, Hooker's soldiers lay in the midst of the Wilderness of Spotsylvania. Extending over approximately 70 square miles, the Wilderness extended south from the Rappahannock and Rapidan Rivers in an irregular shape to points roughly three miles south and two miles east of Chancellorsville. Few roads traversed this clutching forest, and just a handful of hardscrabble farms offered relief from its choke hold on the gloomy countryside. Once a mature woodland, the Wilderness had been transformed into an ugly, scrub wasteland exploited by loggers in search of fuel to feed a number of small iron furnaces in the region. Choking vines, dense underbrush, thickets of blackjack and hickory, and slender saplings created a nightmarish obstacle to the efficient movement of troops and could nullify Hooker's immense advantage in artillery strength.

Just a few miles east of Chancellorsville, the Wilderness gave way to open, rolling country. If Hooker's grand design were to work, his turning column must break free of the forest's embrace to reach open ground where Federal numbers and equipment could have full weight. Maj. Gen. George G. Meade, who commanded the Federal Fifth Corps, spoke to this fact at Chancellorsville on the afternoon of April 30. Elated when he realized that Hooker had indeed flanked Lee, Meade hoped for a rapid march eastward. "This is no place to stop," he remarked to a fellow officer. "We ought to get into the open country beyond."

Lee responded to Hooker's actions with a series of typically audacious moves. Assigning roughly 10,000 men under Maj. Gen. Jubal A. Early to watch Sedgwick at Fredericksburg, Lee and Jackson hurried the rest of the Army of Northern Virginia westward to stop Hooker. The decisive moment of the campaign occurred on the morning of May 1, when the vanguards of Hooker's and Lee's forces collided near Zoan Church on the road between Chancellorsville and Fredericksburg. The Federals had made good progress eastward that morning, moving out of the Wilderness along both the Orange Turnpike and the Orange Plank Road. As soon as fighting commenced, however, Hooker lost all offensive spirit, immediately ordering a withdrawal to Chancellorsville. With every step the Federals took back into the Wilderness, they forfeited a measure of their superiority in numbers and matériel. Much hard combat lay ahead, but Hooker was a beaten man unwilling to push Lee and Jackson into a decisive confrontation along Zoan Church Ridge. Like a frightened child bravely announcing there are no ghosts in the dark, Hooker told a subordinate that he had "Lee just where I want him; he must fight me on my own ground."

On the night of May 1 Lee and Jackson decided on a bold flanking maneuver of their own. Information from staff officers, local civilians, and cavalrymen who had probed the Union position indicated that Hooker's right flank was vulnerable. If enough infantry could march undetected across the Federal front and strike the exposed flank, Lee might fashion a tactical victory. Key information about possible routes for the flank march came from an area resident who knew the network of narrow woods roads along which wagons carried ore to the iron furnaces. Lee decided to commit all 28,000 men of Jackson's Second Corps to the flank attack; he would watch the bulk of Hooker's force at Chancellorsville with the 14,000 men of Maj. Gen. Lafayette McLaws's and Maj. Gen. Richard H. Anderson's divisions of Longstreet's First Corps.

Jackson's column marched for most of the day on May 2, glimpsed by sharp-eyed Federals through a vista in the woods early in the morning but shielded by the forest for most of the way. At about 5:00 p.m., Jackson's corps burst out of the tree line on the Federal right flank, advancing astride the Orange Turnpike and routing Maj. Gen. O.O. Howard's 11th Corps. Howard graphically described the effect of the rebel offensive on his command: "More quickly than it could be told, with all the fury of the wildest hailstorm, everything, every sort of organization that lay in the path of the mad current of panic-stricken men had to give way and be broken into fragments." A North Carolinian recalled the assault in a description that combined humor and more than a hint of ethnic dismissiveness toward the many German-speaking soldiers in Howard's corps: "We captured piles of fat knapsacks and piles of fatter Dutchmen. Private Alexander Faw...remarked that the thick woods through which we were passing was like a strainer, letting the lean and the lesser Dutchmen escape, while we secured the fat ones." Darkness and confusion came early to the forest, and Jackson's attack soon lost steam. Riding forward in an attempt to mount another round of assaults, "Stonewall" was struck down by fire from a North Carolina regiment unaware that he and his staff had reached a point in the woods to their front.

As fighting sputtered to a halt on the night of May 2 the bulk of Hooker's army remained between Jackson's and Lee's forces. Hooker could have struck each part of the rebel army in turn but failed to exploit this opening, pulling his men into a tighter defensive position near Chancellorsville. In the process, he relinquished control of Hazel Grove, a high, cleared plateau that afforded one of the few good sites for artillery in the Wilderness. On May 3 the Confederates resumed their attacks. The most brutal combat of the campaign raged through the smoke-filled forest on both sides of the Orange Plank Road. Applying pressure in a vast semicircle around Hooker's position at Chancellorsville, Lee's and Jackson's soldiers, the latter commanded by Maj. Gen. James E.B. "Jeb" Stuart, slowly gained the upper hand amid smoke-filled woods that often made it difficult to identify friend from foe. "It was an ugly give and take," wrote a Pennsylvanian in reference to the soldiers' restricted field of vision in the dense growth. "We could not see the enemy, but the whizz and ting of the bullets proved they were not far away." Several dozen pieces of Confederate artillery at Hazel Grove helped tip the balance in favor of Lee, whose veterans captured the Chancellorsville crossroads about 10:00 a.m. Lee surveyed a scene of unlikely triumph, as Hooker withdrew into a large V-shaped position closer to the Rappahannock.

Within minutes of riding into the clearing at Chancellorsville, Lee learned that Sedgwick had breached Early's line at Fredericksburg. He divided his army a third time, leaving 25,000 men under Stuart to confront Hooker and concentrating the balance of his men several miles west of Fredericksburg at Salem Church. The Confederates won a fumbling victory against Sedgwick on May 4, and by the morning of May 6 the Army of the Potomac had retreated back across the Rappahannock. The strategic situation had returned to precisely where it had been at the outset of the campaign.

Lee had crafted a victory often termed his masterpiece but at a cost of more than 12,500 casualties, including Stonewall Jackson, who died on May 10. Hooker's losses totaled more than 17,250, a much smaller percentage of his army. Chancellorsville spread optimism throughout the Confederacy and cemented a bond between Lee and his soldiers unrivaled in any other army during the Civil War. Lee believed his men could accomplish the apparently impossible—a circumstance that would influence his actions two months later at Gettysburg. On the Union side, many officers and soldiers in the Army of the Potomac, disgusted with Hooker's decision to withdraw on May 1, believed they had not been given a chance to win the battle. On the home front, Abraham Lincoln realized on May 6 that Hooker had failed. A newspaperman recorded the anguished President's reaction: "My God! my God! What will the country say?"

It is difficult to imagine Lee's winning against Hooker had the armies confronted one another in more open terrain. Hooker later blamed the defeat on several of his subordinates, most notably Sedgwick for not moving more aggressively from Fredericksburg to Chancellorsville. But Sedgwick's actions would have been irrelevant had Hooker not abandoned all offensive thoughts after the first clash at Zoan Church on the morning of May 1. Having handed Lee the initiative, Hooker issued his misguided orders to concentrate the flanking element of his army in the Wilderness. There, unable to monitor his opponent's movements and hampered in the use of his superior artillery and more powerful infantry force, he presided over an unfolding panorama of failure. Hooker's decisions allowed the dense growth of the Wilderness to envelop his mighty army. This combination of commander and geography yielded a result that prompted one New York editor to remark, "It is horrible—horrible; and to think of it, 130,000 magnificent soldiers so cut to pieces by less than 60,000 half-starved ragamuffins."

Oil painting of Belleau Wood by Barry Faulkner, 1920

Edward Robinson, a director of the Metropolitan Museum of Art, commissioned this painting as a tribute to his son, Capt. P.B. Robinson, who died at Belleau Wood. In 1920 artist Barry Faulkner completed the oil on canvas painting, which measures approximately five feet square.

Devil Dogs
Belleau Wood, France, 1918

AGOSTINO VON HASSELL

Belleau Wood had been a traditional hunting preserve of French royalty and in 1918 would witness a very different, and decidedly less decorous, kind of bloodletting.

Belleau Wood, lying among the rolling hills of the Marne Valley and bordered by three hamlets: Belleau, Bouresches, and Lucy-le-Bocage, was dark, densely wooded, slashed by deep ravines, and dotted with major rock outcrops. A nursery song comes to mind—"Don't go into the woods today, you're sure of a big surprise." It had that kind of foreboding aura.

In 1918 Gen. Erich Ludendorff, Germany's prime strategist, knew he had to win the war right now: The balance was shifting and his time was running out. The Americans had arrived. They had started coming in 1917, and by 1918 there were 325,000 of them and the numbers were rising rapidly. Unlike their French or British counterparts they had not been exhausted by years of trench warfare. They had not been through a Passchendaele or a Verdun. If they were green, they were also full of sap, and had an eagerness for the fight that the Europeans had not seen since 1914, when they too had marched into battle as though it were a game.

Ludendorff launched his offensives in March 1918 against the British in the Somme and then in April up around Ypres, almost breaking through to the Channel ports. After all those years of static warfare he had managed to open it up. No longer were the gains in yards; the Germans punched huge holes in the Allied lines, miles deep. Each time, though, desperate defenses had held them; that and the Germans' own speed, outstripping supplies and reinforcements. By the end of April they had been blocked and Ludendorff needed to find another way. He had to the win now and he had to win it fast. Where to strike next?

It was the Americans who saw it coming. Maj. S.T. Hubbard of the AEF's Intelligence section warned his French and British counterparts that Ludendorff would launch his next attack on the quiet sector between Reims and Soissons, just north of the Marne. In his estimation it would come between May 25 and 30. It was here, argued Hubbard, that the Germans could strike with greatest surprise; there was simply nowhere else on the Western Front with as much potential.

The American warning went to the French General Headquarters but was disregarded. After all, what did these upstart Americans know that the war-tested intelligence services of the French and British did not? It was presumptuous, naive. At 4:40 a.m. on May 27, 1918, the Germans opened up with a massive barrage from 3,719 guns on the French and British precisely where Hubbard had predicted.

French General Duchêne was in charge of the Marne front and, despite warnings from the British contingent under his command, decided to put all his eggs in one basket, and that basket was the formidable ridge of the Chemin des Dames, running east-west between Reims and Soissons, north of the River Aisne. There he massed his troops, leaving the hinterland behind the Chemin with little by way of reserves to stem a breakthrough. The German barrage, almost unprecedented in ferocity, pulverized the Allied defenders. Soon after, wave after wave of German assault infantry were pouring over the Chemin. They streamed down the reverse slope, brushing aside French and British divisions. In the French rear areas there was unalloyed panic. In one day the Germans had created a pocket 13 miles deep, and before them lay the road to Paris, a mere 50 or so miles away. French and British forces were in full retreat, and in Paris the French government began burning documents in preparation for a hasty flight. The French were in bad shape: "There were French soldiers in the rout, too. Nearly all were wounded, or in the last stages of exhaustion," wrote Marine Corps Capt. John W. Thomason, Jr., who fought at Belleau.

By May 29 Soissons in the west of the pocket, and Château-Thierry in the southeast, were in German hands. Belleau Wood lay between them at the southernmost extremity of the German advance. Although Ludendorff had exceeded his wildest expectations his army was running out of steam. They had come far and fast and now needed to regroup. After the initial panic the French and British had reacted well, containing the western and eastern flanks of the pocket.

Under tremendous pressure, the French and British high commands conceded to Gen. John "Black Jack" Pershing's insistence that his American army be kept as a coherent fighting force rather than be split up piecemeal among the Allies. Pershing was also well aware that the main quality of his troops would be shown in open fighting, not hunkered down in trenches. They had already proved they could fight when the First Division had gone into the line at Montdidier and Cantigny on the Somme in March. Now, they were going to get another chance to prove themselves.

If the French and British commanders had a prejudiced view of the AEF, its own command was not without prejudices of its own. One of these was the low regard, even disdain, in which the Marine Corps was held, particularly by Pershing himself. He did not believe they had the tradition, experience, or leadership to be used as a large fighting unit, and the Corps was dismissed as "a landing party that had gotten out of hand." Even the commander of the Marine brigade that formed part of the U.S. Second ("Indian Head") Division (Brig. Gen. James G. Harbord) was an Army officer, not a Marine. His Marine brigade was made up of the Fifth and Sixth Regiments. The Fifth was commanded by Col. Wendell C. Neville, the Sixth by Col. Albertus W. Catlin, and Sixth Machine-gun Battalion by Maj. Edward B. Cole. They were untested in battle and had no artillery to speak of, and only a few trench mortars.

Belleau Wood offered the Germans a perfect defensive position, and by June 3 the Bavarian 237th Division was well dug in and soon had machine-gun nests artfully concealed among the ravines and outcrops. "Across this wheat field [on the south of Belleau] there were more woods, and in the edge of the woods the old Boche, lots of him, infantry and machineguns," wrote Captain Thomason. Fields of fire were prepared and artillery emplacements constructed. What had been a peaceful wood was now a formidable bastion.

On June 5 the French directed the Marines to move toward Belleau and support the defensive line just north of Lucy-le-Bocage. Confusion and defeatism reigned among the French, who were flooding back, and they advised the Marines in no uncertain terms that they had better hightail it too. Their advice elicited the now legendary response from Marine Capt. Lloyd Williams: "Retreat? Hell, we just got here!"

The battle for Belleau began June 6, 1918, a day that would go down in history as one of the most catastrophic in Marine history. Not realizing how well dug in the Germans were, Marine commanders planned two assaults. No preliminary reconnaissance was carried out. The first attack went in at 5:00 a.m. as First Battalion/Fifth Regiment attacked from the west, capturing Hill 142. Despite this local success the Marine organization and tactical communication were abysmal. There was no artillery, no reconnoitering, and very little by way of command and control. The Germans, on the other hand, were in timber-rein-forced trenches, had a plethora of machine guns and heavy artillery in support, and used air balloons to spot Marine emplacements and movements.

At 5:00 p.m. the second attack was launched by the Third Battlion/Fifth Regiment and the Third Battalion/Sixth Regiment in an attempt to capture the east side of the wood. The approach, across an open wheat field, was poorly coordinated and executed. "Platoons—very lean platoons now—formed in small combat groups, deployed in the wheat, and set out toward the gloomy wood....It was late afternoon; the sun was low enough to shine under the edge of your helmet," wrote Captain Thomason.

There was no supporting artillery, and the Marines were cut down in swaths, the Third/Fifth being decimated. "The air snapped and crackled all around. The sergeant beside the lieutenant stopped, looked at him with a frozen, foolish smile, and crumpled into a heap of old clothes. Something took the kneecap of the lieutenant's right knee and his leg buckled under him. He noticed, as he fell sideways, that all his men were tumbling over like duck-pins...." wrote Captain Thomason.

It was like a grisly replay of the killing-fests of the early battles of 1914 or the courageous assault of the old Confederacy against entrenched Yankee lines during Pickett's Charge at Gettysburg. But in it there was a kind of magnificent bravery that amazed not only the French but also the Germans. At one point in the assault, Gunnery Sgt. Dan Daly was reputed to have led his men across the wheat field with the words now immortalized in Marine lore: "Come on ya sons-of-bitches, ya want to live forever?" Floyd Gibbons, a reporter who accompanied the Fifth Regiment of Marines in this assault, wrote that day: "Major Berry had advanced well beyond the center of the field when I saw him turn toward me and heard him shout, 'get down everybody.' We all fell on our faces…withering volleys of lead swept the tops of the oats just over us.…"

By the end of that first day the Marines held the hamlet of Bouresches, but the cost had been enormous. Not until the landings on Tarawa in World War II would they take such a hammering. One thousand eighty-seven were killed or wounded, 31 of them officers. It was only the beginning.

June 7 was quiet, and a new assault was planned (it failed the next day). The 10th saw the first use of heavy artillery from the American side, and the Marines made several successful probes into the wood, rousting some of the machine-gun nests, but by the end of the day they had to withdraw to the southern end to avoid German counter fire. On the 11th they reentered the wood and managed to take about two-thirds, although the casualty rate was again very high.

"Day and night for nearly a month men fought in its corpse-choked thickets, killing with bayonet and bomb and machine-gun. It was gassed and shelled and shot into the semblance of nothing earthly," wrote Thomason. One of the problems was that German machine-gun emplacements that had supposedly been knocked out were reactivated, causing havoc as the Marines tried to move forward. "Machine guns were everywhere, in the ravines, behind rocks, and sometimes in the trees…we had to rush each gun crew in turn, in the face of their deadly fire. It was a furious dash from one next to another," reported Capt. Martin A. Gulberg. It was a case of taking and then retaking ground they thought had been won. By the 12th Harbord was forced to accept that his men were on the point of total exhaustion but his request for urgent reinforcement could not be met.

The Germans now started a series of counterattacks that very nearly re-captured Bouresches. Here, for the first time, Americans had to deal with phosgene gas. It resulted in heavy casualties, one of whom, Sergeant Stockham, was to receive a posthumous Medal of Honor for giving his gas mask to a stricken Marine while he went on to assist others. He died a few days later. The Marines held on at Bouresches until they were relieved by the U.S. Army's 23rd Infantry.

On June 18 the Marines, now reinforced by the U.S. Army Seventh Infantry Brigade, made a series of attacks, finally seizing it on July 25, 1918. It had been an extraordinarily brutal and bloody affair marked by what could be called military naivety, but also marked by the grit and guts that would be forever honored in Marine Corps lore.

COASTS

Amphibious assaults on defended beaches have never been easy propositions for military commanders, as Julius Caesar's account of his landings on the south coast of England in 54 B.C. illustrates: "The natives, however, perceived the designs of the Romans. So they sent forward their cavalry and charioteers...and following up with the rest of their forces, they sought to prevent our troops from disembarking. Disembarkation was a matter of extreme difficulty for the following reasons. The ships, on account of their size, could not be run ashore, except in deep water; the troops, though they did not know the ground, had not their hands free, and were loaded with the great and grievous weight of their arms—had nevertheless at one and the same time to leap down from their vessels, to stand firm in the waves, and to fight the enemy." He could have been talking about any number of amphibious assaults in World War II. As Caesar pointed out, one of the other major factors is the landing craft themselves. Before World War II there were few if any vessels specifically designed for the task. At Gallipoli in World War I, as Peter A. Huchthausen shows here, keeled rowboats could not land troops on the beaches. The World War II development of specialized motor landing craft with flat bottoms and drop-down front ramps overcame many problems, but even they could be grounded by reefs (as Agostino von Hassell's account of Tarawa illustrates), forcing their human cargoes to disembark into uncomfortably, sometimes lethally, deep water and wade with agonizing slowness through the bullet- and shell-lashed shallows. After a beachhead has been established it still has to be exploited. For example, at Anzio in Italy in 1944 the Allied landing was unopposed, but failure to move out of the beachhead almost condemned the whole operation in the face of German counterattacks. Matthew Bennett's account of the Battle of Marathon is included here as just such an example of a successful landing being extinguished in the breakout phase. Even the D Day landings at Normandy on June 6, 1944, despite months of training and the massive forces the attackers could assemble, were no cakewalk, as anyone who was on those bloody beaches knew all too well.

Marathon, Greece, 490 B.C.

The long coastline stretching across the northern part of the Bay of Marathon and away from the Greek camp made an ideal harbor for the Persian vessels. However, when the Persians advanced to Soros, they were unable to stand up to the Greek counterattack.

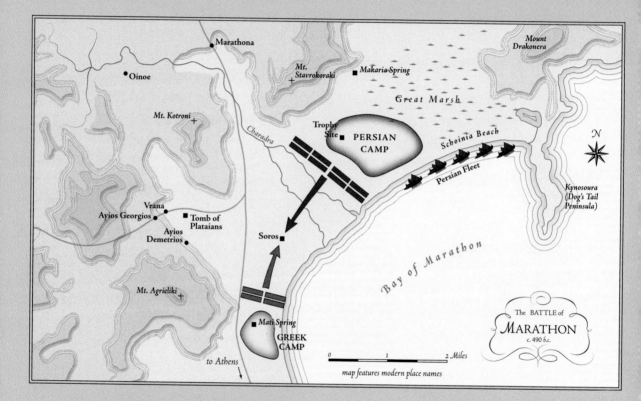

Beachhead Victory
Marathon, Greece, 490 B.C.

MATTHEW BENNETT

Five hundred years before the birth of Christ, the greatest empire in the world was that of the Persians. Originally based in what is now Iran, it had expanded under three great conquerors to extend from the Mediterranean to the Himalaya. It had been founded by Cyrus in the 550s B.C., who at his death in 530 B.C. ruled territories consisting of modern Turkey, Syria, Iraq, Iran,and Afghanistan. His son Cambyses added Egypt, and his successor, Darius I, conquered much of modern Pakistan and crossed the Bosporus into Europe for the first time in 513 B.C., overrunning Thrace and Macedon—almost all of northern Greece.

At this time there were many Greek colonies on the western coast of Asia Minor, which also fell under Persian sway. They joined an empire that was centrally organized but tributary in nature; as long as subject peoples paid taxes and provided contingents to the Persian Army and Navy, they enjoyed a certain amount of local independence. This was not enough for the Greeks, however, who, in 499 B.C., launched the Ionian Revolt against their overlord. They received assistance from the cities of mainland Greece with whom they shared a common culture and language. But the Persians proved too powerful, and by 495 B.C. the rebellion had been crushed. In 492 B.C., a force under Darius's son-in-law, Mardonius, was sent across the Hellespont into northern Greece. A further extension to the Persian Empire seemed inevitable.

Darius had been angered by the mainlanders' support of the revolt, especially that of Athens, and was determined to take his revenge. In 491 B.C. he sent envoys demanding "earth and water," the traditional symbols of submission. Their reception by the Greeks certainly lacked diplomatic decorum. The Athenians threw them into prison and the Spartans hurled them down a well, an ironic indication that they were most likely to find their demands at the bottom. The following year, Mardonius moved to occupy the island of Euboia (off the east coast of Attica) and specifically the city of Eretria.

The Persian force consisted of as many as 600 ships, with about 25,000 fighting men, of whom 1,000 were cavalry. They were accompanied by siege engineers who were capable of reducing sophisticated fortresses, as they had proved in Asia Minor. Eretria's defense lasted only a week before the besiegers stormed the walls, and the city was sacked and burned and its citizens enslaved. This same fate now awaited Athens, which at this time was not properly fortified. Because Mardonius possessed an amphibious capacity with which he had conquered Cyprus a few years earlier, he could maneuver by sea and land wherever he wished. In the late summer of 490 B.C. he chose to disembark and set up camp on the plain of Marathon, 24 miles northeast of Athens. (The famous 26-mile distance of the modern race was erroneously taken from Marathona village, beyond the plain.) Perhaps made overconfident by both the size of his forces and his mobility, Mardonius gave no instructions to fortify his beachhead.

The Athenians felt themselves very exposed. Many Greek city-states were either busily submitting to the Persians ("medizing") or keeping a low profile for fear of suffering a punishment similar to that threatened against Athens. Sparta, the definitive warrior-state, was not interested in temporizing, but when approached by Athens for aid, its rulers declared that the army could not move for religious reasons: It was an inauspicious time of the month. So the Athenians had a choice: either to wait for the Persians to attack, or to advance against them and block the road to the city. The Assembly made the decision to take the bolder course.

The citizen-levy, "10,000" strong, divided into ten units, all under the command of the War Archon Kallimachos, marched out and set up camp on the southern edge of the plain of Marathon, around the Mati spring. The Athenians' only allies were another 1,000 men from the city of Plataia. There was no immediate battle. The Persians were either unprepared or overconfident, and do not seemed to have skirmished against or even reconnoitered the Greek position. This is surprising, because the strength of their army lay in a mobile cavalry, capable of showering an opposing line with javelins and arrows, while their infantry were also primarily equipped with the bow. Although some wore body armor, they carried only light wicker shields and were considered by the Greeks to be "unarmored." In contrast the Athenian fighting man of this era wore a "corslet" (covering his torso) made of stiffened linen or leather, sometimes with small metal platelike scales attached. On his head was a bronze helmet, his legs were covered with bronze greaves from knee to ankle, and he carried a three-foot-wide bronze shield lined with leather called a hoplon, from which the soldier derived his name—hoplite.

The hoplites fought in a phalanx, a close-order formation, usually eight ranks deep, attacking the enemy with ten-foot spears. So tightly were the men packed, and so well were they protected, that hoplite battles usually became shoving matches, until one side gave way. Apart from the Spartans, who were devoted to drill, there is no evidence that hoplites had much training, so they needed flat terrain on which to maneuver and fight to best effect. This is what the plain of Marathon offered, and why the Athenians had chosen the risky strategy of advancing against a more mobile enemy. Also, a swift attack offered the opportunity to pinch out the Persian beachhead and strangle at birth their attempt to march on Athens.

The topography of Marathon has changed somewhat over the past 2,500 years. The sea has retreated, and the ground level has risen in the intervening period. Yet certain crucial factors are still quite clear. At the southern end of the battlefield lies Mount Agrieliki, to the west of the Athens road, while to the east of the road was the sea, essentially creating a bottleneck that was stoppered by the Greek camp. This narrow gap was probably only half a mile wide. Farther north the plain broadened out to a couple of miles' width, with a long shingle beach arcing to the east. This is what made the bay such a good harbor for the shallow-drafted Persian vessels, which were beached or anchored close to shore. Their own camp is believed to have been situated near the Makaria spring, and what is now called the Great Marsh, four miles to the north of the Greeks.

One of the Athenian commanders was Miltiades, who had served with a Persian army in Thrace. He may have initially cautioned against an advance, because he was aware that Persian tactics involved a storm of missiles to disorganize an enemy line, while their cavalry maneuvered around the flanks, looking for gaps to exploit. A hoplite phalanx, inflexible as it was, would suffer grievously if its formation was disrupted, as its men could not support one another in close combat. Neither side seemed keen to attack: The Greeks were waiting for the Spartans, and the Persians were intriguing with potential "medizers" in Athens. After a few days, however, the Persian force advanced to a position now believed to be marked by the Soros, a memorial burial mound to the Greek dead, about a mile away from the Greek camp. Then the Athenians did something remarkable: Miltiades ordered them to advance in the face of the Persian arrow-storm. It was daring to the point of recklessness when one remembers that the Greeks had never beaten the Persians on land before.

Because of the disparity in numbers, the Greeks spread out to match the length of the Persian front, about a mile wide, which resulted in a thinning-out of the center of their phalanx to only four men deep. (Some historians see this as a deliberate attempt to create a pincer movement in from the flanks; but such tactical sophistication was probably beyond hoplites.) Not only did the Greeks advance, but they advanced "at the double," which probably meant a brisk trot. This was a very difficult maneuver for largely untrained men to perform, because it is very difficult to keep a line abreast, even at a slow pace. Now we need not imagine the heavily equipped hoplites charging a full mile: It would have exhausted them, and they would have arrived in ones and twos against a composed enemy formation. The "doubling" probably did not begin until the phalanx came within range of the Persian arrows, at about 200 yards, with an effective range of perhaps 100 yards.

The Persians may well have been taken by surprise. The Greek historian Herodotus describes them as amazed when they saw "a mere handful of men coming on at the run without either horsemen or archers." The center of Mardonius's army was composed of native Persians and their best allies, the Sakae, both renowned for their use of the bow. When the two forces clashed, the weakened Greek center broke under the attack of these experienced soldiers.

But on the flanks, where the hoplite phalanx was at its proper depth, and the less enthusiastic Persian allies stood, the Greeks triumphed.

One mystery is why the Persian cavalry is not mentioned as playing any part. A (very) late source describes them as being absent from the battle, but this may not be reliable. To charge horse with foot soldiers is usually futile, as the cavalry can simply evade contact. Whatever the case, the wings of the phalanx then swung in upon the Persian center and crushed it. This again shows remarkable initiative for troops unused to such maneuvers. The lightly equipped Persians proved no match for the heavily armored hoplites in the melee, and the entire Persian force broke in flight to their ships. Herodotus claims that 6,400 Persians died, as against only 192 Athenians, although one of them was their general, Kallimachos. The fugitives mostly escaped, though, and the Athenians captured only seven vessels. Yet this signaled the effective end of the Persian campaign, and Athens could breathe again.

The Greek victory at Marathon has been viewed by historians as a triumph of democracy over oriental tyranny, and to a modern reader it might almost seem inevitable that free men will defeat the servants of an oppressive regime. Yet this is to operate with hindsight, in the light of the defeat of a second Persian invasion, launched ten years after Marathon, and Alexander the Great's conquest of their empire almost two centuries later. In 490 B.C., it was far from certain that the Greek city-states were going to retain their independence.

Map of Gallipoli, published in London 1936
Found in a history book released by the British government, this map shows the British frontline at the end of April 1915. The uncompromising cliffs that rose from Gallipoli's shoreline,
coupled with ineffectual British leadership, finally led to the demise of the seven-month campaign near the end of the year.

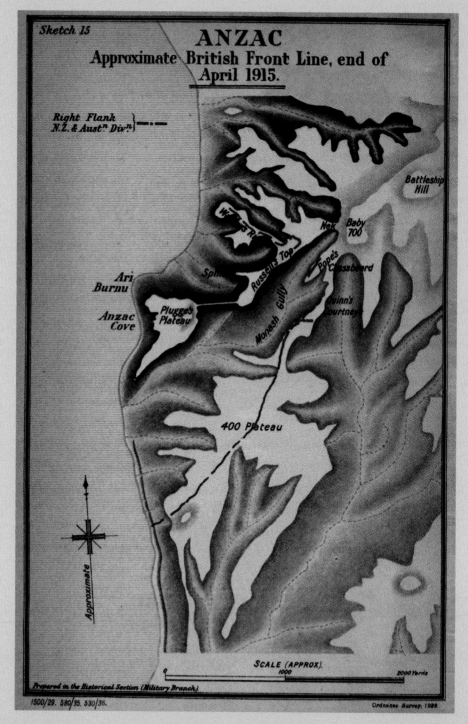

Sketch 15

ANZAC
Approximate British Front Line, end of April 1915.

Right Flank
N.Z. & Austⁿ Divⁿ⁾

Battleship
Hill

Nek   Baby
700

Pope's
Crossboard

Ari
Burnu

Spin

Russell's Top

Quinn's
Courtney

Anzac
Cove

Plugge's
Plateau

Monash Gully

400 Plateau

Approximate

SCALE (APPROX).
1000   2000 Yards
0

Prepared in the Historical Section (Military Branch).

1500/29. 580/35. 530/36.

Ordnance Survey, 1928.

Buried on the Beaches
Gallipoli, Turkey, 1915

PETER A. HUCHTHAUSEN

The Gallipoli Peninsula on the European side of Turkey stands, sentry-like, over the southern entry to the Dardanelles, a narrow, fast-flowing channel connecting the Aegean Sea and the Sea of Marmara. At the head of the Sea of Marmara sits Constantinople (modern Istanbul), bestriding Europe and Asia and the guardian of the Bosporus, the gateway to the Black Sea.

In October 1914 Turkey sided with Germany and the Central Powers and promptly sealed off the Bosporus, thus slamming the door on Allied aid to beleaguered Russia. In addition, Turkey attacked Russia itself in the Caucasus at a time when Russia was being battered by Germany on its eastern front (the five-day battle of Tannenberg in August 1914 had alone cost Russia over 200,000 casualties). Desperate, Russia pleaded with her western allies, Britain and France, to open a second front.

Add to this scenario the static yet horrific killing ground that was the Western Front, and the search for a bold outflanking movement that might help restore an aggressive war of maneuver became one of the highest priorities. Winston Churchill, Britain's First Lord of the Admiralty, was a firebrand member of an otherwise stolidly unimaginative war cabinet. Assisted, somewhat tentatively, by the brilliant but erratic naval commander in chief, Adm. Sir John "Jackie" Fisher, and supported by Lord Kitchener, Churchill marshaled his brilliantly persuasive powers behind a plan to smash through the Dardanelles.

At a stroke, the plug would be pulled from the Bosporus, supplies would flow to Russia, Turkey would be knocked out of the war, Bulgaria would mobilize for the Allies, and the bite would be put on the Central Powers in the Balkans. The plan was bold though it was probably achievable, but, like so many brilliant plans, it depended on flawless organization, resolute leadership, and immaculate execution. At Gallipoli all were conspicuous by their absence.

The operation was first thought of primarily as a naval action: Blast through the Dardanelles and take Constantinople (which British intelligence predicted was ready to fall like a ripe plum). Leading the charge would be Vice Adm. Sir Sackville Carden at the head of his Anglo-French fleet (mainly obsolete pre-dreadnoughts with the exception of the super dreadnought, *Queen Elizabeth*). On February 19, 1915, Carden's fleet moved into the lower reaches of the Dardanelles. The Turks had mined the channel and Carden had with him a flotilla of civilian trawlers and their less-than-enthusiastic crews to act as minesweepers, a technique that was then in its infancy. The fleet pounded away at the shore emplacements but could never satisfactorily find an effective range or trajectory (even when hit, the emplacements were quickly repaired and back in action). The Turks, on the other hand, used highly mobile horse-drawn field artillery whose dropping shots began to make Carden a very nervous man indeed. This was hit-and-run warfare with a vengeance. Driven to the point of distraction, Carden withdrew (he actually had a nervous breakdown) and was replaced by the more aggressive Adm. John de Robeck. But like Carden, he too was heading for a very bloody nose, this time at the hands of Turkish mines. After losing four battleships (including the French *Bouvet* with the loss of over 700 hands) de Robeck stood off and passed the poisoned chalice on to the soldiers. They would have to seize the Gallipoli Peninsula, immobilize the forts, and provide security for the navy to open the straits.

British Gen. Sir Ian Hamilton was chosen for the task. He commanded a force of British, Empire (Australian-New Zealand Corps, known as Anzacs), and French elements. It numbered four divisions in all, a smaller force than that of the Turkish defenders who, apart from the natural advantage defender enjoys over attacker (for example, in World War II amphibious assaults planners aimed for odds of 10 to1 in favor of the attacker), also benefited from the cliffs and bluffs (often as much as 200 feet high) of the rocky coastline Hamilton was forced to attack. The Turks had been given plenty of warning in a general way about Allied intentions. Hamilton had spent a month in Alexandria feverishly trying to pull his command together. Liman von Sanders, the brilliant German general brought in as the head of the German military mission to Turkey to reorganize the Turkish army and plan its defense of Gallipoli, had prayed, "If only the English will leave me alone for eight days." The English left him alone for four weeks. What von Sanders did not know was exactly where the landings would be, and he was forced to keep most of his troops in the center of the peninsula, ready to be deployed as the occasion might demand. However, as the battles unfolded, the geographic advantage of commanding the heights above the beaches more than offset any element of surprise.

It is also important to note that the sneering sense of Allied superiority ("poor old 'Johnny Turk' is just a peasant of a corrupt and derelict nation: the 'sick old man of Europe'") was later to cost them dearly. Underestimating your enemy is never a good idea, especially one with a proud military tradition that is defending its homeland, and some months and many of thousands of casualties later "Johnny" would wipe the smirk off many a face.

On April 25, 1915, Hamilton sent in the British 29 Division at Cape Helles on the southern tip of the peninsula, and the Anzacs some 15 miles farther up the west coast at Gaba Tepe (Anzac Cove). The southern landing beaches formed an arc around the toe of the peninsula: S, V, and W on the eastern shore, X and Y on the western.

Neither the Anzacs nor the British at S and X met much resistance at the shoreline. V and W, however, were a very different story. At W the Turks were well dug in and held their fire until the rowboats that served as assault craft hit the beaches. Then they opened up a murderous fire that caused heavy casualties. The bloodied remnant of the British force managed to make the shelter of the bluffs and established a toehold.

The experience on V beach was to be one of the most horrific of the whole campaign, if not the whole war. The British had adapted an old collier, the *River Clyde*, as a crude proto-landing craft with ports cut in her bows to allow the attackers to disembark onto barges and thence to the beach. Only one company of Turks with four machine guns held the heights overlooking V beach, but that geographic advantage was to spell death to hundreds of British infantrymen as they debouched from the Clyde onto the congested killing ground of the barges: sitting ducks for the Turks above them. Within moments the barges were filled with the dead and dying, their scuppers awash with blood. Others, carried to the shore in rowboats, met a similar fate, "running," says the great military historian Sir Basil Liddell Hart, "like gladiators into a gently sloping arena designed by nature and arranged by the Turks—themselves ensconced in surrounding seats—for a butchery." A few survivors clung to the beaches or cowered in the *Clyde,* waiting for nightfall to release them from their hell.

While the slaughter ground on at V, the attackers at Y, three miles north, had found a sweet spot and landed unopposed. They could have cut across the peninsula, relieved V beach, and in all probability won the whole campaign. In fact they spent the day swimming or sauntering around: "What had been an idle stroll on the 25th could not be had for blood in the days thereafter."

Within a very short period the Turks, courageously and energetically led by Mustafa Kemal (destined to become Atatürk, "the father of modern Turkey") had locked down all the bridgeheads and at some points, like Anzac Cove, invaders and defenders were so close that trenches had to be roofed to prevent grenades from landing in them. The fighting was often brutally hand to hand, with men leaping into enemy trenches "where they hacked and stabbed and died in the dark and the dust and the powder smoke." So, ironically, Gallipoli became nothing more than a scorchingly hot version of the Western Front, the very bloody stalemate it had been designed to break.

On August 6 Hamilton made a supreme effort to break out of his shoreline imprisonment. The British in the south and the Anzacs in the west made courageous but futile attempts to break out. The men were utterly spent, physically and mentally, by the months of grueling warfare they had already endured. Farther up the western coast at the wide and beautifully unspoiled Suvla Bay British Gen. Sir Frederick Stopford (his last military service had been as Sir Redvers Buller's military secretary during the Boer War) landed his 35,000 men. Facing them was the laughably small force of 1,800 Turkish gendarmerie, with reinforcements at least 30 hours away. Yet again, administrative muddle and lethargic leadership gave the Turks time to bring up their reserves. Suvla also went into the bag.

Although Hamilton was to send Stopford home in ignominy, he too was relieved by Gen. Sir Charles Munro, of whose defeatism Churchill was to fume: "He came, he saw, he capitulated." The seven-month campaign was over at a cost of 250,000 Allied casualties. By the end of 1915 Gallipoli was evacuated, ironically one of the only Allied successes of the whole campaign, when 115,000 men were extracted at night only meters from the Turkish positions. Only in defeat did the Allies exhibit the careful planning and brilliant execution that could have won them the campaign.

The whole sorry debacle was to be a disaster for Churchill, and one that dogged him long after. He was first demoted to an obscure cabinet post, then took himself off to France to lead an infantry battalion, condemned to wander in the political wilderness for many years. Hamilton's reputation was in irreparable tatters, his career demolished. He was never again given a command.

Gallipoli has become synonymous with a type of bumbling British leadership that paid for its mistakes with the lives of its soldiery, many of whom came from Australia and New Zealand where resentment has not died to this day. Lions led by donkeys. But Gallipoli is also one of the most tantalizing "what-ifs'" of history. Had the campaign been successful and Contantinople taken, had Russia been relieved and the Central Powers attacked up through the Balkans, could the Russian Revolution have been avoided? If the heights above the beaches had proved less intractable, what would have been the shape of the postwar world?

Navy map of Tarawa, Gilbert Islands, from the records of the Hydrographic Office
The U.S. Navy used this aerial map of Tarawa as a target chart in their first amphibious attack
of World War II. Naval forces targeted the deepwater port at Betio, as shallow coral reefs prevented them from landing on the majority of the island's coastline.

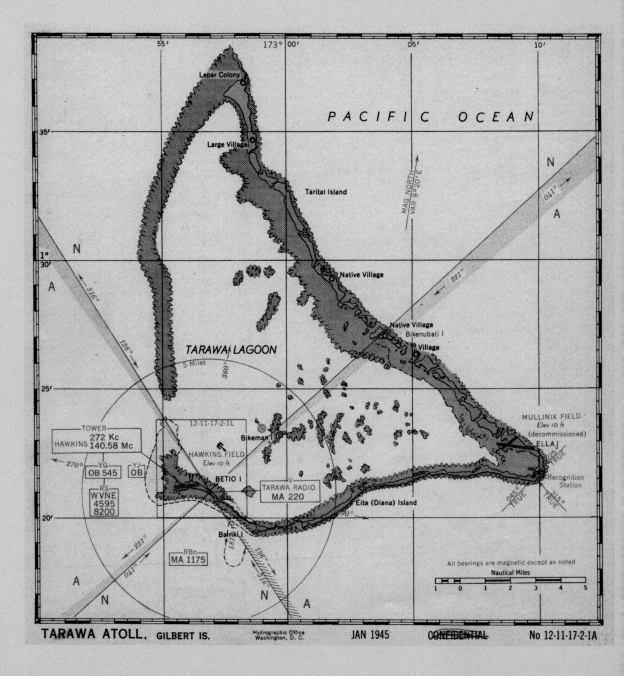

TARAWA ATOLL, GILBERT IS.   Hydrographic Office Washington, D. C.   JAN 1945   CONFIDENTIAL   No 12-11-17-2-1A

A Bloody Brawl
Tarawa, Gilbert Islands, 1943

AGOSTINO VON HASSELL

The Tarawa Atoll, 20 miles square and created entirely from coral, is part of the Gilbert Islands (today called Kiribati), a 16-island group located in the central Pacific at 1.25° north latitude and 173° east longitude, straddling the Equator about one-half of the distance from Hawaii to Australia. The vicious 76-hour battle that started on November 20, 1943, was the first U.S. amphibious assault of the Second World War and would drastically change how the U.S. military regarded the Japanese as a foe.

The Gilberts were first recorded by British Commodore John Byron in 1765, but they got their name from Royal Navy Capt. Thomas Gilbert, who sailed the Pacific with Capt. John Marshall in 1788. The two spent over a year exploring and mapping the Gilbert and Marshall Islands. Subsequent to their explorations, Great Britain made the Gilbert Islands a British protectorate in 1892 and began colonization in 1915. The island has been populated for thousands of years, although no one knows definitively when people of Micronesian descent began the first colonies. The original settlements are believed to have been on Betio, a small island adjacent to Tarawa, which has a deepwater port and through the years has evolved into a commercial center. Betio was to see much of the bloodiest fighting of the battle.

The Japanese military viewed Tarawa as an important strategic outpost from which it could launch air and naval attacks on other islands, and its nearby deepwater port of Betio was ideal for maintaining and provisioning ships. Even small ships had difficulty navigating the seas surrounding Tarawa because of the coral reefs and unpredictable tides. With this in mind, and recognizing that they would need a midpoint from which to launch air attacks and use as a supply depot, the Japanese attacked and occupied Tarawa on December 9, 1941, just two days after Pearl Harbor. The very speed with which they did so underlines the strategic importance they gave to the island.

The U.S. "island-hopping" campaign that started with Guadalcanal and would end with Iwo Jima and Okinawa was much dictated by both geography and technology. These small islands such as the Tarawa Atoll provided strategically crucial airfields, as few military aircraft in World War II were capable of covering the enormous distances of the Pacific.

Japanese Rear Adm. Keiji Shibasaki was charged with turning the island into a fortress. He is quoted as having said it would "take a million men a thousand years" to take Tarawa from the Japanese, and in order to guarantee his prediction, he imported 1,000 Japanese workers and 1,200 Korean laborers to aid his 2,600 Imperial Marines and another 2,400 Japanese soldiers to convert Tarawa and Betio into an impenetrable fortress. Recognizing that much of the island was already unassailable from the sea because of shallow coral reefs, Shibasaki located 14 coastal defense guns around the island's perimeter; 40 strategically located artillery guns were sited at every vulnerable approach.

He had laborers build a four-foot-high coconut-log seawall that lined the entire lagoon and then sited 100 machine-gun emplacements behind it. The armament surrounded an island that was only one mile long and less than 400 yards wide and had limited access from the sea. Similar care was taken by the Japanese to protect Betio Island with coconut-log walls, shelters protecting machine guns and antiaircraft guns under corrugated iron roofs protected by six feet of sand and logs. They may have been rustic, but they were surprisingly tough.

U.S. forces quickly recognized that Tarawa was an important strategic island for the Japanese, but following the devastation of U.S. ships at Pearl Harbor, an attack could not be planned until naval forces could be restored, giving Admiral Shibasaki time to build up his formidable fortifications around the island. Moreover, American forces realized that in order to capture the Marshall Islands, some 100 miles north of the Gilberts, it would be necessary to eject the Japanese from the Gilberts.

U.S. naval planners were severely hampered by a lack of modern maps of the atoll (many they used were 100 years old!) and in order to obtain up-to-date information they sent several reconnaissance groups ashore to reconnoiter the island and develop new maps. A key concern was the depth of water over the surrounding reefs at high tide. In fact, new maps provided by reconnaissance showed the atoll was really a triangular group of islands that were no higher than ten feet above sea level at the highest point. Betio, the most strategic of the islands because of its deepwater access, would be a tactical key to any battle. U.S. reconnaissance forces also learned that the barrier reef provided insufficient water depth for landing craft, and where there were opportunities to traverse the reef, the shoreline was heavily mined.

Operation Galvanic, the code name for the Tarawa invasion, was unlike later U.S. amphibious assaults on Pacific islands in that there was no intense air or naval bombardment prior to the landings. The strategy was to take Betio quickly, gain access to the deepwater port, and move inland. What preliminary fire there was fell all over the island in an attempt to confuse the enemy.

On November 20, 1943, ships began to fire on the island in an attempt to provide cover for the Second Marine Division. LVTs (Landing Vessel Troops) were chosen as the primary assault craft because their shallow draft would carry them over the coral reefs. The problem was that there were not enough for the entire assault force, and there were concerns that the first Marines to land might have difficulty in being reinforced because the much larger support assault vessels (Higgins boats) needed deeper water.

The assault concentrated on Betio's northwest shore, which was divided into Red Beach 2 and Red Beach 3. It would also extend north into the lagoon just beyond the reef: one of the most heavily defended areas of the island. A short western area was designated Green Beach. The strategy was to have three battalions of Marines land on the Red Beaches and move inland quickly across 600 yards of terrain and pin the enemy down. In doing so the Marines planned to capture the airfield and keep the enemy concentrated on the west side of the island. Naval gunfire and air support allowed the first three waves of Marines to land ashore virtually unscathed.

But things were not to remain that way. Once the Marines were ashore, naval gunfire support was limited. Nevertheless, Marines surprised the Japanese at Betio, overcame the sniper fire, and took the deepwater port. On Red Beach 2 and 3 it was a different story. As the first waves of the Third Battalion, Second Marines landed on Red Beach 2 they found a Japanese stronghold and lost 50 percent of their men to machine-gun fire. Red Beach 3 was next. Second Battalion, Eighth Marines got as far inland as the airstrip before Japanese resistance stopped them. This unit took only 25 casualties in landing and moved several hundred yards inland. Second Battalion, Second Marines encountered the most resistance when it landed at Red 2. In fact, few got ashore at Red 2 and were forced to land on Red 1 under heavy machine-gun fire.

Although the first three waves of assaults went pretty much according to plan, the Marines' worst fears were to be realized later. As the tides began to change, subsequent waves of troops, tanks, and artillery grounded on the reefs—sitting ducks for the enemy. Many Marines were forced to abandon their boats and wade 400 to 500 yards in chest-deep water carrying whatever they could under withering Japanese fire. The situation became chaotic as many became separated from their units and had no idea where to go once ashore. Marines had no time to regroup and as the tide went out, so did hopes of getting more troops and artillery ashore. This may have been the way Admiral Shibasaki planned it, knowing that a large enough force could not have landed on the island even under the best conditions because of the coral reefs and irregular tides. By evening of D Day there were about 5,000 Marines on land.

Confusion reigned. Many Marines were cut off from their units and continued to fight individually. However, it was their ability to improvise in the face of a logistical disaster that prevailed. Col. William K. Jones, commanding the First Battalion, Sixth Marines, later recalled, "I do not believe that heroism alone would have sufficed—although without it in extraordinary amounts Tarawa would never have been captured. What tipped the scales in our favor was the traditional ingenuity and flexibility which Marines have called upon many times in the past....Decimated units were regrouped into new and efficient fighting organizations, not on orders of higher authority but simply through the initiative of those officers and men in the vicinity."

Most men were centered on the pier at Betio, occupying a piece of real estate about 500 yards wide and 150 yards inland. A Japanese counterattack on that first night would have been devastating, but it never came. It was a golden opportunity squandered, for historians speculate that if the Japanese had counterattacked on that first night they would have been able to repel the landing forces. The fact was, the Japanese command had been decapitated very early in the battle. Shibasaki and his key staffers were killed by U.S. naval gunfire when they given up their heavily fortified command bunker on Betio for use as a hospital.

In the meantime, Marines succeeded in their initial goal of taking the pier at Betio and were able to hold it overnight until high tides the next morning allowed landing craft of the First Battalion, Eighth Marines, who had been in boats for over 20 hours, to come ashore. As they landed they fought to reinforce Red Beach 1, encountering heavy fire. Numerous Japanese snipers had placed themselves among the sunken hulks of landing craft that lay on or near the beach and they found easy targets as the Marines attempted to land.

By noon of the second day, yard by yard, Marines managed to gain control of the southern coast of the island, splitting the defenders into two groups. With naval support fire and Sherman tanks, which were used here for the first time in battle in the Pacific, Third Battalion, Eighth Marines took Green Beach on the western side of the island, securing a vital beachhead for landing artillery and reinforcements.

The second half of the first day was spent expanding the beachhead at Green Beach, and by evening Col. David M. Shoup, senior commander ashore, called for more reinforcements. Before nightfall Marines from the First Battalion, Sixth Marines, landed on Green Beach with hardly a shot fired, and Colonel Shoup (who was awarded the Medal of Honor for his actions at Tarawa) had his first fully equipped fighting force ashore.

A key factor in winning the battle was the taking of Green Beach on D+1, but the massive offensive on D+2 emphatically decided the outcome. Marines started early in the morning on a broad sweep eastward, with Sherman tanks clearing the path ahead while flamethrowers routed the enemy from caves and pillboxes. By now, the Japanese had been forced back to the eastern end of the island where they held strong positions just inland from Red Beach 1 and the eastern end of the airfield. But they were becoming desperate.

Near nightfall there was a last-ditch attempt by the Japanese to retake Betio, but after a day's fierce combat they were completely spent and had lost most of their armament. On the eastern end of the island, they made three attempts to charge two companies of First Battalion, Sixth Marines. All three failed as Marines thwarted them with artillery and gunfire from the destroyers USS *Schroeder* and *Sigbee*. The fact that U.S. warships could patrol and support Marines ashore with such ease was another battle-winning factor that would play a significant part in future amphibious assaults.

By the morning of the fourth day (D+3), Marines estimated there were 500 Japanese still alive on the island, most of them concentrated on the eastern end. Third Battalion, Sixth Marines stormed the only remaining Japanese stronghold, and by the end of the day Tarawa was in U.S. hands. Of the 2,800 Japanese assigned to defend the island, only 17 lived to surrender. The Korean construction troops also fared poorly. Of the 2,000 brought to the island as slaves, only 129 survived. Of the total Japanese forces on the whole atoll, 97 percent—4,859—were killed.

Marine Corps and U.S. Navy losses were also extreme and had a profound effect back in the U.S.A.: 990 dead and 2,311 Marines wounded in action. The Navy lost 644 men with the sinking of the carrier USS *Liscomb Bay* (sunk by a Japanese submarine), and a further 43 men when one of the 16-inch gun turrets aboard the battleship USS *Missouri* exploded.

The battle for Tarawa had considerable significance for the U.S. and the opening of its war in the Pacific. Strategically, it was important because it provided a base from which Marines could go on to take the Marshall Islands. Tactically, however, the battle was even more significant. It defined the means by which the war in the Pacific would be fought and won, over and over, island by island. Marines learned how the Japanese would react to certain tactics and gained much insight into the types of defenses they would meet on other islands. It was an invaluable lesson, and one learned the hardest way—in blood.

HIGHGROUND:
HILLS, MOUNTAINS, RIDGES

Throughout the history of warfare holding the high ground has been seen as a strategic and tactical imperative. It was no accident that most medieval castles were built on mounds or hilltops, from which the surrounding land could be surveyed and controlled. The seven battles in this chapter cover a variety of high grounds. Matthew Bennett's account of the Roman conquest of the Jewish hilltop garrison at Masada in A.D. 73/74, is a classic tale of siegecraft in the ancient world. The defense of the Little Round Top, a strategically crucial hill on the left flank of General Meade's Union line at the battle of Gettysburg, 1863, would have, as Professor Gary Gallagher points out, a profound effect not only on the outcome of the battle, but on the whole war. Two ridge battles are included: the great assault by the Canadians of the forbiddingly defended Vimy Ridge in northern France in 1917 was, as Nigel Cave relates, one of the great feats of arms during World War I. The aptly named "Bloody Nose Ridge" on the Pacific island of Peleliu in 1944 prompted Gen. Roy S. Geiger USMC, the commander of the American attackers, to declare: "The battle for Peleliu was the toughest in the entire war." And within that battle there was no tougher nut to crack than "Bloody Nose Ridge." Mountain warfare is represented by two battles that, although different in many specific ways, are united in the massive difficulty of fighting in such radically inhospitable terrain. Whether it was among the rock-strewn slopes of Monte Cassino in Italy, 1944, or among the frozen Taebeck Mountains of Korea at the Chosin Reservoir in 1950, geography and climate together conspired to have a lethal impact on the soldiers unlucky enough to fight there. The siege of Khe Sanh in Vietnam, 1968, saw two geographic characteristics—hills and jungle—combine to give this crucial battle its specific identity. Like an earlier Vietnam siege, at Dien Bien Phu in 1954, Khe Sanh was overlooked by hills held by a skilled and determined enemy. Like the French at Dien Bien Phu, the Americans also faced the master tactician of the North Vietnamese Army, Gen. Vo Nguyen Giap. But, as Col. Joseph Alexander here relates, the outcomes of the two battles were to be very different.

Masada, Israel, 73 A.D., from *The Survey of Western Palestine* by Capt. C.R. Conder
This map of Masada depicts the casemate walls surrounding the town, as well as the Roman camps outside of it. The "snake path," the main entrance to Masada, is indicated here by "the serpent" on the northeast side of the diamond-shaped fortress.

MASADA.

General Plan.

Scale

Silva's Camp

White Promontory

410 feet above Mediterranean Sea

The Serpent

Large Camp

ROMAN WALL OF CIRCUMVALLATION

The Chosen Few
Masada, Israel, A.D. 73–74

MATTHEW BENNETT

The huge rock fortress known as Masada rises some 1,300 feet above the east-ern shore of the Dead Sea. Now part of a desert wilderness, 2,000 years ago it was home to a palace complex constructed by the ruler of Judaea, Herod the Great (ruled 37-4 B.C.). Herod had gained power with the support of the Romans, who arrived in the region in the mid-first century B.C., and specifically with the aid of Mark Antony's legions. After his patron's suicide, following defeat at the naval battle of Actium in 31 B.C., Herod made an accommodation with Octavian, who, as Augustus, became the first Roman emperor.

Yet Herod never felt entirely secure as ruler of the Jews. He was a Roman puppet of mixed lineage (his mother was of the Hasmonean lines of kings, his father an Indumean from the southern part of the country) and a convert to a Greek-Roman lifestyle that offended against Jewish orthodoxy. So he constructed a series of fortifications throughout his kingdom as places of refuge in case of rebellion. Masada was the remotest and most formidable of these fortresses.

The rock is roughly diamond shaped, almost half a mile long and 250 yards across at its widest part. A casemate wall (double thickness, with rooms within the dividing space) some 4,250 feet long runs around the summit. Within this circumference, there was a western palace, with a throne room, and numer-ous smaller domestic structures. At the northern end, a complex of buildings formed a palace-villa of three stories, descending outside the walls to provide a spectacular belvedere. Behind and above it lay large storerooms and a Roman-style bathhouse. For although the region sees little rain for most of the year, heavy downfalls cause flooding. Furthermore, when the fortress was constructed, Herod's engineers dammed a couple of nearby wadis, water from which was carried to the rock via an aqueduct and stored in a series of cisterns capable of holding an estimated 1.4 million cubic feet.

Access to the site was chiefly via a northeastern entrance standing at the top of a zigzag route known as the "snake path," which entailed a three-hour climb from the valley bottom. Halfway down the western side, another gate gave onto a much shallower, 300-foot cliff. Fortified as it was, Masada was all but impregnable to any except the most determined besieger. In the Romans it found just such determination and skill in the art and science of siegecraft.

Emperor Augustus had been content to rule the newly acquired eastern provinces through a system of puppet-kings, of which Herod was just one. After his death there was a succession dispute that threw Judaea into turmoil. In A.D. 6, the country was taken under direct Roman rule, although the dynasty continued. The Jews found the Roman cult of emperor worship deeply offensive, and complained that the local Roman official appointed the high priest, which meant that any religious festival might become the occasion for a riot in Jerusalem. Also, the Jews began to look for a messiah who would save them from ungodly oppression. The Roman response was harsh and unimaginative: Their reaction to the predictable riots was massacre and the execution of anyone seen as the possible leader of rebellion. One such victim was Jesus of Nazareth.

In the face of Roman repression (despite some periods of conciliation) a Jewish resistance movement known as the Zealots began to gain ground. When Nero became emperor in A.D. 54, repression returned and intensified, forcing the Zealots to go underground. A militant splinter group, the Sicarians, named after the short curved daggers they carried, began a program of assassination of Jewish leaders sympathetic to Roman rule. The Romans could keep order only by even more severe repression, leading in A.D. 66 to a general rebellion. The Zealots seized Masada, killing the Roman garrison, while in Jerusalem they took control of the high priest and conduct of Temple affairs. The Antonia citadel was stormed and the garrison massacred. Cestus Gallus, governor of Syria, brought a force to besiege the city but was foiled by the onset of winter. In attempting to retreat, his troops were ambushed and suffered heavy losses, including the entire siege train.

Nero now appointed the vastly experienced commander Vespasian (who had commanded a legion in the conquest of Britain 20 years earlier) to suppress the revolt. He advanced south from Syria with the Sixth and Tenth legions, while his son Titus brought the 15th from Alexandria in Egypt: a force of up to 15,000 men. The Romans also collected a similar amount of auxiliary infantry and 5,000 auxiliary cavalry, while local rulers, including Agrippa II of Judaea, provided 4,000 cavalry and 10,000 archers: some 50,000 men in total.

It was inconceivable that the Jews could face such numbers in pitched battle, so they determined to rely upon fortifications. The defenses of Jerusalem were strengthened and the invaders were first opposed at Gabara, near the Sea of Galilee. The city was stormed, its male inhabitants killed or enslaved, the buildings burned to the ground. This was meant to be a salutary lesson to those who opposed Rome. The Romans then moved a few miles farther west to Jotapata, where the defenders were led by a certain Joseph who, as the historian Josephus, later chronicled the rebellion. The ensuing siege was to provide a chilling preview of events at Masada.

Jotapata was built on the spur of a hill and could be approached from only one direction. Vespasian deployed his stone-throwing artillery to put down a barrage of missiles, while his men labored day and night to construct a ramp up to the height of the walls. In response, the defenders raised the walls even higher, but eventually the Roman engineers completed the ramp and broke into the town, supported by fire from siege towers that over-topped the walls. The siege had lasted eight weeks, and the entire population was massacred. Josephus escaped, having hidden in a cave with other leaders, and then engaged in a suicide pact from which he emerged as the sole survivor. He then promptly joined the Romans.

By the end of A.D. 67, Vespasian had recovered Galilee, and in the spring of 68 he overran Samaria and began a blockade of Jerusalem. But later in the year came the news that Nero was dead. Vespasian had an interest in the succession and departed for Rome, leaving Titus to complete his campaign.

The siege of Jerusalem in A.D. 70 involved three (later four) legions, plus supporting troops, and lasted five months. Eventually, the Temple, the scene of last resistance, was stormed, and the heart was torn out of the Jewish rebellion. The sacred treasures were robbed to be displayed in Titus's triumph and the population dispersed. What could there be left to fight for?

The Zealots of the Sicarian faction who occupied Masada numbered about 1,000 men, women, and children, led by Eleazar ben Yair. They could depend upon vast storehouses of grain and the huge, water-filled cisterns with which Herod had provided the fortress. The Romans were nothing if not thorough, though, and in A.D. 73 the governor, Flavius Silva, set out with the Tenth legion, numerous auxiliaries, and a slave workforce to besiege the remote rock citadel.

As at Jotapata, Jerusalem, and many other sites, Flavius began with a blockade, surrounding the rock with fortifications (circumvallation) and establishing camps for his troops. Remarkably they can still be seen on the ground today, identified by archaeology and aerial photographs. The siege walls extended for nearly two miles, six feet thick and with 12 towers on the eastern side, about 100 yards apart. In addition, there are two large camps (one 140 x 180 yards, the other 130 x 160 yards) outside the walls to east and west, which housed the legionaries, and another six much smaller sites around the perimeter, for the auxiliary troops. Because of the remote site and climatic conditions, the rubble walls that formed the bases of the soldiers' tents (they slept and ate in groups of eight) and even the stone benches are still visible. In all, the camps could have accommodated up to 5,000 legionaries and a similar number of auxiliaries. Another 5,000 were Jewish prisoners responsible for carrying the food and water, while an unknown number of camp followers tending to the soldiers' needs also accompanied the besiegers.

Unlike the city sieges, Flavius could not expect hunger or thirst to play a part in reducing the defenders' resistance, so he set about constructing a ramp some 300 feet high against the lower, western cliff. The normal construction method was layers of stones, earth, and timber. It used to be assumed that the wood had to be brought from a great distance, although archaeological work in the 1990s found evidence of the use of (presumably local) tamarisk trees. It may be that the climate was more suitable to their growth 2,000 years ago, and indeed was generally wetter, making the terrain rather less inhospitable than it is today.

The huge ramp—one of the greatest feats of military engineering in history—can still be seen at the site, although it has slumped from an originally much wider top into a narrow ridge. Josephus tells us that it was over 25 yards wide, supporting a platform of large stones onto which the siege engines were wheeled. These included an iron-plated tower 90 feet high, from which Roman artillery and missiles kept the defenders at bay, and a battering ram. When the ramp was close enough, the ram was brought into play and eventually created a breach. Anticipating this, the defenders had already started upon a secondary wall. Faced in stone, but largely of timber and earth construction, it was built as a kind of box of interlocking beams with soil poured into the gaps. Because this structure gave under the blows of the ram, the impact was reduced.

Flavius Silva gave instructions to set fire to the second wall and torches were hurled into it and set it ablaze, but the wind blew the flames back on to the Roman siege engines, threatening to consume them. Then, as the turncoat Josephus puts it, the wind veered "as if by divine providence" in the direction of the wall, turning it into a blazing mass from top to bottom. The defenders' last resort was now destroyed.

At this point Josephus, writing later in Rome, has the attackers withdraw. It is difficult to see why they would give up the initiative at this point (unless the fire was so intense as to prevent any further advance). Also, Josephus may have had a political agenda in demonstrating the folly of those who continued to oppose the Romans. So, in two long imaginary speeches, Eleazar is depicted as urging suicide upon his remaining 960 followers, but sparing the food stores to show they had made a conscious decision to prefer "death to slavery." Next day, discovering the bodies, the Romans are represented as admiring the Zealots' determination. The only recorded survivors were two women and five children who had hidden in the aqueducts. Recent research has cast doubt upon the suicide story, but whatever its validity, it is too deeply embedded in Israeli mythology to eradicate. And even today, soldiers of the armored units of the Israeli Army swear their military oath at the rock.

The Little Round Top, Gettysburg, 1863, from *Civil War Maps* (2nd ed.)

This 1863 sketch by T. Ditterline shows troop, cavalry, and artillery positions during July 1–3, the three days of the Battles at Gettysburg. The Rebel line is indicated by red dashes; the Union line by blue. The Little Round Top is the hill at the southern end of the Union line (depicted on the last two days of fighting). Residents' houses are marked with their names.

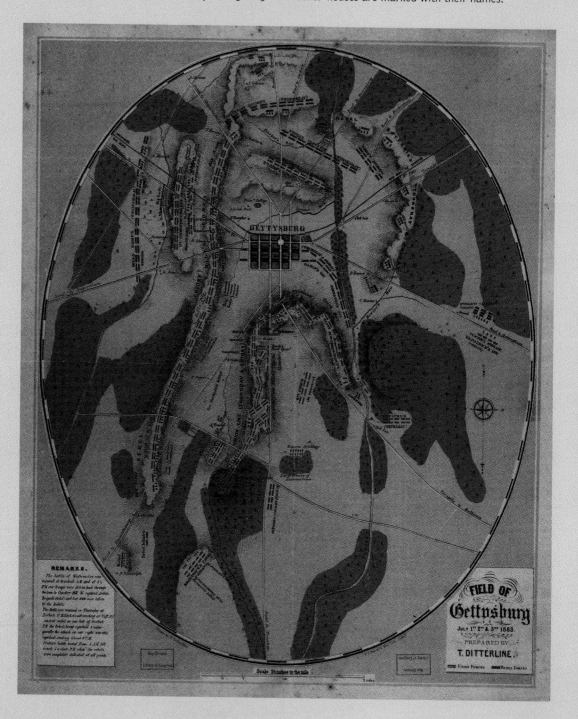

"Fix Bayonets"
The Little Round Top, Gettysburg, 1863

GARY GALLAGHER

The Battle of Gettysburg, bloodiest of all actions during the Civil War, featured a series of struggles for ridges and hills. On July 1, 1863, the first of the three days of fighting at Gettysburg, Gen. Robert E. Lee's Confederate Army of Northern Virginia won a striking tactical victory by driving the First and 11th Corps of Maj. Gen. George G. Meade's Army of the Potomac off McPherson's Ridge and Seminary Ridge. The Federal Army made a stand that night on high ground south and southwest of the town. Meade's line extended from Culp's Hill on his right, to Cemetery Hill in his center, and south along Cemetery Ridge on his left. Lee's army occupied Seminary Ridge opposite Meade's left and faced the Federal center and right from positions on lower ground. Beyond Meade's left, Cemetery Ridge terminated at the northern slope of Little Round Top, a knob outside the scope of the fighting on July 1 but at the center of action on July 2 that ranked with the most dramatic episodes in U.S. military history.

Robert E. Lee's tactical plan for July 2 ensured that Little Round Top would come into play as a critical piece of terrain. Hoping to apply simultaneous pressure against Meade's flanks, Lee instructed Lt. Gen. James Longstreet to assault the Federal left with two divisions of his First Corps, and Longstreet launched his offensive about 4:00 p.m. Maj. Gen. John Bell Hood's division swept eastward from the Emmitsburg Road, clearing Federal defenders from Maj. Gen. Daniel E. Sickles's Third Corps out of Devil's Den, a boulder-strewn hillock separated from Little Round Top by a stream called Plum Run. As the Confederates reached the top of Devil's Den, they gazed toward Little Round Top, which rose to a height of 650 feet and dominated the valley of Plum Run. Although many Confederates described Little Round Top as a "mountain," it was 135 feet lower than Round Top, an eminence a short distance to the south. The crucial difference between the two was that trees covered the slopes and summit of Round Top, rendering it useless as a possible artillery position. In contrast, the western half of Little Round Top had been cleared, making it the vital point on the southern end of the field. Whoever controlled it would be able to command the entire Federal line along Cemetery Ridge.

Although Little Round Top had not been defended early in the day, Federals had taken positions along its southern and western slopes shortly before the Confederates seized Devil's Den. General Meade had instructed his chief engineer, Brig. Gen. Gouverneur K. Warren, to check the far Federal left, and Warren had found nothing but a group of signalmen on the hill. Little Round Top was "the key to the whole position," realized Warren, a potential anchor for the Federal Army's left, and so he prudently requested troops to hold the position. Presently a brigade from Maj. Gen. George Sykes's Fifth Corps ascended the hill. Commanded by 26-year-old Col. Strong Vincent, the 1,350-man brigade consisted of the 44th New York, 16th Michigan, 83rd Pennsylvania, and 20th Maine regiments. Vincent examined the ground, decided the southern slope of the hill was most vulnerable, and placed his regiments (from right to left the 16th, 44th, 83rd, and 20th) on a line that dropped from the military crest toward a spur that faced the northern slope of Round Top. That spur represented the likely target for any Confederate effort to turn Vincent's flank, and the 20th Maine, led by Col. Joshua L. Chamberlain, a college professor before the war, occupied it. Chamberlain observed in his official report that Vincent "indicated to me…that this was the extreme left of our general line, and that a desperate attack was expected in order to turn that position, concluding by telling me I was 'to hold that ground at all hazards.'"

The Confederates who strove to seize Little Round Top belonged to the brigades of Brig. Gen. Evander M. Law, who commanded five regiments of Alabamians, and Brig. Gen. Jerome B. Robertson, whose three Texas regiments and one Arkansas regiment were justly celebrated as the finest shock troops in Lee's army. Six of the nine regiments—the Fourth, 15th, 47th, and 48th Alabama and Fourth and Fifth Texas, numbering perhaps 2,250 in all, would carry the burden of the assaults. These regiments had marched a considerable distance during the day but, like the men of Vincent's brigade, had been spared any serious fighting. They had crossed Plum Run, progressing eastward, whereupon the Fourth and Fifth Texas and Fourth Alabama, in that order from left to right, shifted their front to the north in woods along the base of Round Top. From there, they moved toward open ground at the southwestern base of Little Round Top while the 47th and 15th Alabama, led by Col. William C. Oates of the 15th, continued straight ahead toward the peak of Round Top.

The epic struggle for Little Round Top began on the Federal right. The Fourth Maine Infantry, after being engaged in Devil's Den, had gone into line astride Plum Run to prevent any Confederate advance against the western face of Little Round Top. The Fourth and Fifth Texas, a short distance southeast of the Fourth Maine, cleared the woods and started to climb toward the positions of the 44th New York and 83rd Pennsylvania. Col. James C. Rice, commanding the New Yorkers, reported that the Texans "approached in three columns, with no skirmishers in advance. The object of the enemy was evident. If he could gain the vantage ground occupied by this brigade, the left flank of our line must give way, opening to him a vast field for successful operations in the rear of our entire army." "Upon their first appearance, we opened a heavy fire upon them," commented another New York officer, "which was continued until they were compelled to retire." The Confederates, wrote Col. R. M. Powell of the Fifth Texas, faced an "ascent so difficult as to forbid the use of arms" during the climb. One of Powell's soldiers left a vivid description of the attack: "As we start up the mountain we got a plunging volley from the enemy, who are posted behind the rocks on the crest....Their first volley was most destructive to our line. Every line officer of my regiment is shot down except one man—the major."

The fighting surged back and forth along the rocky shelf of the hill, with the Confederates making at least three major attempts to carry the position. Although the Texans achieved little coordination with the Fourth Alabama to their right, the three southern regiments exerted considerable pressure on the

44th New York, 83rd Pennsylvania, and 16th Michigan. Late in the action, stern pressure from the Fifth Texas and the 48th Alabama, together with a confusion of orders on the Federal side, triggered a momentary collapse of the Michiganders' right. The timely appearance of the 140th New York, clad in bright Zouave uniforms and ably led by Col. Patrick O'Rorke, who had graduated at the head of his West Point class of 1861, helped restore the line. O'Rorke was killed outright and Col. Vincent mortally wounded in this phase of the battle.

With the restoration of Vincent's right flank, the focus of the battle shifted to the spur occupied by Chamberlain's 20th Maine. Col. Oates's 15th Alabama, following a tiring climb and descent of Round Top, had maneuvered with the purpose of turning Chamberlain's left. The 47th Alabama had suffered from the loss of its commander and a stinging fire from Federals in its front, which rendered the regiment largely ineffective and denied Oates support on his left. Oates's soldiers, who counted 499 muskets against 386 in the 20th Maine, faced the prospect of driving their opponent from higher ground. But the disparity in elevation was less pronounced than on the Texans' end of the line, and Oates skillfully sought to extend his line to the right in such as way as to get around Chamberlain. The two regiments alternated probing the other's position and suffered a significant number of casualties in the process.

Alarmed by Oates's steady progress toward his unsupported left flank, Chamberlain reconfigured his line into the shape of a flat V. "Mounting a large rock, I was able to see a considerable body of the enemy moving by the flank in rear of their line engaged, and passing...toward the front of my left," explained Chamberlain after the battle. "I immediately stretched my regiment to the left, by taking intervals by the left flank, and at the same time 'refusing' my left wing, so that it was nearly at right angles with my right...."

Oates's soldiers mounted heavy attacks soon after Chamberlain redrew his line. "The edge of the fight rolled backward and forward like a wave," recalled Chamberlain, and the fighting often was viciously hand to hand. Confederate pressure against the remainder of Vincent's brigade remained such that no reinforcements could buttress the 20th Maine, whose casualties were mounting toward a third of the regiment. Ammunition was running low, and

Chamberlain doubted that his men could withstand another assault from Oates's Alabamians. For his part, Oates believed that his men, after marching more than 25 miles and fighting a bloody uphill battle, had reached their limits. At first deciding to "sell out as dearly as possible" on the side of the hill, he thought better of it and opted for a withdrawal to Round Top, where he hoped to re-form his exhausted regiment. Chamberlain decided on a more aggressive solution to his problems. If he could not be sure of holding his line, he would try to smash his enemy's. He ordered his soldiers to "fix bayonets" and charge, with the 20th's left swinging down the slope into line with the right and the whole regiment advancing as rapidly as possible. The charging Federals cleared the Confederates from their front, taking many prisoners and ending the threat to the Federal flank. Oates denied that his men were driven from the field but admitted they "ran like wild cattle" when he ordered them to retreat.

After a few final spasms of fighting along Vincent's brigade front, the onset of darkness cloaked the retreat of the Texas regiments to the slope of Round Top. Vincent's brigade, assisted by the 140th New York and other reinforcements, had withstood Law's and Robertson's determined attacks. Confederate casualties amounted to about one-third of those engaged; the Federals, fighting with the advantage of high ground, suffered roughly 20 percent casualties. Chamberlain's regiment, which led the Federal units in terms of percentage lost, counted 125 killed, wounded, and missing. Losses in the Fifth Texas exceeded 50 percent, those in the 15th Alabama 34 percent. On a day when thousands fell in places such as the Wheatfield, the Peach Orchard, East Cemetery Hill, and Culp's Hill, the action at Little Round Top counted for a relatively minor portion of the overall casualties. Yet the contest for this modest hill loomed large as part of the Federal Army's successful repulse of Lee's offensive blows, reversing the momentum Confederates had generated the day before and setting up the climactic action of July 3.

Vimy Ridge, France, 1917, Canadian barrage map

The precipitous drop on the east side of Vimy Ridge impaired the Germans' ability to launch counterattacks. Having lost land to the west of the ridge in 1915, the Germans no longer had the option of keeping reserves in the rear and lacked sufficient ground area to maneuver effectively. The Canadians used this barrage map during the assault.

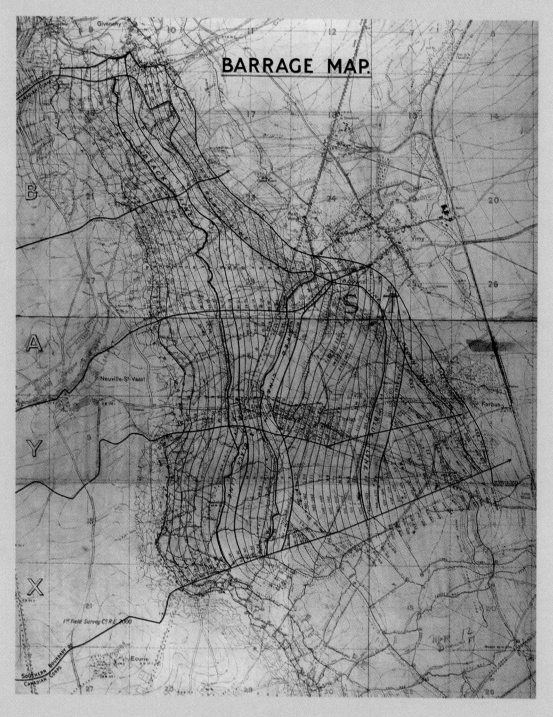

BARRAGE MAP.

The Canadians' Great Assault
Vimy Ridge, France, 1917

NIGEL CAVE

The area around Arras has seen a great deal of warfare over the centuries. Arras itself formed part of the Burgundian dominions of Philip II in the 16th century and only came directly under the French crown in the middle of the 17th century. Marlborough spent much of the campaigning season of 1711 in a fruitless attempt to break through the French defenses in the area, and in 1940 the British Frank Force managed to launch a limited offensive, based on Vimy Ridge, to delay the inexorable advance of the German panzers, and win valuable time for the evacuation from the beaches around Dunkirk.

Vimy Ridge lies a few miles to the north of Arras, an ancient cathedral city 95 miles north of Paris. The Ridge runs from the southeast to the north-northwest for several miles, reaching its highest point almost at the northern end, about 450 feet above sea level. The summit of the Ridge, especially to the north, offers dramatic views across the Plain of Douai to the east, which in 1917 was studded with numerous coal mines. To the northeast it overlooks the great industrial city of Lens. On a clear day the hills south of Ypres are visible, including Messines Ridge, a significant proportion of which was to be blown sky high by the biggest mining operation of the war as part of the successful British offensive that commenced on June 7, 1917.

After the final throes of the 1914 campaign in the west, culminating in the race for the open flank and the desperate struggles around Ypres, the

Germans occupied the high ground around Arras. They took up positions some distance forward of Vimy Ridge, based on the defenses and viewpoints offered by the equally high ground of the neighboring Lorette spur, which runs in a broadly east-west direction and is separated from Vimy Ridge by the Souchez Valley. This secured the important mining and industrial area east of the Ridge. Successive French offensives in 1914 and 1915—collectively known as the Battles of Artois—succeeded in pushing the Germans back to the summit of the Ridge at its northern end. Indeed, for one glorious moment in May 1915, the Moroccan Division managed to secure its summit. However, the Germans pushed the French off. Jostling for position, both sides settled down to holding on to the best positions that they could and began to engage in a massive campaign of underground warfare, making use of the chalk substratum, which was ideal for tunneling.

The French made no further attempts to seize the Ridge, and in February 1916, soon after the German attritional offensive at Verdun commenced, the sector was handed over to the rapidly expanding British Expeditionary Force (BEF). The British confined their activities here to winning the underground battle and set about a systematic campaign to take the initiative. Along the Ridge it was said that you could almost set your watch by the 7:00 p.m. mine explosion—one British staff officer noted in his diary on May 1, 1916, "For once in a way a mine did not go up in the evening so had a quiet night."

This situation became of so much concern to the Germans that toward the end of May they launched a massive limited offensive to seize the mine heads toward the northern part of the Ridge, and to advance their line by several hundred yards, thereby strengthening their hold on the summit. After this excitement, and with the continuation of mine warfare, the focus of the Allied campaigning switched south, to the Battle of the Somme (July 1 to November 18, 1916). It was there that all four divisions of the Canadian Corps saw action (the fourth division arrived in France in August 1916); and from there they gathered, for the first time all together, in the line opposite the Ridge.

As part of the spring campaign for 1917, Field Marshal Haig, commander of the BEF, had agreed to cooperate with the offensive proposed by the dynamic and persuasive new French commander, Robert Nivelle, who had mesmerized both French and British politicians with his vision of a decisive victory in the west, to be launched in the Champagne region. The British commanders were far from convinced, but undertook to support his offensive by making a major attack around Arras. This would be spearheaded by Allenby's Third Army, situated to the east and south of Arras. It was decided that General Horne's British First Army, immediately to the north, would contribute by seizing Vimy Ridge, which would provide security for the left flank of the attack and dominate the Plain of Douai, to the east below.

This part of the battle came under the command of General Byng, a British cavalry officer who had become the Canadian Corps commander at the end of May 1916. In October 1916, almost as soon as the whole Corps had assembled, he set about planning a careful and complex operation to take the Ridge, taking full advantage of the developments in operational warfare. Staff officers were sent to investigate how the French had managed to recover most of the territory lost to the Germans in the first months of the fighting at Verdun; others were sent to study heavily mined parts of the Somme battlefield to work out how well troops could move across the mined landscape along Vimy Ridge and beyond. New developments in artillery technology were adapted and used, such as sound ranging and flash spotting. The ease of working in the chalk below the ground was used to construct a series of subway accesses from the rear to the front-line positions.

The transformation of munitions production in the U.K. meant that at last there was a sufficiency of artillery of the right type and caliber and an ample supply of shells to go with them, along with the new 106 "Fuze instantaneous." Excellent staff work meant that the huge quantities of ordnance supplies could be brought forward to maintain such a sizeable force. Because it was the only First Army formation going into action on the day, the Canadian Corps could borrow significant elements of the army artillery and some from the corps to the north. Above all, it had the advantage of a Corps whose composite Canadian divisions and support elements—engineers, artillery, and so forth—would almost always in future work together, and not be moved around, as was the case for their equivalent British formations. In addition, because of the nature of the task, the Corps was given the British Fifth Division. Indeed, the additional

British engineers, gunners, tunnelers, and men of Fifth Division represented over 40 percent of the men under Corps command or in its area.

The German generals faced a considerable problem. Because of the loss of ground west of Vimy Ridge in 1915, they had little room at the northern end of the Ridge to maneuver effectively. In particular, the policy of keeping reserves in the rear and bringing them forward as the enemy artillery fell out of range and when the attacking troops had lost cohesion was not really an option here because the deep escarpment on the east side of the Ridge, at least at the northern end, made it extremely difficult to launch counterattacks. General Falkenhausen, commanding the defending Sixth Army, placed his reserves 15 miles to the rear instead of close behind his Second Line, as doctrine required—convinced that his frontline troops were capable of holding up the assault long enough for him to bring up his reserves. In any event, they were too far back to take any effective part in the onrush that swept over the Ridge.

This should not underestimate the achievement of Byng and his planners in carrying out a complex maneuver that over 12 hours of infantry battle succeeded in taking all the objectives on a 7,000-yard front (except Hill 145 to the north, which fell the following day). This achievement was due to a considerable extent to the effective use of counter-battery work, a technique introduced by the French and developed by the British (particularly V Corps) on the Somme. Over 80 percent of German heavy artillery was knocked out before the battle commenced.

In the two weeks before the battle the Germans—artillery, infantry, airmen, and supply—were harried. Rations to the front were inordinately delayed, and ration parties that used to take 15 minutes took anything up to six hours—if they arrived at all. In the cold April of 1917 this had a devastating effect on the morale of the soldiers in the line. Artillery positions and crossroads, trench junctions, and communications systems were relentlessly targeted.

Smooth operating logistics, effective control, limited objectives under artillery cover, and the quality of the troops, hardened and experienced by the months on the Somme, as was much of the BEF, resulted in complete success. This was crowned by the taking of the Pimple, a prominence at the northern extremity of the Ridge, on April 12. To be added to the capability of the fighting men was "General" Luck. Easter Monday, April 9, was a miserably cold day, with snow being blown into the faces of the German defenders. In this case, poor visibility was a definite advantage for the attackers.

The capture of Vimy Ridge was an outstanding success—as indeed, by and large, was the whole of the British attack on April 9. Indeed the farthest advance of the day, well over three miles that included the vital high point known as the Point du Jour, was made by the British XVII Corps.

The Canadian success came at a heavy cost—over 10,000 casualties to the Corps in the fighting between October 9-14, though most of fell on the 9th. Not only had the Germans been thrown off the Ridge, but the Canadian Corps (including the British Fifth Division), had pushed them deep into the Douai Plain. The Ridge remained in Allied hands throughout the rest of the war, despite considerable pressure during the German Spring Offensive of 1918.

But April 9, 1917, was Canada's day. Censorship regulations had by then been relaxed enough so that individual corps operations could be made public. Vimy Ridge was already a well-known feature in the world's press: The subheading of almost every newspaper proclaiming the start of the Battle of Arras referred to the Canadians capturing Vimy Ridge. Congratulations flowed from Allied governments around the world.

The Canadian Corps went on to win more important battles, and more technically complex ones. General Currie (the Canadian appointed Corps commander in June 1917 when Byng was promoted to command the Third [British] Army) was quick to point this out when the question of siting memorials in the postwar years arose. The brilliant crossing of the Canal du Nord in September 1918 immediately comes to mind. But for many Canadians—then and since— it was here at Vimy that Canada fought the action that placed it in the ranks of nations: It marked her coming of age. It was at Vimy that Canada's great Memorial to the Missing was erected, unveiled in 1936, recording on its stones the names of over 10,000 Canadian solders who died in France with no known grave (those in Belgium are on the Menin Gate in Ypres). And the shell-ravaged ground—250 acres in all—with its mine craters and trench lines, its subway system and below that several miles of tunnels, remains one of the most important and deeply moving testaments to the Great War in France.

Peleliu, 1944, from *The Assault of Peleliu,* by Maj. Frank O. Hough, USMCR, 1950
Peleliu is an island, but the aspect of its topography that proved most daunting in this WWII
battle was the Umurbrogal, a labyrinthine network of ridges, caves, and crevasses. "Bloody
Nose Ridge" is located in the southwest region of the Umurbrogal mountains, which stretch
along the western coast of the island. The U.S. Marine Corps used this map during the attack.

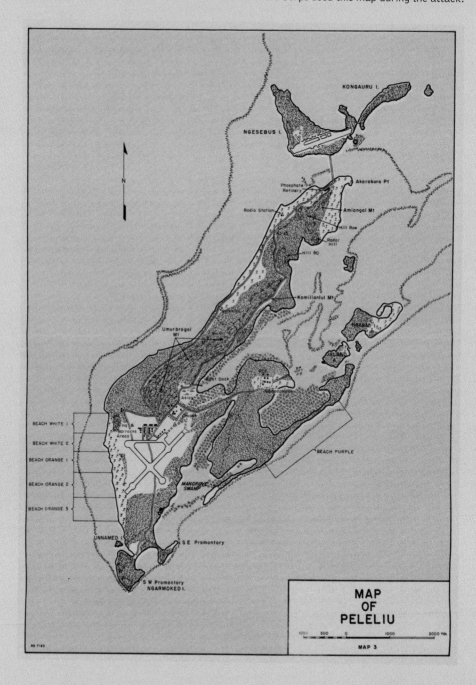

Haunted Highlands
"Bloody Nose Ridge," Peleliu, 1944

COLONEL JOSEPH H. ALEXANDER, USMC (RET.)

Two unexpected factors made the 1944 Battle of Peleliu so costly for the invading U.S. III Amphibious Corps: the island's convoluted topography and the resourcefulness of the Japanese defenders in converting that terrain to their tactical advantage. The American troops at Peleliu encountered one of the most disciplined infantry regiments in the Imperial Japanese Army, a unit recently redeployed to the Pacific theater from the Soviet border in Manchuria. The Japanese found Peleliu's coral limestone ridges, cliffs, and caves in the northwestern highlands to be ideal for a defense in depth. The natives called this mountain complex Umurbrogal. The Marines, misled by aerial photographs depicting a gently undulating hill covered by scrub jungle, would ruefully nickname it "Bloody Nose Ridge."

As one surviving participant reported, "Our language just does not contain the words that can adequately describe the horrible inaccessibility of the central ridge line on Peleliu. It was a nightmare's nightmare."

The U.S. Joint Chiefs of Staff selected Peleliu as a campaign objective in their strategic plan to defeat Japan because of its location at the lower end of the Palaus, an 80-mile island chain running north to south and lying equidistant between Guam and the eastern Philippines. The Japanese called the Palaus "the spigot of our oil barrel," because their laden tankers used the islands' protected passage en route to the Empire from oil fields in the Dutch

East Indies. Moreover, the Japanese bomber strip on Peleliu threatened the right flank of Gen. Douglas MacArthur's imminent "return to the Philippines" from his advance bases in New Guinea.

Troops of the First Marine Division and the 81st Army Division composed the landing force for the Palaus under Maj. Gen. Roy S. Geiger, USMC, commanding III Amphibious Corps. The Marines would assault Peleliu; the soldiers, neighboring Angaur, then Ulithi Atoll, north of the Palaus, prepared at all times to reinforce the Marines on Peleliu, the prime target. D Day was set for September 15, 1944.

General Geiger knew he would face at Peleliu a well-armed force of 10,000 soldiers and sailors commanded by Col. Kunio Nakagawa. But Geiger knew nothing of Nakagawa's exceptional leadership and resourcefulness. Nor did any U.S. commanders know that Imperial General Headquarters in Tokyo had just ordered a radical change to their counter-landing doctrine. No longer would Japanese commanders defend their islands at the water's edge, followed by a sacrificial banzai charge, as had proved so unsuccessful at Tarawa and Saipan. Beginning with Peleliu—and extending sequentially to Iwo Jima and Okinawa—the island commanders would "disrupt" the U.S. landing while preserving their main forces in underground caves and bunkers, waging a protracted battle of attrition to "bleed" the attackers and discourage the American home front.

Significantly, Geiger also lacked information about Peleliu's distinctive topography, especially the daunting terrain of the Umurbrogal. Neither aerial photographs nor periscope reconnaissance by offshore submarines revealed the cliffs that lay shielded by the scrub jungle. Geiger accordingly approved he assault plan that assigned a single regiment, Col. Lewis B. ("Chesty") Puller's First Marines, to assail the Umurbrogal after D Day.

Blissfully unaware of these critical shortfalls, Puller declared to his veteran troops, "This is going to be a short one, a quickie….We'll be through in three days. It might take only two."

Hubris and ignorance produced a painful reality for the Marines on D Day. The Japanese withstood a final flurry of naval gunfire and dive-bombers, then unleashed a deadly crossfire against the U.S. assault waves from artillery and heavy mortars hidden in the highlands and 25mm machine cannon emplaced in concrete-reinforced coral outcroppings along the flank of the landing beaches. The effect was murderous. Within the first hour the Marines lost 60 landing vehicles and amphibious trucks, and more than 1,100 Marines became casualties by nightfall. In the grim calculus of amphibious assaults to date in the Pacific, only Tarawa and Saipan exceeded the D Day butcher's bill at Peleliu. General Geiger, who would face the Japanese in campaigns ranging from Guadalcanal to Okinawa, later admitted that "the battle for Peleliu was the toughest in the entire Pacific War."

On D Day, hearing the urgent reports of his assault commanders and observing the landing vehicles burning in the shallows from the flagship, Geiger decided to go ashore and see for himself what had disrupted the assault plans. Landing a full day before the division commander, Geiger surveyed the battlefield from the captured Japanese antitank ditch that marked the inland extension of the Marines' beachhead. By this time the naval bombardment had burned off much of the jungle screening the contours of the Umurbrogal. Geiger was appalled. The highlands dominated both the beachhead and the nearby airfield. Moreover, the topography revealed itself to be an ungodly jumble of sheer cliffs, crevices, spires, and canyons. Enemy muzzle flashes emanated from dozens of caves and fissures. One large-caliber, direct-fire shell nearly took Geiger's head off, the shock of the near miss tumbling him on his back in the ditch. His heart sank at the realization of how difficult it was going to be for his Marines to seize the high ground.

Geiger's chief of staff, Col. Merwin H. Silverthorn, described Peleliu's terrain as "abominable...the most horrible terrain I'd ever encountered. It was as though several submerged reefs had been forced up out of the water with their jagged sharp edges...the ridges were as steep as the roof of a house."

The island of Peleliu had indeed been formed by volcanic upthrusts from the ocean floor. But where the pressure had proved strongest, according to historian Frank O. Hough, "the ground had buckled and cracked to form a maze of ridges and defiles, the whole littered with jagged boulders and rubble which had been torn apart by the violent action."

Brig. Gen. Oliver P. Smith, USMC, the assistant division commander, landed early enough on D Day to be able to greet Geiger in the tank ditch. Smith recorded his observations of the terrain in his journal: "Ravines...actually had sheer cliffs for sides...There were dozens of caves worked into the noses of the ridges and up the ravines. It was very difficult to find blind spots as the caves and pillboxes were mutually supporting." The contemporary First Marines Regimental Narrative recorded another aspect of the punishing terrain: "It was impossible to dig in...casualties were higher for the simple reason it was impossible to get underground away from the Japanese mortar barrages. Every blast hurled chunks of coral in all directions."

Col. Nakagawa, given a three-month respite when the U.S. chose to invade the Marianas before the Palaus in 1944, used the expertise of the miners and tunnel builders in his naval construction battalion—in addition to backbreaking work by his riflemen with pick, shovel, and dynamite—to expand Peleliu's natural limestone caves, dig secondary entrances, and develop mutually supporting firing positions. One elaborate cave proved to be four stories deep, capable of holding more than 1,000 men.

"The ruggedness of the terrain was almost indescribable," recalled Pfc. Eugene B. Sledge, a 60mm mortarman with the Fifth Marines. "The crazy-contoured coral ridges and rubble-filled canyons [were]...like no other battlefield on earth. It was an alien, unearthly, surrealistic nightmare like the surface of another planet."

It was a credit to the veteran Marines—and to the ship's gunners and carrier-based dive-bomber pilots who supported them—that the landing force fought its way ashore through such a vicious crossfire. The three regiments seized a beachhead, maintained their tactical integrity, repulsed a spectacular tank-led counterattack, and prepared to advance inland.

The most desperate fighting in the initial phase took place at "The Point," a fortified promontory on the left flank of the landing beaches, seized by Company K of the First Marines in what became one of the classic small-unit assaults in Corps history. The remnants of the company, cut off from their regiment, defended their gains against heavy counterattacks the ensuing two days and nights. Capt. George P. Hunt, commanding the stout-hearted company, described the small battleground as "a rocky mass of sharp pinnacles, deep crevasses, [and] tremendous boulders." (As recently as 1999 it was still possible to slither into the aperture of the main Japanese casemate, sight down the rusty barrel of the 25mm machine cannon, and marvel at the shooting-gallery field of fire the gunners must have enjoyed against the Marine landing vehicles.)

Chesty Puller's First Marines launched a five-day assault against the south-western ramparts of the Umurbrogal, the cluster of peaks most specifically addressed as "Bloody Nose Ridge." The attacks were as brave as they were costly. Lt. Bruce Watkins, commanding a platoon that would lose three-fourths of its numbers in the steep assaults, recalled how Japanese gunners hidden in the caves made sitting ducks of his advancing Marines. "They could see us so clearly from their dark caves, and we were so blinded by the bright coral," he said, "that until we got right on top of them it was like a Civil War advance—better intervals, maybe, and very wary, but terribly exposed."

Puller's men surpassed themselves, overwhelming peaks and crests that seemed unassailable, capturing ten ridgelines and neutralizing 155 caves. Yet by September 20 the proud regiment was shot to pieces—one battalion sustained 71 percent losses—and had to be redeployed to the Russell Islands for rehabilitation. Sequentially, the Seventh and Fifth Marines would take their turns in the Umurbrogal, followed by the regiments of the 81st Army Division, fresh from their victories at Angaur and Ulithi. Each would pay a high price.

The succession of regiments gradually constricted the Japanese resistance in the highlands to a pocket roughly 900 by 400 yards, yet the Japanese continued to defend their remaining caves and canyons for week after week. The troops, scrambling over the rugged terrain in skull-cracking heat, chronically short of drinking water, and always at risk of being shot in the back from a cave previously deemed neutralized, became fatalistic about the battle. "Many of us thought the Japs would fight on for years," said Eugene Sledge. The highlands' bizarre cliffs and declivities took on foreboding nicknames: the Five Sisters, the China Wall, the Five Brothers, Death Valley. As the Second Battalion, Fifth Marines reported on the 13th day of the battle, "The hill we were taking was honeycombed with caves, and we used everything in the book in closing them. (Hand grenades, five-gallon cans of gas, composition C [explosive] wrapped around 81mm WP [white phosphorus] mortar shells, flame throwers, and finally a 155mm gun)." And still the fighting raged on.

General MacArthur validated his promise to return to the Philippines, landing in great strength on the island of Leyte on October 20, 1944. On that same date, the First Marine Division, having suffered more than 6,500 casualties to protect MacArthur's right flank during that strategic deployment, turned over the battle for Peleliu's Umurbrogal Pocket to the 81st Army Division and steamed back to the Russells to prepare for the Okinawa campaign.

The Army resorted to siege tactics to break the deadlock. Over the next five weeks the soldiers made a valient effort to deliver sandbags from the beach to the highlands, winched artillery to the heights for direct fire against adjacent cave mouths, built large ramps to provide access for tanks into Colonel Nakagawa's final canyon redoubt, and interdicted the enemy's efforts to replenish their water supply by illuminating and barricading the few remaining sumps.

Colonel Nakagawa committed ritualistic suicide—later receiving a posthumous promotion to lieutenant general from his appreciative emperor—and by November 27 all organized resistance ended. Some ordnance officer calculated that it took the U.S. forces 1,589 rounds (bombs, shells, bullets) to kill each of the 10,900 Japanese slain in the battle, a reflection of the enemy's superb use of the terrain in defending the island.

Peleliu's caves continued to shelter die-hard bands of Japanese survivors for years. On April 21, 1947, Lt. Ei Yamaguchi formally surrendered the last 26 of his men to U.S. authorities.

The Marines who survived Peleliu remained bitter about their losses and the dubious strategic benefits attained, arguing with considerable logic that MacArthur no longer needed Peleliu and its dearly bought bomber strip by the time the Marines stormed ashore. Yet the battle was not devoid of benefits. Six months after leaving Peleliu, the First Marine Division would find itself extremely well prepared for the longer, costlier Battle of Okinawa, especially in terms of tank-infantry coordination, the tactical use of flame-throwers, and the employment of combined arms to overcome Japanese ridge-and-cave defenses.

Fittingly, in the final month of the war, it was a Peleliu-based U.S. Navy search plane that found the 316 waterlogged and delirious survivors from the torpedoed cruiser *Indianapolis* on the fourth day of their incredible ordeal.

Crown of Thorns
Monte Cassino, Italy, 1944

STEPHEN BADSEY

The famous monastery on the heights of Monte Cassino (17 miles inland from the Gulf of Gaeta, south of Rome) was founded about 529 by St. Benedict. Almost 1,000 years later the historic monastery and its 1,600-foot mountain became the setting for one of the epic battles of the Second World War. When the Allies landed in southern Italy on September 3, 1944, the Italian government surrendered (Italy declared war on Germany on October 13, and Italian troops fought alongside the Allies later in the war) and a rapid Allied advance through Italy to the Alps beckoned. But against a determined German defense, the Allies did not reach Naples until October 1. Hitler ordered his commander in Italy, Field Marshal Albert Kesselring of Army Group C, to establish strong defensive lines across the peninsula from the Adriatic to the Tyrrhenian Sea, blocking the way to Rome some 120 miles farther north.

The Apennine mountain range forms a spine running almost the length of Italy, and about four-fifths of the country is either mountains or hills, giving way to plains along both coasts. Just under halfway from Naples to Rome, across the narrowest part of the Italian Peninsula, the Germans established the "Gustav Line" from the Gulf of Gaeta to the Adriatic, ordered by Hitler to be strengthened to fortress status in December 1943, and defended by Tenth Army under Col. Gen. Heinrich von Vietinghoff. To the east, the Gustav Line was constructed along the mountains above the River Sangro that come almost down to the

Monte Cassino, Italy, 1944, 36th Infantry Division WWII campaigns
This pictorial map, which shows Rome and its vicinity, chronicles the events in the Italian campaign
of the U.S. Army's 36th Infantry Division from 1943 to 1944. The "T" Patch in the upper-right
corner represents the 36th, and the two red stars beside it stand for the two Italian campaigns.

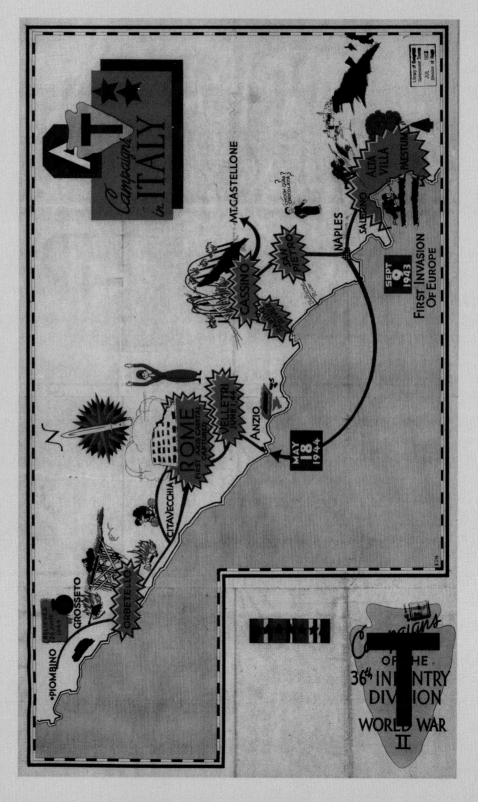

sea, and with no open plain beyond there was little point in the Allies attacking this terrain. To the west, there were two historic routes from Naples to Rome, both defended by the mountains of the Gustav Line. The Appian Way (Via Appia), the coast road running between the sea and the Aurunci Mountains known to the Allies as Route 7, crosses the River Garigliano as it flows into the sea near Monte Girafino. Inland from the Aurunci Mountains, the Via Casalina—or Route 6, to the Allies—crosses the River Rapido, a tributary of the Garigliano, and passes directly under the heights of Monte Cassino, a sheer peak that overlooks completely the road and accompanying rail track. This road runs through the valley of the River Liri, which flows roughly parallel to the coast and into the Rapido just before its confluence with the Garigliano. A flat and fertile plain about 5 to 10 miles wide between Monte Girafino and Monte Cassino at the start of the Apennine massif, the Liri Valley originated as an inland lake, with Monte Cassino as a crag rearing up from its shoreline, surrounded by water from the south and east. This lake had drained naturally over geological time, leaving marshlands, mudflats, and floodplains on either side of the Rapido and the Liri itself.

Dominating the Liri Valley, Monte Cassino is itself overlooked by the next peaks in the Apennine massif that formed part of the Gustav Line, the Colle Sant' Angelo and Monte Castellone, and then Monte Cairo. For the Allies in 1944, the only route for a frontal attack on the monastery was across the Rapido, through Cassino town at the foot of the mountain, and then by a tortuous and steeply ascending path that doubles back on itself several times, passing under the lesser peaks of Castle Hill and Hangman's Hill on its way upward. Allied attacks south of Monte Cassino had to be made across the floodplain of the Rapido at Sant' Angelo and into the Liri Valley, under full observation from the mountains on either side, or up onto Monte Girafino. Attempts to outflank Monte Cassino from the north also required assault crossings of the Rapido, fighting up onto the heights of Monte Castellone, and then for a farther 5,000 yards of bare mountain along the twin saddle of Phantom Ridge and Snakeshead Ridge before reaching the monastery.

The mountains themselves were formidable. Fred Majdalany, who fought as an infantry officer at Cassino, describes the terrain: "The mountains were rocky, strewn with boulders and gorse thickets, laced with ravines and gullies on which you would come suddenly: and where there had been clumps of trees there were by this time only stumps blasted by shellfire. Digging was out of the question on these hard volcanic slopes. Only the Germans—who had had three months in which to blast holes in the rock, enlarging existing caves and dynamiting new ones—could man their guns in secure cover. The attackers in this country would have to forget about their spades, and rely for cover on the loose stones they could scrape together with their bare hands and build into some kind of breastwork."

Slopes of over 45 degrees were not unusual, and ridges that appeared smooth and bare from a distance turned out to be a jumble of knolls and hollows, with sheer cliffs or great slabs of rock blocking the way. A promising line of advance would end overlooked by another commanding ridge, or in an impassable obstacle or ravine. Under shellfire, the boulders shattered like broken glass and shards and pebbles flew through the air, forming a natural shrapnel; head and eye injuries were particularly prevalent among the troops.

The Germans strengthened these natural defensive positions by damming the Rapido and the Garigliano, reflooding the plain on either side and turning it into a muddy marsh, defended by minefields and belts of barbed wire. To cross the swamps, tanks and vehicles had to use steel-matting trackways so that the loss of one vehicle blocked any movement, whereas on the mountains, vehicles could hardly be used at all. Cassino town itself was a maze of defensive emplacements and bunkers. Old stone houses were reinforced with steel girders and concrete. Armored casemates weighing three tons each were placed on the heights, holding a two-man machine-gun crew. Mortar positions, machine-gun nests, and sniper holes were everywhere. Attacking Allied troops had the choice of muddy marsh or of steep mountain crags, so that all stores and equipment had to be carried long distances on foot. Fighting in the bare mountains meant the return to foot-soldiering of a previous era. Hitler himself referred to the attritional nature of the battle as something out of the First World War.

At Monte Cassino the German defenders, mainly from First Parachute Division, had one of the world's best natural observation posts, and could see and report every move that the Allies made, moving reinforcements or bringing down artillery fire. To the Allied troops the monastery became an evil, malignant monster, watching their every move: "...by the time you cross the Rapido to enter the outskirts of Cassino you barely notice the river or the buildings but only the great mountain towering above the far end of the town half a mile ahead, like a gigantic flying buttress to the mountain mass stretching away to the right. And by this time the cream-colored building on its crest is seen to be grotesquely huge, and there is a fine arrogance in the way it appears to be looking down over its shoulder on the town far below" (Fred Majdalany).

Despite the strength of the German positions, the Allies could not wait through the winter until the better weather of the spring before mounting their attacks. Allied 15th Army Group under Gen. Sir Harold Alexander consisted of U.S. Fifth Army to the west under Lt. Gen. Mark Clark, and British Eighth Army to the east under Lt. Gen. Sir Oliver Lees. Despite their names both armies were multinational; troops from 17 nationalities took part in the battles for the Gustav Line, including New Zealanders, Indians, Poles, Frenchmen, and Canadians. Their first hopes were that a sudden attack could quickly break through the German lines and provide support for the Allied landing at Anzio, just south of Rome, which had gone in on January 22; later the attacks continued chiefly as part of the preparations for the Normandy landings in June, to maintain pressure on the Germans and prevent them moving reserves to France.

Despite the Allied strengths, their persistent problem throughout the bleak winter was getting enough troops and firepower close enough to overcome the enemy defenses in such impossible terrain. Conditions were bleak: "Bad weather," reported the historian of the Second Gurkha Rifles, "has made life almost unbearable at times. For weeks on end we have sat on a draughty mountain top in heavy snow and rain, with one's clothing and blankets soaked through in the first five minutes...." Starting on January 17, 1944, Allied troops began the first of several unsuccessful attempts to break the Gustav Line on either side of Monte Cassino. Faced with such a formidable obstacle, the Allies also tried seapower and airpower. The Anzio landings came to nothing after the initial surprise, as the Germans contained the beachhead. On March 19 the Allied air-forces began Operation Strangle, a bombing campaign against road and rail transport north of Rome, to starve Tenth Army of supplies and ammunition.

A German soldier recorded in his diary: "Mar. 22. What we are going through here is beyond description. I never experienced anything like this in Russia, not even a second's peace, only the dreadful thunder of guns and mortars and there are planes over and above. Mar 25. There has been a heavy fall of snow. It is whirling into our post. You would think you were in Russia. Just when you think you are going to have a few hours' rest to get a sleep, the fleas and bugs torment you. Rats and mice are our companions too." It was the last entry he was ever to make.

Although holding both Cassino town and the mountain strongly, the Germans had refrained from placing troops in the monastery itself. Not knowing this, on February 15 the Allies bombed the monastery for four hours, so the Germans occupied the ruined buildings and rubble, which, ironically, made excellent cover for German snipers, machine gunners, mortar teams, and the dreaded Nebelwerfers, multibarreled rocket launchers. Should the Allies have bombed the monastery? Brig. Howard Kippenburger, commander of the Second New Zealand Division, had little doubt: "It was impossible to ask troops to storm a hill surmounted by an intact building such as this, capable of sheltering several hundred infantry in perfect security from shellfire and ready at the critical moment to emerge and counterattack. I was in touch with our own troops and they were very definitely of the opinion that the Abbey must be destroyed before anyone was asked to storm the hill." The bombing was followed by an attack by New Zealand and Indian troops against Cassino town. After waiting for better weather, a further attack by the same forces on March 15, supported by 1,400 tons of bombs and 190,000 shells, pulverized the town and got up to Castle Hill, but could not push past Hangman's Hill.

Amid the carnage and vicious house-by-house fighting there were extraordinary incidents, like the one described by Lt. E.D. Smith: "Later that afternoon a direct hit by a heavy German shell caused one of the castle walls to collapse, engulfing and burying several Essex soldiers under the rubble. Without hesitation their comrades, British, Indian and Gurkha, began tearing at the stones in an attempt to save their lives. After a few minutes came German paratroopers from foxholes, some only 75 yards away, to join in the rescue operations side by side with our soldiers. In the middle of the Cassino battle there began an unofficial and very local "ceasefire." Friend and foe worked together, talked, and exchanged cigarettes. My company commander spoke German fluently and he learned that the enemy's view of Cassino was very similar to ours—it was Hell, the weather bloody, and the end impossible to predict."

By the end of March the Allies gave up their attacks, waiting for better weather and more troops.

After a month's preparation, 15th Army Group planned for a major push with both its armies on either side of the Liri Valley, pinning down and wearing out the German forces, and so breaking through. On May 11 the fourth and last Battle of Cassino began, a coordinated offensive from the Gulf of Gaeta to Monte Cairo, in which Canadian and French forces at last broke through into the Liri Valley. As Polish troops took the Colle Sant' Angelo, Monte Cassino could no longer be held; on May 17 the German paratroopers abandoned the ruins of the monastery, which the attacking Poles found unoccupied. Fred Majdalany wrote the battle's epitaph: "Cassino, so costly in human life and suffering, and thus deprived at the last of the full victory that would have made it worthwhile, was in the end little more than a victory of the human spirit: an elegy for the common soldier: a memorial to the definitive horror of war and the curiously perverse paradoxical nobility of battle."

North Korea, 1950, from the U.S. Marine Corps Historical Center

This topographical map of the Changjin ("Chosin") Reservoir area was used by the U.S. Marine Corps during the 1950 campaign in the mountains of North Korea. It is likely that a Marine Corps officer marked the distance to Machuria from the Reservoir.

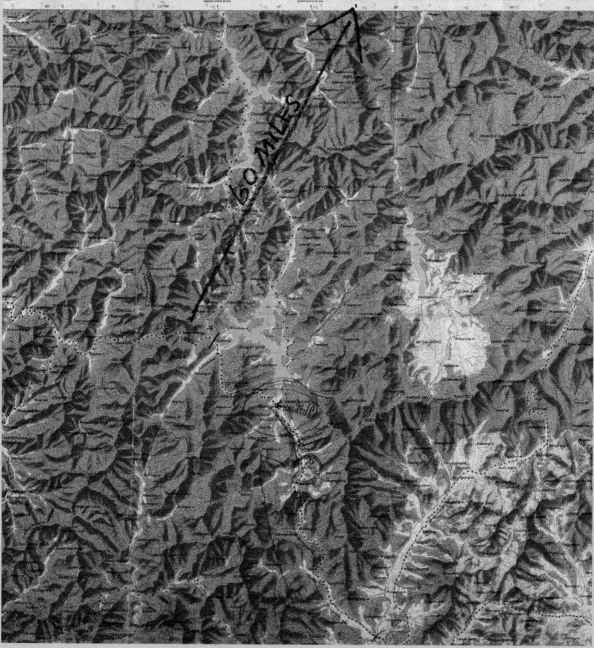

Frozen Chosin
North Korea, 1950

COLONEL JOSEPH H. ALEXANDER, USMC (RET.)

Few military campaigns have been fought under worse conditions of winter weather and rugged terrain than the breakout of the First Marine Division from surrounding Chinese Communist forces in the Taebaek Mountains of North Korea during November 27 to December 11, 1950.

The Marines called the large reservoir in north-central North Korea Chosin, in part because that was the name found on the Japanese military maps in use at the time, and later because the name handily rhymed with "Frozen." The reservoir's correct Korean name is Changjin, for the river that flows north from the lake to join the Yalu River along the Manchurian border, 50 miles away.

The epic battle of 1950 erupted among the hills that loom over the lower reaches of the Changjin Reservoir when the 150,000-man Ninth Chinese Communist Forces Army Group sprang a trap to surround the First Marine Division and other elements of the United Nations X Corps far removed from their fleet base at Hungnam.

The Americans had advanced 78 miles north-northwest of Hungnam along a single-lane gravel road in the Taebaek Mountains in November just as the harbingers of an early winter occurred. The Taebaeks compose the major north-south mountain chain along the "spine" of the Korean Peninsula. The mountains average 4,000 to 6,000 feet in height and rise more steeply, often precipitously, along the eastern coast near the Sea of Japan.

The Marines called this route from Hungnam to the village of Yudam-ni on the southwest arm of the Changjin Reservoir the "MSR" (Main Supply Route). In 1950 the road was particularly tenuous as it zigzagged through Funchilin Pass between Chinhung-ni and Koto-ri. This 10-mile stretch, with its many switchbacks and sharp drop-offs, proved especially vulnerable to Chinese interdiction. Another critical point occurred near the hamlet of Sinhung-ni where the road twisted through 4,000-foot Toktong Pass en route from Hagaru-ri to Yudam-ni. Each of these exotic names became the site of savage, desperate fighting.

Gen. Douglas MacArthur's surprise landing of the X Corps at Inchon on September 25, 1950 outflanked the North Koreans besieging the Eighth Army around the "Pusan Perimeter" in the southeast corner of the peninsula. The North Korean Army dissolved and fled northward, leaving small units to delay the advance of the resurgent U.N. forces.

In his ebullience over the Inchon masterstroke, General MacArthur (and the Joint Chiefs of Staff) altered the war's objectives from restoring the prewar borders at the 38th parallel to forcibly reuniting the two countries. In October, MacArthur unleashed his major commands across the parallel—the X Corps along the east coast, the Eighth Army along the west—in an unbridled "race to the Yalu." MacArthur predicted an early and total success, and "Home by Christmas" became a common mantra.

The assault elements of X Corps consisted of the First Marine Division, commanded by Maj. Gen. Oliver P. Smith and the Seventh Army Division, commanded by Maj. Gen. David G. Barr, plus a British Royal Marine Commando (in battalion strength) and two Republic of Korea infantry divisions. These forces advanced in relative proximity to each other at first, the Koreans along the coast road, the Marines entering the Taebaeks to the west, and the Seventh Division in between. Then their axes of advance began to diverge as the forces entered the widening expanse of North Korea north of its narrow waist along the Pyongyang-Wonsan corridor.

Both the Soviet Union and the People's Republic of China watched these developments with concern. Neither could countenance the potential loss of a key ally or the presence of a U.N. army on their borders. With the approval

of Soviet dictator Joseph Stalin, Chinese chairman Mao Zedong decided to intervene militarily once the United Nations crossed the 38th parallel. In one of
the greatest strategic surprises of the 20th century, enormous numbers of Chinese "volunteers" began crossing the Yalu into the mountains of North Korea,
largely undetected. By the second week of November, the Chinese Communist
Forces (CCF) reported 250,000 men assembled just north of the Eighth Army
in the west and another 150,000 men hiding north of the Changjin Reservoir
in the east. Their mission was to lure certain U.N. units into pre-selected
"killing zones" for annihilation.

The Marines, strung out along 40 miles of bad road below the reservoir,
were particularly vulnerable. Learning of this, Chairman Mao telegrammed his
field commander in North Korea, suggesting that since "the American Marine
First Division has the highest combat effectiveness in the American armed
forces," its destruction should take top priority.

Gen. O.P. Smith experienced his own concerns. His vanguard regiment,
the Seventh Marines, fought a pitched battle with a division-size Chinese unit
at Sudong as early as November 2-6, after which the Chinese mysteriously
vanished into the higher mountains. Ten days later, Smith received orders to
attack in two directions—north to the Yalu, and west across the Taebaeks to
link up with the Eighth Army. With growing uneasiness he wrote the Marine
Commandant, "I believe a winter campaign in the mountains of North Korea
is too much to ask of the American soldier or Marine." Unaffected by reports
that the Seventh Division to the northeast was approaching the Yalu at two
sites, Smith slowed his division's advance, consolidated his two lead regiments,
and took the precaution of building an emergency airstrip on the outskirts of
the mining town of Hagaru-ri. By the third week of November the gap between
the Seventh Division and the Marines had grown to 100 miles.

Smith's operations officer, Col. Alpha L. Bowser, Jr., expressed even greater
uneasiness about the wide gap to the west. "We never established contact with
the right flank of the Eighth Army," he said, "and we had a great void out there
which I at one time estimated to be in the neighborhood of 85 to 100 miles."

Winter hit the Marines before the Chinese did. Members of the Seventh
Marines emerged from Funchilin Pass on November 10 to encounter intense

cold and wind on the open plateau near Koto-ri. "Our men were not conditioned for it," reported Col. Homer L. Litzenberg. "The doctors reported numerous cases where the men came down to the sickbay suffering from what appeared to be shock."

General Smith supervised the distribution of cold-weather clothing, giving first priority to his riflemen. The bulky garments reduced the shock of cold weather, but the waterproof "shoepacs" proved woefully deficient. Designed to protect hunters' feet in a wintry duck blind, the boots proved dangerously unsuitable for cross-country hiking in the Taebaek Mountains. The exertion caused the Marines' feet to sweat, and the waterproof material could not exude moisture, too often causing frostbite. Temperatures plummeted as the Marines climbed warily north by northwest, and the artillery regiment's thermometers registered nightly lows of 20 to 25 degrees below zero. The Marine rifle companies, standing watch on 5,000-foot hills and exposed to the full force of the northwestern winds, experienced wind-chill factors exceeding 60 below zero.

The Chinese sprang their trap against the First Marine Division during the night of November 27-28, howling winds masking their approach through the snow. Elements of three divisions struck the outposts of the Fifth and Seventh Marines near Yudam-ni. Another division attacked a composite Army regiment from the Seventh Division (renamed Task Force Faith after its intrepid commander, Lt. Col. Don C. Faith) operating east of the Reservoir. Other divisions hit the First Marines at Koto-ri and cut the MSR in a dozen places. A Chinese regiment also struck Fox Company of the Seventh Marines, detailed to defend Toktong Pass, the vital link between the exposed regiments at Yudam-ni and the forward division headquarters and supply base at Hagaru-ri.

It was a brilliantly conceived and executed attack, and the Chinese overran many Marine outposts and forward command posts. Task Force Faith suffered grievous casualties, including the death of its commander, and the remnants had to escape across the frozen arm of the Reservoir to embattled Hagaru-ri. Meanwhile, Task Force Drysdale, another cobbled-together unit, composed of Royal Marines, U.S. Marines, and U.S. Army soldiers, tried to force its way up the MSR from Koto-ri to reinforce Hagaru-ri, but lost half its men and many vehicles to a series of Chinese ambushes in "Hellfire Valley."

Yet not all the news was bad. Fox Company, under the superb leadership of Capt. William E. Barber, grimly held Toktong Pass, one decimated rifle company defending the high ground above the road throughout six successive nights of Chinese assaults. Likewise, Col. Lewis B. ("Chesty") Puller's widely scattered First Marines held both Hagaru-ri and Koto-ri against repeated attacks. Each nighttime penetration attained by Chinese forces would be subject at daybreak to attack by low-flying Marine, Navy, and Air Force aircraft with napalm, bombs, and rockets.

The critical focus shifted back to where the battle had begun, the attacks of the three divisions of the 27th CCF Army against the Fifth and Seventh Marines at Yudam-ni. The two regiments could hold their own as long as the MSR through Toktong Pass remained open. On the other hand, with the Eighth Army in full retreat to the west, and with a chagrined MacArthur's orders to the X Corps to pull back to Hungnam, the Marines realized they had to extricate themselves—with their wounded and dead—as quickly as possible. Breaking the Chinese siege against Toktong Pass became critical.

Lt. Col. Raymond G. Davis, commanding the First Battalion, Seventh Marines, undertook the mission to relieve Fox Company. With the high ground along the MSR thoroughly interdicted by the Chinese, Davis led his battalion through the mountains north of the road in an arduous, all-night march during the worst weather of the campaign. Davis estimated the wind-chill factor to be 75 below zero. "We would freeze if we didn't move," he said. His men lurched and stumbled through the snow for hours, eventually surprising and defeating a large force of Chinese preparing to launch another attack on Fox Company. Davis led his forces into the Marine perimeter just after dawn, saluting the badly wounded Captain Barber and breaking the siege.

This was the turning point of the battle. Barber had held just long enough for Davis to relieve him, and the way now lay open for the two regiments to fight their way back to Hagaru-ri. Captain Barber and Lieutenant Colonel Davis both received richly deserved Medals of Honor.

General Smith at Hagaru-ri felt confident to refuse the corps commander's offer of an "aerial Dunkirk" in which his men would be evacuated without their combat equipment. "We're not retreating," the reticent Smith told a circle of combat correspondents, "We're just attacking in a different direction."

A mood of dogged confidence settled over the Marines, soldiers, Brits, and Koreans now consolidated under Smith's leadership. They had taken the Chinese Ninth Army Group's worst punch, and they were still attacking toward the sea. Smith ordered his infantry regiments to seize the high ground on both sides of the road, clearing from the flank the hidden ambushes that earlier had sliced up Task Force Drysdale. The weather remained brutal, but the joint force bulled its way down the narrow road. The retreating column hardly slowed when the Chinese blew the bridge at the power station inside Funchilin Pass. Smith asked the Air Force to para-drop Treadway Bridge sections nearby, and engineers assembled them over the petcocks. The column rolled on.

Elements of the First Marines attacked the southernmost Chinese strong-point on Hill 1081 in a blinding snowstorm, holding their ground against repeated counterattacks until the storm cleared, bringing with it the return of the F4-U Corsairs of the First Marine Air Wing.

The First Marine Division fought its way clear of the last Chinese inter-diction efforts in the mountains and returned intact to the port of Hungnam on December 11. The exhausted troops immediately boarded Navy landing craft to embark on designated amphibious ships of the Seventh Fleet, and headed with great relish to their first hot showers and real chow in months. The ships sailed on the 15th, taking the Marines to Masan, South Korea, for recuperation for the next campaign.

The Marines knew they had survived an epic ordeal, one for the ages, a touchstone of the once and future Corps. The cost, however, was sobering: 718 Marines killed in action or dead of wounds, 3,508 wounded, 192 missing in action. An additional 7,000 Marines suffered acute frostbite.

The Chinese suffered equally. Declassified field reports submitted by the Ninth CCF Army Group indicate the loss of up to 40,000 casualties of all cat-egories, including severe frostbite cases. Several of the worst-hit divisions were simply stricken from the records.

The Marines would fight the Chinese Communists often in the remaining two and a half years of the Korean War, but never again under such awful con-ditions of weather and terrain as experienced by both sides at "Frozen Chosin."

Jungle Highlands
The Siege of Khe Sanh, Vietnam, 1968

COLONEL JOSEPH H. ALEXANDER, USMC (RET.)

In early 1968, as the war in Vietnam entered its fourth year, a substantial force of the North Vietnamese Army (NVA) laid siege to a regiment of U.S. Marines defending the remote highland outpost called Khe Sanh. It was to last 77 days, from January to April, and the nightly television news reports of the dramatic battle mesmerized millions.

At the height of the siege, President Lyndon B. Johnson and other public officials expressed grave concern that Khe Sanh might turn out as disastrously for the Americans as the French loss of Dien Bien Phu to besieging Viet Minh forces in 1954 during the Indochina War.

There were indeed certain similarities between Khe Sanh and Dien Bien Phu. Both campaigns represented efforts by Western powers to force a set-piece battle against shadowy hit-and-run opponents. Both involved the defense of a remote outpost by elite forces—French Legionnaires and paratroopers at Dien Bien Phu, the 26th Marines, with its regimental legacy of Iwo Jima, at Khe Sanh—under attack by the master tactician, Gen. Vo Nguyen Giap. And in both cases the defenders could be resupplied only by air. But Dien Bien Phu fell and Khe Sanh survived because the Americans seized just enough of the commanding terrain around their airfield to keep the daily aerial resupply pipeline functioning.

Yet the news of Khe Sanh in February and March seemed to foreshadow

Khe Sanh, Vietnam, 1968, Associated Press map

Released by the Associated Press on February 6, 1968, this map shows the U.S. base at Khe Sanh and its vicinity. According to the accompanying press release, one Marine officer said of Khe Sanh, "This is the cork right here. If they get past us, they can tear up the countryside way over to the coast."

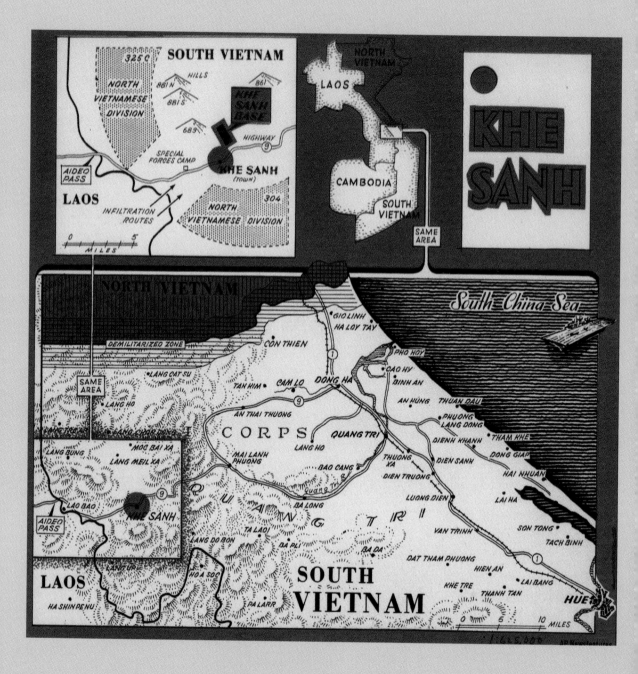

an unmitigated disaster. The NVA pounded the Khe Sanh combat base and its outposts each day with heavy mortars, artillery, and rockets. They shot down scores of U.S. aircraft, attacked the hill outposts, overran neighboring villages, and dug zigzag approach trenches against the Marine perimeter.

At one point President Johnson grimly asked the Joint Chiefs of Staff (JCS) to consider employing tactical nuclear weapons against the besiegers. Cooler heads prevailed. Despite the nonstop shelling and frequent raids, the NVA never launched a full-fledged ground attack against the main base.

The siege of Khe Sanh occurred in an exotically beautiful corner of South Vietnam rarely seen by Westerners. Lt. Gen. Victor H. Krulak, USMC, a presidential adviser during the early years of the Vietnam War, inspected the area in 1964 and found it "an impressively wild area, beautiful in its rugged simplicity—and definitely remote."

Despite its remoteness, Khe Sanh in 1967-68 attracted both the North Vietnamese and the Americans because it was the nexus of a spidery maze of jungle trails that led into the northwestern corner of South Vietnam from the storied Ho Chi Minh Trail in Laos.

Khe Sanh is situated eight miles east of the Laotian border and 40 miles from the mouth of the Cua Viet River on the South China Sea. A poorly maintained and easily interdicted national road, Route 9, wound its way westward from the coast, eventually passing the village of Khe Sanh and proceeding into Laos. The French built a dirt airstrip atop a rectangular plateau north of the village in 1949. Here in 1962 U.S. Army Special Forces established a camp to train indigenous Montagnard tribesmen. By 1967 Navy SeaBees had converted the French strip to a 3,900-foot, hard-surface, all-weather airfield capable of accommodating transport aircraft as large as the C-130 Hercules. Marine forces assumed responsibility for defending the airfield, and by 1968 Khe Sanh represented the westward terminus of a string of Marine outposts just below the Demilitarized Zone (DMZ) that included Gio Linh, Con Thien, Cam Lo, Camp Carroll, and "The Rock Pile."

The Khe Sanh combat base occupied a 300-foot plateau overlooking the Rao Quan River. Steep hills dominated the plateau, and it was surrounded by dense undergrowth of triple-canopy foliage, bamboo thickets, and stands of elephant grass that provided excellent cover and concealment for approaching invaders.

As at Dien Bien Phu, the hills surrounding the airfield at Khe Sanh would decide the fate of the siege. The most militarily significant of these included two pairs of hills with identical heights, Hills 881-South and 881-North, and Hill 861 and its adjoining spur, Hill 861-A (heights are in meters), all lying within a five-mile arc from the combat base. "The Khe Sanh plateau is a hard place to defend," commented General Krulak. "Hills, rising to altitudes of 3,000 feet, look down on the airstrip just as the top-row seats in a football stadium look down on the playing field."

In the spring of 1967 the Third Marines fought a vicious series of battles against infiltrating NVA elements along these hilltops, eventually wresting control of each summit. The NVA melted away in the jungle, but their willingness to risk high casualties for control of the high ground above Khe Sanh indicated the likelihood of a return engagement.

Gen. William C. Westmoreland, the senior U.S. commander in Vietnam, concluded in late 1967 that the NVA would attack Khe Sanh as a prelude to a major effort to cut off the two northernmost provinces of South Vietnam. "The virtually unpopulated Khe Sanh Plateau, which lay astride the enemy's principal avenue of approach from his large base areas in Laos, was obviously an initial objective of the North Vietnamese Army," he said. Westmoreland saw the opportunity to blunt this advance and at the same time lure large NVA forces into killing zones by positioning the 26th Marines at Khe Sanh as an irresistible target. He authorized reinforcement of the regiment by two additional infantry battalions, including one of South Vietnamese Rangers, but he would allow no additional buildup for fear of being unable to resupply the outpost by air, another reflection of Dien Bien Phu's long shadow.

Westmoreland and the Marines figured the NVA would move against Khe Sanh in the winter months when the weather would favor their advance. The region averaged 80 inches of rain per year, much of it falling during the monsoon season. Khe Sanh was also subject to dense and persistent fog, a product of the plateau's location slightly above the river and the adjoining rain forests. Both the fog and the rain would shield NVA movements and restrict US air activities.

Col. David E. Lownds commanded the 6,000-man regiment. He assessed the closest circle of hills, realized that 881-North was beyond his reach, and decided to invest one-fifth of his command to outpost Hills 881-South, 861, 861-A, and 558 (near the Rao Quan River). Lownds determined that 881-South, overlooking the west end of the runway, represented the most critical terrain, and along its sprawling summit he posted a composite force of two rifle companies, reinforced with 105mm howitzers, 106mm recoilless rifles, 81mm mortars, machine guns, snipers, and a forward air controller—all under the command of Capt. William H. Dabney.

The Marines were shock troops, aggressive and impatient, and they chafed at the mission of sitting at Khe Sanh as passive targets, waiting for the NVA to initiate the assault. "Tethered bullocks baiting the enemy tiger," snorted combat photographer and former Marine David Douglas Duncan disapprovingly.

As anticipated by Westmoreland, the NVA began infiltrating two divisions with heavy weapons into the jungles around Khe Sanh from Laos in December 1967.

Captain Dabney's troops flushed a large force of NVA during a daylight patrol near 881-South on 20 January 1968. At the height of the fighting, Dabney received orders from Colonel Lownds to return immediately to his hilltop. The Marines at Khe Sanh had captured an NVA officer near the perimeter who willingly revealed that the North Vietnamese stood poised to attack that night. Lownds placed his command on full alert.

Early the next morning an NVA battalion attacked the Marine outpost on Hill 861 and overran a sector of the position. The Marines counterattacked, engaged the NVA in hand-to-hand combat, and eventually drove off the survivors.

At dawn the North Vietnamese gunners in the distant hills opened a suffocating barrage of the Khe Sanh combat base. One of their first rounds hit dead center in an ammo dump, causing a chain reaction of fires and explosions that rocked the base for the next 48 hours.

During January 29-30 the Tet Offensive began with major NVA attacks against many of the cities and villages throughout South Vietnam. Most of the penetrations fizzled out within days—Tet was a military disaster for Hanoi—but the political effect was incalculable.

Yet the NVA never relinquished their pressure on besieged Khe Sanh during Tet. An NVA battalion attacked Hill 861-A during the night of February 5, overran a platoon position, then succumbed to a savage counterattack. A larger force, accompanied by Soviet-built T-76 tanks, overran a neighboring Special Force camp on the Seventh and an outpost near the combat base suffered a penetrating attack the following night. That same week NVA gunners destroyed a Marine C-130 with mortar fire just as it landed on the runway.

Later in February the base was hit by a single-day record of 1,307 rounds of artillery, mortar, and rocket fire. The Marines hated most the NVA's 120mm mortars, which, armed with superquick fuses, would leave a crater no deeper than a soup bowl but whose blast would kill exposed men within 30 meters and badly wound others in a circle 30 meters beyond that. "The Marines lived like prairie dogs, in and out of their vast colony of bunkers," reported photographer Duncan.

Some of the fiercest firefights occurred during the daily efforts to resupply the hilltops by helicopters. Said Captain Dabney of his experiences on Hill 881-South, "No helicopter could approach the hill without being fired upon. And no helicopter could stay on the hill more than 25 seconds without a real risk that a mortar round would hit it. The first 30 days of the siege we lost seven helicopters up there."

Never in any previous campaign had Marine riflemen been so lavishly supported by aviators of every service. Each day the skies over Khe Sanh resembled a thunderhead of circling jet aircraft flying holding patterns and cycling ever lower in the queue to deliver their bombs and rockets.

Most awesome of all the considerable firepower delivered in support of the Marines at Khe Sanh were the Air Force B-52 Strato-fortress "Arc Light" missions. Each plane carried a payload of 27 tons of high-explosive bombs, typically released from a height of six miles. A formation of bombers could destroy an entire ridgeline. Marine outposts in proximity of the impact learned to force their mouths open by clenching socks in their teeth to prevent their eardrums from bursting from the overpressure. Montagnard tribesmen reported hundreds of NVA bodies stacked for burial in the jungle. Often there were simply no bodies to be found.

Yet still the zigzag trenches of the NVA wormed their way ever closer to the Khe Sanh perimeter each night. One morning the shell-shocked troops discovered a fresh NVA trench within 300 meters of the barbed wire. The Marines began placing their ears to the ground, listening for subterranean tunneling. The strain of the siege was becoming manifest.

On April 1, General Westmoreland launched Operation Pegasus, a joint Army-Marine effort to clear Route 9 and break the siege of Khe Sanh. But the linkup proved anticlimactic. The NVA shelling and probing had diminished perceptibly in the last weeks and there were intelligence reports of NVA units exfiltrating back into Laos. The enemy seemed to have lost heart, or lost interest.

The Marines gladly assumed the offensive. A reinforced battalion assaulted the NVA stronghold on Hill 881-North, location of many of the rocket launchers and heavy mortars that had bedeviled the base for so long. This was the final battle of the siege.

Four days later the entire 26th Marines departed for Dong Ha. The Khe Sanh combat base, defended so desperately for so many weeks, was abruptly abandoned, almost as if it had been a giant boxing ring, rented by the antagonists for a title bout, then deserted after the final bell.

It had been a hell of a fight. The JCS estimated 10,000 North Vietnamese soldiers died from the combined firepower inflicted by the Americans. Somewhat fewer than 1,000 Marines died in the fighting. The beautiful landscape of the Khe Sanh plateau that had charmed General Krulak four years earlier now resembled a denuded and dying planet. The shredded jungles reeked with the smell of death.

A number of unanswered questions remained. What was General Giap's real objective at Khe Sanh? Was it to tie up as many American forces and supporting arms as possible during the strategically more rewarding Tet campaign? Or was he in fact tempted at Khe Sanh to replicate his epic victory against the French at Dien Bien Phu? How did he justify to President Ho Chi Minh the deaths of 10,000 of their countrymen for the dubious ploy at Khe Sanh? And for all his siege expertise, why did Giap fail to order the cutting or poisoning of the Marines' water supply from the Rao Quan River?

For his part General Westmoreland later stated that the decision to hold

Khe Sanh "was to my mind militarily sound and strategically rewarding." General Krulak disagreed: "When it was all over nothing had changed—nothing."

Captain Dabney, whose company sustained 90 percent casualties on Hill 881-South during the siege, shrugged off his regiment's reassignment. "The subsequent abandonment of Khe Sanh didn't bother me," he said. "It was purely a tactical position. This was never a war of geography."

DESERT

The desert does not have a single face. It may encompass the drifting soft-sand dunes of popular imagination, but it is just as likely to be an arid, rock-strewn plain of hardened earth, perhaps broken by low ridges and rocky outcrops, and slashed with wadis—the dry beds of flash-flood runoff. The two battles in this chapter—Omdurman in the Sudan, 1898, and Desert Saber, 1991 (the land-war component of the first Gulf War)—illustrate some defining characteristics of open-terrain warfare. As with plains warfare (see Chapter 1), maneuverability and numbers were traditionally critical factors. In the past, it was the ability of one army to bring a critical mass to bear on the enemy, usually by enveloping a less mobile force, that decided the outcome. For example, one of the greatest military disasters ever to befall the Roman Army took place in the semi-desert plain of Carrhae (near modern Harran, Turkey) in June 53 B.C. As the Roman commander Marcus Licinius Crassus, at the head of 39,000 infantry and cavalry, moved into the desert his army was swarmed by Parthian horse-archers. The Romans, outnumbered, formed a square, essentially abdicating maneuverability. Once Crassus had opted for a static response, the end was inevitable. Crassus and most of his command paid with their lives. The advent of firearms changed the ancient equation. As Bryan Perrett shows in his account of the Battle of Omdurman, a small and massively outnumbered Anglo-Egyptian army inflicted what a war correspondent at the time described as "not a battle but an execution." As Will Fowler (who served there) recounts, Coalition forces in Desert Saber, with their vastly superior military technology, also inflicted an "execution." But even in modern warfare desert fighting is never easy. Soldiers in North Africa during World War II broiled under a sun that was "a burning metallic monster in a cloudless blue sky," and endured sandstorms that "struck us with terrific force and fine sand got into everything, including the hair, eyes, ears, and throat. It turned day into night...a truly unpleasant experience," remembered a participant. But above all it was the monotony of the terrain itself that got to you. Private Crimp recalled: "The desert, omnipresent, so saturates consciousness that it makes the mind as sterile as itself."

Sudan, 1898, "Battle of Omdurman, the Khalifa's Attack; Time 9:40 a.m."
This map appears in Winston Churchill's 1899 book, *The River War: An Historical Account of the Reconquest of Sudan*. Having fought in the war, Churchill wrote about his experiences in Sudan when he returned in 1899, at age 25.

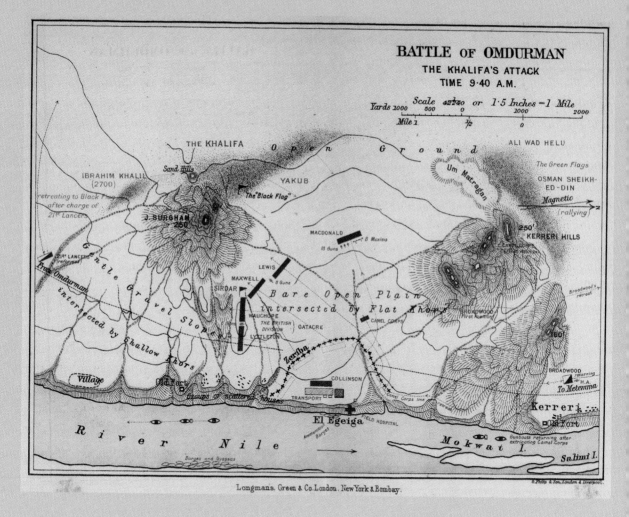

A Desert Storm
Omdurman, Sudan, 1898

BRYAN PERRETT

The Sudan, like Egypt, is the gift of the Nile in that its primitive agriculture benefits from the annual inundation that brings down rich mud from Equatorial Africa and provides irrigation. In other respects the climate and topography are among the harshest on Earth. The average annual temperature is about 90° Fahrenheit. At noon in the midsummer months it can soar to 130 degrees, the heat thrown down by a brazen sky reflected upward from the stony ground. Rainfall, largely confined to the months of July, August, and September, is approximately one-tenth that of New York.

Away from the river the terrain is mainly desert, punctuated by rocky outcrops and dotted with thorn bushes, the only vegetation the arid landscape can support. The country possesses very few natural assets. Omdurman lies on the left bank of the Nile, below the confluence of the Blue and White Niles, in the inner angle of which is the city of Khartoum. Downstream, in descending order, are the Sixth, Fifth, Fourth and Third Cataracts, which are rock-strewn rapids difficult to negotiate when the river is at its lowest.

During the 19th century, the Sudan's ruler was the khedive (viceroy) of Egypt, who owed a nominal loyalty to the Sultan of Turkey but, in effect, was controlled by Britain (the commander in chief of the Egyptian army, the sirdar, was a British appointee). By 1885 a religious rising, led by the Mahdi Mohammed Ahmed, having inflicted several defeats on the Egyptian Army, set the seal on its victories by overwhelming British Gen. Charles Gordon's garrison at Khartoum, in the Sudan. In response, Britain decided to withdraw the remaining garrisons in the Sudan and simply defend Egypt's southern frontier. The Sudan was left to be ruled by the mahdi's successor, the Khalifa Abdullah.

In 1896 Britain decided to reconquer the Sudan, partly because, following a recent Italian defeat at Adowa in Abyssinia, it was considered necessary to maintain the prestige of the European Powers, and partly to discourage an unwelcome interest the French were showing in the headwaters of the Nile. Geographic considerations apart, this was no easy undertaking, for the khalifa's army numbered over 60,000 fanatical dervishes. It also possessed 40,000 rifles, of which 22,000 were comparatively modern Remingtons captured from the Egyptians, 61 cannon including six German-made Krupp field guns, and eight machine guns. However, much of the captured ammunition had been shot off during the recent war with Abyssinia, and the mechanism of the machine-guns had suffered seriously from the attentions of untrained hands. In fact, the dervishes preferred to regard fire-power as simply a prelude to the decisive charge with spear and sword, pressed home with religious fervor.

The khalifa and the sirdar of the Egyptian Army, British Gen. Horatio Herbert Kitchener, both believed that the climactic battle of the coming campaign would be fought close to Omdurman, but for different reasons. The khalifa took the traditional view that in desert warfare the farther an army advanced from its base, the weaker it became, and that if his forces offered only token resistance to the Anglo-Egyptian advance they would be at their strongest, whereas Kitchener's would be stretched to the limit. Kitchener, on the other hand, was a sound logistician who was prepared to use the most modern means of transport available, not only to keep his army supplied, but also to reinforce it with fresh British troops shortly before the decisive battle, during which his army would be at twice the strength it had at the beginning of the campaign. He would also have the support of a squadron of gunboats, shipped out to Egypt in sections and transported forward by rail to their assembly point. These, armed with 12- and 6-pounder guns, machine-guns, and searchlights, would prove to be a vital source of firepower.

As one dervish outpost after another fell, the confidence of the Anglo-Egyptian troops grew steadily. Following the capture of Dongola on September 21, 1896, Kitchener took the decision that was to win him the campaign. This was nothing less than to build a railway across 235 miles of desert from Wadi Halfa to Abu Hamed, thereby cutting an arc across the upper portion of the Great Bend of the Nile. Some doubted whether sufficient water could be found for steam locomotives in this vast expanse, but adequate quantities were discovered 77 and 126 miles out from Wadi Halfa. Work started on January 1, 1897 and proceeded at the rate of one mile per day.

Meanwhile the Anglo-Egyptian army, supported by the gunboats, continued its remorseless advance around the Great Bend. Abu Hamed was captured in August 1897, followed by Berber the following month. The railway reached Abu Hamed on October 31 and was extended southward. As a result, those dervishes in the eastern Sudan found their position untenable and were forced to retire on Omdurman. At this point the British government agreed to the immediate dispatch of one British brigade up the line, to be followed shortly by another. The first of these reinforcements reached Kitchener in January 1898.

The khalifa knew nothing of railways, but when his spies told him how they worked and described the mountains of stores that daily reached the enemy army he decided that the line must be destroyed and dispatched the Emir Mahmud and 16,000 men to complete the task. Mahmud, however, understanding the nature of the opposition better than his master, simply dug himself trenches inside a thorn zariba (barricade), beside the dry bed of the River Atbara. Tired of waiting for him to attack, Kitchener stormed the zariba on April 8, inflicting heavy loss and capturing Mahmud.

The road to Omdurman was now open, but Kitchener was not inclined to move until the second British brigade had joined him. When he renewed his advance in August he crossed to the west bank of the Nile.

On September 1 his gunboats engaged the defenses of Omdurman, blasting holes on the town's walls and the dome of the mahdi's tomb. Meanwhile, having decided to fight a defensive battle, he detailed his troops to construct a large thorn zariba seven miles to the north of Omdurman and centered on the village of El Egeiga, around which it curved in a half-moon with both ends resting on the river. Outside the zariba lay a wide, featureless plain devoid of cover but intersected here and there by shallow *khor*, or depressions. About two miles to the southwest was a rocky feature, Jebel Surgham, and a similar distance to the northwest was a broken ridge known as the Kerreri Hills.

At dawn the next day the khalifa led out his army, swinging round Jebel Surgham for an immediate assault on the Anglo-Egyptian zariba. He personally commanded 21,000 men on the right of the attack, while the center consisted of 8,000 under Osman Azrak and 28,000 under Osman Sheikh el Din, and the left of 5,500 under Ali Wad Helu. A battery of guns was also on its way forward but does not seem to have caught up with the fighting.

At Kitchener's disposal were 25,000 men (8,200 British and 17,600 Egyptians) with 44 guns and 20 Maxim machine guns, plus ten gunboats with 36 guns and 24 Maxims in support. The British held the left of the line and the Egyptians the right. Winston Churchill, a lieutenant with the 21st Lancers, described the scene from his vantage point on the Jebel Surgham: "It was a quarter to six. The light was dim, but growing stronger every minute. There in the plain lay the enemy, their numbers unaltered, their confidence and intentions apparently unshaken. Their front was now nearly five miles long, and composed of great masses of men joined together by thinner lines. Behind and near to the flanks were large reserves. From the ridge they looked like dark blurs and streaks, relieved and diversified with an odd-looking shimmer of light from the spear points" (*The River War,* 1899).

At 06:25 a.m., with the dervishes some 2,700 yards distant, the artillery opened fire, using high explosive and shrapnel. The effect of shell bursts on the stony terrain was doubly devastating. Not only did steel fragments kill and mutilate but the very rock itself was turned into lethal projectiles. (Churchill reported that when his regiment was fired on, "their bullets struck the hard gravel into the air, and the troopers, to shield their faces...bowed their helmets forward....") The gunboats joined in, followed by the Maxims. Ten minutes later, with the range down to 2,000 yards, the infantry began firing volleys: "The infantry fired steadily and solidly, without hurry or excitement...the soldiers were interested in the work and took great pains. But presently the mere physical act became tedious...The rifles grew hot—so hot they had to be changed for those of the reserve companies. And all the time out on the plain on the other side bullets were shearing through flesh, smashing and splintering bone...." By 6:45 a.m. the whole of Kitchener's line was engaged. The dervishes pressed their attack to within 800 yards of the British and 400 yards of the slower-firing Egyptians, but were unable to come closer and at 7:30 a.m. retired, leaving the desert plain carpeted with their dead and wounded.

Meanwhile, Osman Sheikh el Din had allowed himself to be distracted by the Egyptian cavalry and the Camel Corps, which were operating to the south of the Kerreri Hills. He launched an immediate attack against them and was drawn away from the main battlefield and over the hills toward the river. The cavalry experienced no difficulty in executing their diversionary role, but the slower Camel Corps would have been in real danger of being cut off and wiped out had not several gunboats brought concentrated fire to bear on the enemy's packed ranks.

Kitchener may have been a good strategist and a fine logistician, but he was an indifferent tactician. Believing the battle to be won, he ordered a general advance on Jebel Surgham, which was taken without difficulty, and continued to push the remnants of the defeated enemy out into the desert. On the left of his line the 21st Lancers mounted a charge against some 2,000 dervishes concealed in a khor. It was to be the last full-fledged cavalry charge in British history. Churchill's description is mesmerizing: "A deep crease in the ground—a dry watercourse, a khor—appeared where all had seemed smooth, level plain; and from it there sprang, with the suddenness of a pantomime effect and a high-pitched yell, a dense white mass of men nearly as long as our men and about twelve deep. A score of horsemen and a dozen bright flags rose as if by magic from the earth. Eager warriors sprang forward to anticipate the shock. The rest stood firm to meet it...the British squadrons struck the fierce brigade with one long furious shout. The collision was prodigious....Stubborn and unshaken infantry hardly ever meet stubborn and unshaken cavalry. Either the infantry run away and are cut down in flight, or they keep their heads and destroy nearly all the horsemen by their musketry. On this occasion two living walls had actually crashed together. The Dervishes fought manfully. They tried to hamstring the horses. They fired their rifles, pressing their muzzles into the very bodies of their opponents. They cut reins and stirrup-leathers. They flung their throwing-spears with great dexterity....Within two minutes every man was clear of the Dervish mass. All who had fallen were cut with swords till they stopped quivering."

On the right, however, a dangerous situation had developed. Here, Col. Hector Macdonald's First Egyptian Brigade was engaged with Ali Wad Helu to the west when, suddenly, to the north, thousands of Osman Sheikh el Din's men came streaming back from their abortive foray into the Kerreri Hills. Macdonald thus found himself engaged in two directions simultaneously. Appreciating that if his brigade were overrun the rear of Kitchener's advancing army would become vulnerable, he coolly wheeled back three companies of his right-hand regiment so that his frontage became a right angle. Then, as the threat from Ali Wad Helu decreased, he transferred regiments from left to right across the brigade's inner angle. The Camel Corps came up to extend his right, followed by the Fourth Egyptian Brigade, which had been guarding the zariba, and Kitchener sent back the First British Brigade. Despite this, some of the Dervishes managed to close to within 30 yards, and by the time their attack had been beaten off, Macdonald's men were down to six rounds of ammunition apiece.

By 11:30 the battle was over (a war correspondent, G.W. Steevens, described it as "not a battle but an execution"). Over 9,700 dervishes had been killed and twice that number wounded. Anglo-Egyptian losses amounted to five officers and 43 other ranks killed (almost all during the charge of the 21st Lancers), and 428 wounded. Kitchener redeployed his army for the final stage of the march to Omdurman, which fell during the afternoon. The khalifa, his power broken, escaped but was hunted down and fought to the death.

Fire Storm: Desert Saber
Kuwait/Iraq, 1991

WILL FOWLER

The desert has many forms. It is not only the romantic image of miles of sand dunes over which trudged the Beau Gestes of the Foreign Legion. It can just as well be rock, gravel and sand, or dotted with salt marshes that, when soaked by rain, become quagmires. Temperatures may vary from extremes of heat by day to intense cold at night. When rain falls it can be very intense, creating local flooding and turning the normally dry wadis, or gullies, into raging watercourses. The Coalition operations in Kuwait, Saudi Arabia, and Iraq also had many faces: Desert Shield (the buildup), Desert Storm (the air campaign), and Desert Saber (the ground war).

Prior to their deployment to Saudi Arabia in 1990 to combat the Iraqi invasion of Kuwait and the threat to Saudi Arabia, the U.S. Army had become familiar with deserts through its training at the National Training Center at Fort Irwin, California, and in Egypt and Sudan in the Bright Star exercises. However, the terrain in southern Iraq, Kuwait, and northern Saudi Arabia was unknown. Analysis showed that on the coast there were good roads connecting ports and cities, while off-road there were sand dunes, some over 20 feet high, and, more significantly, the saltwater marshes known as *sabkhas*, with their thin crust that could support men on foot but, following rain, turned to a mushy mix of sand and mud that could engulf a vehicle up to its axles in minutes.

Kuwait/Iraq, 1991, West Point map

Used for education purposes at West Point Military Academy, this map shows the ground units involved in the Gulf War, as well as the oil fields and airstrips in the region. Listed on the right and left respectively are Coalition naval and air forces; total Coalition forces eventually numbered over 500,000 and included Arab allies such as Syria and Egypt.

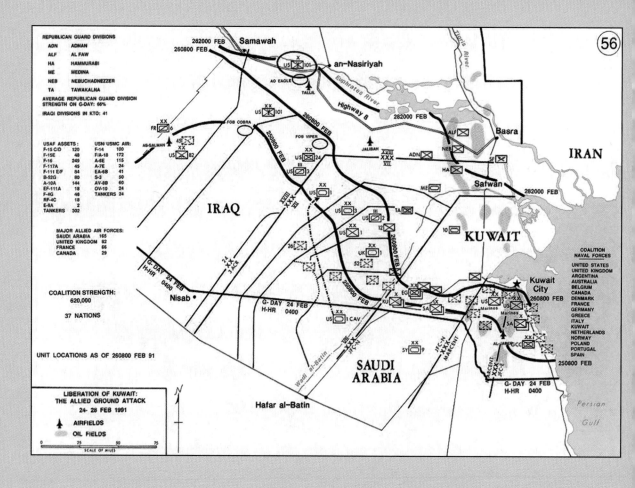

Moving west along the Saudi Arabian—Iraqi border from about ten miles inland to Wadi al-Batin the land becomes flatter with fewer dunes, but numerous small rocks. The wadi itself marks the western border of Kuwait and is only an obstacle in the winter rainy season. To the west of the wadi the going is rockier—hard on tires and the track-pads of tanks.

For the planners, weather was also a key factor. Temperatures between August and September can reach 140°F. Since there was a known chemical threat from the Iraqis, soldiers would be wearing protective suits and might have to mask up with respirators. Under these conditions it would be exhausting to simply walk, let alone fight. Between November and March the temperatures moderate and soldiers were to find that nighttime frosts were common. An added problem was winds that, combined with rain and sand, could reduce visibility to levels that could not be penetrated even by sophisticated thermal imagers. When there was cloud cover, the desert at night could be so dark that image intensifiers fitted to weapons and vehicles had insufficient ambient light with which to operate.

A planning team under Lt. Col. Joe Purvis, U.S. Army, examined the terrain and identified four "Mobility Corridors." The most obvious was along the road network into Kuwait. The second was west of Wadi al-Batin and the third farther to the west which took vehicles through terrain that was classified as "slow-go" until As-Salman, an area that was "intermittent slow-go." The fourth corridor ran roughly east-west, south of the Euphrates Valley.

Operation Desert Shield, the buildup of U.S. and Coalition forces in Saudi Arabia, began in 1990 and was completed early in 1991. When negotiations had failed and military operations began against Iraq they were phased, beginning on January 17, 1991, with Desert Storm air attacks against a range of targets in Iraq, Kuwait, and the waters off Kuwait. Desert Storm began with a low-level precision attack by U.S. Army Apache helicopters against Iraqi air-defense radar, and when these were destroyed or neutralized, a gap was created through which Coalition aircraft streamed into Iraq. Among the first targets was the headquarters and offices in Baghdad, with the aim of destroying command-and-control facilities. Also high on the list were the suspected chemical and biological warfare facilities in the country.

The weather, which had been growing cooler, deteriorated into rainsqualls with low clouds, and by mid-February Coalition forces began to move westward in what their commander, Gen. Norman Schwarzkopf, U.S. Army, drawing on a football analogy, called his "Hail Mary" move. On the extreme western flank were the lightly equipped French Sixth Light Armored Division. The formidable US 101st Airmobile and 82nd Airborne Divisions were in position to make a helicopter assault deep into Iraq and hold position in the Euphrates Valley near Talil airfield. Weather permitting, this massive helicopter lift capability could defeat any terrain barriers.

Eastward from the French force on the Iraqi border were the Third Cavalry Regiment, 24th Infantry Division, First Armored Division, Second Armored Cavalry Regiment, Third Armored Division, First Cavalry Division, and the British First Armoured Division. On the Kuwaiti border were joint forces drawn from Saudi Arabia, Syria, Egypt, Kuwait, and Pakistan. The U.S. First Marine Division, the Tiger Brigade of the Second Armored Division, and the Second Marine Division were on the Kuwaiti border, while on the coast road were Joint Forces drawn from Saudi Arabia, Kuwait, Oman, and the United Arab Emirates. On February 15 Iraq offered to withdraw from Kuwait, but this was dismissed as a "cruel hoax" by President Bush in Washington.

On February 18 the Coalition began "artillery raids," engaging Iraqi batteries and troop concentrations with MLRS (Multiple Launch Rocket System) and artillery barrages. Air attacks with supporting psychological warfare operations hit positions along the border. The terrified Iraqi conscripts in the trenches and bunkers were warned that they were next in line for a massive air attack and encouraged to surrender. Some, seeing low-flying unmanned target-locating drones, emerged from their trenches and stood unarmed with their hands raised.

U.S. and British Special Forces were now operating inside Iraq tasked with the location of Scud missiles and the destruction of Iraqi command, control, and communications centers. The cold and wet weather came as a surprise to many of them and some British troops received an issue of shaggy traditional sheepskin coats—a nonregulation garment that would not have been out of place in the First World War and would at times prove a surprisingly effective disguise—a case of wolves in sheep's clothing. One of their key roles was to examine the desert and establish if it could support an attack by massed armored formations, or if the surface would break up under the wheels and tracks.

On February 22 Washington urged Baghdad to comply with a U.N. resolution to withdraw from Kuwait by 5:00 p.m. on February 23 or face a land war. The Iraqis stalled and hung on; a pathetic bluff. Preceded by massive air and artillery bombardment, Operation Desert Saber, the ground attack on Iraq and Kuwait, was launched at 1:00 a.m. on Sunday, February 24, 1991. It was a day earlier than many experts had predicted, and in many respects resembled the "Blitzkrieg" tactics developed by the Germans in World War II. While the U.S. Marine and Joint Forces launched attacks on the strongly held Kuwaiti border—confirming what Iraqi staff officers had assumed would happen, the U.S., British and French forces launched a huge attack into Iraq. The Kuwait attack held the Iraqi attention while the powerful armored forces delivered the left hook.

In the air war phase the bridges across the Euphrates had been destroyed with laser-guided bombs, and this meant that the river, lakes, and marshland would prevent any Iraqi reinforcements' reaching the theater from the north. Iraqi convoys approaching the front were now set upon by low-flying U.S. Army H-64 Apache attack helicopters, the pilots and gunners hovering to the flank and working their way down the line of vehicles, hitting only the tanks and armored personnel carriers, since trucks had no offensive capability.

In the first 48 hours the French reached the Iraqi base at As-Samawa and U.S. heli-borne troops carried in H-60 Blackhawks in a two-stage attack reached Objective Gold and established a firebase in the Euphrates Valley. The theater was now sealed off to the west. The huge armored thrust pushed through the sand berms that Iraqi engineers had constructed on the border and northward into Iraq. By the end of two days, tanks and armored infantry had begun the maneuver that would take them eastward to smash Iraqi forces on the anvil of Kuwait.

In the final phase the Joint Forces had penetrated into Kuwait to liberate the city with the U.S. Task Force "Ripper" driving hard to capture the city's airport; the Second Marine Division reached Al Jahrah, and the Tiger Brigade swung north to trap the fleeing Iraqis at Mutla Ridge. The road north across the gently rising Mutla Ridge was soon clogged with looted vehicles from Kuwait, as well as tanks and trucks, as Iraqi soldiers attempted to flee the country. It became a killing ground for ground-attack aircraft, and the smashed and burned vehicles and charred bodies a grim testament to the destructiveness of modern war.

To the west, the U.S. VII Corps had crossed the Kuwaiti border. To the north, the key battle of the campaign was being fought near Basra, where the U.S. XVIII Corps had entered the Rumaila oil field near Safwan where Iraqi leader Saddam Hussein had husbanded his Republican Guard Division (the brigades within the division had grandiloquent titles like Al-Faw, Nebuchadnezzar, Adnan, which were meant to invoke recent battles against Iran, as well as the heroes of Babylonian history).

Trapped against the Hawr al-Hammar Lake in the Euphrates Valley, the T-72 tanks of the Hammurabi Division straddling Highway 8 were hammered into destruction by the guns of the M1-Abrams tanks. The superior fire-control and target-acquisition systems of the Abramses enabled them to locate and engage the Iraqis at longer ranges. Prisoners reported that in darkness sometimes the first they knew that they were under attack was when their own tanks around them exploded and burned.

On February 25 the Coalition reported that the Iraqis had set fire to more than 600 oil wells in Kuwait. It was in part an act of revenge and in part an attempt to screen Iraqi movements from satellite and aerial reconnaissance— it was a man-made ecological disaster. On February 27 President Bush declared victory and Coalition forces were ordered to cease operations at 5:00 a.m.

On February 28 a temporary cease-fire was initiated, and on March 3 this was confirmed when an Iraqi delegation accepted the terms at a meeting at Safwan, an Iraqi air base just north of Kuwait. The Iraqis had lost control of the situation so comprehensively that they were unaware how much territory was in Coalition hands and were shocked when it was shown on a map display.

After 26 days of air war, Iraq admitted that 20,000 had been killed and 60,000 injured. By the end of the war the Coalition estimated that Iraq had suffered 150,000 casualties, of whom a third had been killed. The U.S. lost 79 killed, the British 17 (9 by U.S. fire), France 2, and the Arab forces 26. It had not been "the mother of all battles," as threatened by Saddam Hussein, but rather a staggering victory for the Coalition.

JUNGLE

Like the desert, jungle is defined as much by its climate as by its other physical characteristics (almost all horrible for the soldier who had to fight in it). The two representative battles in this chapter—Buna in Papua New Guinea, 1942–43, and the Ia Drang Valley, Vietnam, 1965—illustrate how jungle fighting changed, even within a relatively short space of time. Buna was an infantry battle devoid of sophisticated military technology in what is generally considered the most vile climate and terrain of the Pacific war. The Ia Drang was a close-run battle, but one in which geography and tactics were transformed by advances in air mobility. Jungles are extreme environments in many ways. An Australian described "the moist and stifling Papuan jungle with its carpet of swamp-ooze and rotting stumps and leaves and its perpetual stench of vegetable decay...this Serborian bog of trees and strangling vines and crazy foliage that shut out the sunlight." Private First Class Connolly of the U.S. 77th Division in the jungles of Guam described it this way: "The distance across the island is not far, as the crow flies, but unluckily we can't fly.... After advancing a few yards you find that the handle of the machine-gun on your shoulder, your pack and shovel, canteens, knife and machete all stick out at right angles and are as tenacious in their grip on the surrounding under-brush as a dozen grappling hooks....You untangle your equipment, retrieve your helmet and move on. The flies, the mosquitoes have discovered your route of march and regard us as nothing but walking blood banks." Pvt. James Jones, later to become the famous novelist, recalled the jungle of Guadalcanal: "The moist humidity was so overpowering, and hung in the air so heavily, that it seemed more like a material object than a weather condition." Even though there had been many medical advances by the early years of World War II, particularly sulfonamides and penicillin, the jungle made it extremely difficult to get the wounded to treatment. A journalist on New Guinea met two wounded men coming down the trail: "One had been shot through the foot, the other through the left eye....The pair had walked 113 miles in 16 days. They expected to reach the roadhead in another five."

Buna, New Guinea, 1942-43, from *The Papuan Campaign,* 1944

Published in 1944, this map shows the attack on Buna that lasted from November 19 to December 14, 1942. Treacherous jungle swamps—breeding grounds for infection and disease—cover most of the terrain on which the battle took place; areas of grassland and coconut trees are marked in smaller regions along the coast. Dashed lines indicate the primitive Papuan trails that were accessible only by foot.

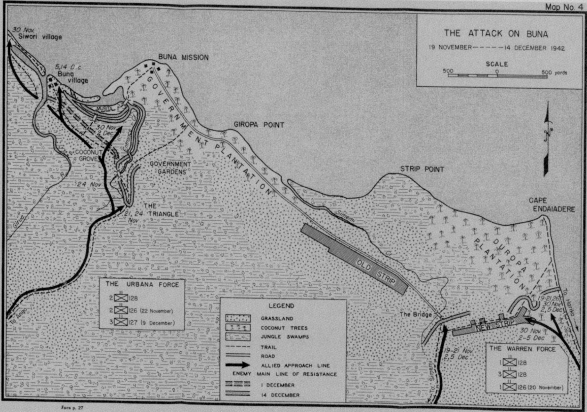

New Guinea Nightmare
Buna, Papua New Guinea, 1942-43

ERIC BERGERUD

In the four months after Pearl Harbor, Japanese forces conquered a vast oil- and mineral-rich area in Southeast Asia. To protect this priceless addition to the Empire, Tokyo also seized a number of islands across the Pacific. In May 1942 the setback in the Battle of the Coral Sea prevented Tokyo from seizing Port Moresby, capital of Australian-controlled Papua New Guinea.

Infuriated by the naval failures at the Battles of the Coral Sea and Midway, the Japanese Army decided to go it alone. In July 1942 transports landed 11,000 Japanese soldiers along a beachhead near the tiny Australian administrative center at Buna on Papua's northeastern coast. Buna was the eastern terminus of the crude Kokoda Trail, the only land route over the rugged Owen Stanley Mountains. One hundred miles down the Kokoda Trail lay Port Moresby. In early August some 7,000 Japanese infantry set off.

The Japanese underestimated Allied resources. Shocked by early Japanese victories, in April 1942 Washington deployed the 32nd and 41st Divisions to Australia, together with a large number of scarce military aircraft. The Australian government recalled the veteran Sixth and Seventh Divisions of the Australian Imperial Force (AIF) from service in the Middle East.

Despite their supreme confidence, a debacle was developing for the Japanese. Just as the expedition began, the Americans landed on Guadalcanal in the Solomon Islands, effectively depriving the Japanese on Papua of support.

More immediately, AIF units were rushed to Moresby by sea and stopped the Japanese advance 20 miles east of the town. In late September Tokyo ordered a retreat back to the Buna area beachhead, pledging to renew the attack after the Americans were smashed in the Solomons. To Tokyo's dismay the Australians turned the Japanese retreat into a near rout. Relieved and elated, MacArthur ordered that the 32nd Division join the battle and help crush the Japanese at Buna.

However, a number of geographic factors coalesced to create a military nightmare at Buna. New Guinea was the last major landmass touched by Western culture or technology. There were no towns, no roads, no civilian services of any kind. Fearing uncharted reefs and Japanese air attack, the Allied navies refused to operate merchant ships in Buna waters. Thus a motley collection of small coastal vessels had to ferry the 32nd Division and basic supplies to a beach 25 miles east of Buna. Ominously, American officers believed it was impossible to debark any vehicles or field artillery. The Americans were crippled before the first shot was fired.

With only crude land and sea communications, air power played a crucial role in the Buna campaign. With the Japanese distracted at Guadalcanal, Allied air forces had air superiority over Buna. Despite high expectations, direct air support proved a great disappointment. The nightmarish terrain made targets invisible by air and forced Allied airmen to attack blind with little effect. Allied airpower did pay off, however, in two ways. First, by preventing Japanese merchant ships from operating, Allied bombers isolated the battlefield and crippled the enemy logistics. Second, the Allies were able to employ military air transport, thanks to a piece of geographic good fortune. On the edge of the Buna swamp, six miles from the battlefield, American engineers found a piece of land with good drainage. By November the rugged C-47 transports were able to land, turning this little strip into the great American air base of Dobodura, the most important piece of real estate in Papua outside of Moresby. It also highlighted the great paradox of jungle warfare: Without the wealth and technology of a modern nation, there could have been no war in Papua at all. Yet because the terrain so limited the employment of advanced weapons, the men were forced to fight the most primitive campaign of World War II.

Almost all of New Guinea was covered by some of the densest jungle on Earth. Directly on the Equator, New Guinea has a climate characterized by searing heat, extremely high humidity, and heavy rainfall. Movement was confined to a bewildering network of crude trails created by the indigenous Papuans. The battlefields there were quite small, confined to a few corridors along the trails and a handful of coastal positions.

The worst place to fight a battle was in a coastal swamp. Such terrain surrounded the Buna area and shaped every facet of the encounter. Rivers flowing north from the Owen Stanley Mountains slowed in the flatlands, breaking up into creeks and creating large mangrove-choked swamps. On the small bits of land above the water table, Papuans had crafted crude trails suitable only for foot traffic. These trails were arteries for battle in the Buna area, and between them soldiers found soggy ground passable for infantry or absolutely impenetrable swamp capable of swallowing a man. On some of this soggy ground tall *kunai* grass grew. The field of vision was rarely over a mere 20 yards, and soldiers huddling in shallow "mudholes" could see only a few feet.

It is best to envision the Buna battlefield as a triangle: Its base was the 11-mile-long Japanese coastal beachhead. The eastern point of the Japanese position lay at a small airfield, built east-west along the Simemi Creek near Cape Endaiadere. Simemi Creek was one of the several mouths of the Girua River that disappeared into swamp five miles inland from Buna. West from Simemi Creek was a coconut plantation and Buna Mission, a prewar station for a handful of Australian officials. A few hundred yards up the coast was the small and abandoned Buna Village with, at its western edge, Entrance Creek, the major mouth of the Girua. A trail ran westward along the ocean to Sanananda Point, which was the final terminus of the Kokoda Trail. A mile farther west was another coastal point at Gona, also connected to the Kokoda Trail.

The apex of the triangle was the village of Soputa, five miles inland from Buna. From Soputa, the lines of battle ran northeast to Gona and southeast, alongside Dobodura airfield, to the Japanese airfield along Simemi Creek.

Three swaths of impenetrable swamp subdivided the battlefield and channeled the Allied lines of advance. Swamp divided Gona from Sanananda. The largest and densest swamp lay along the Girua River-Entrance Creek and effectively isolated Sanananda from Buna Mission. Lateral communications in the Buna Mission area were likewise very difficult, forcing the Allies to attack either along trails running from Soputa or up the coastal trail.

The Japanese prepared accordingly and created a strong line covering the area between the airstrip and Buna Village. Directly in front of Buna Mission, the line followed a creek bend, creating an area American soldiers soon dubbed the "triangle." Inside the Buna Mission perimeter were some 2,000 Japanese, with another 5,000 at Sanananda. Another 800 men protected the flank at Gona, adding up to approximately 8,500 men defending the Buna beachhead.

Skilled Japanese combat engineers fortified the area weeks before the Allied siege began. They constructed bunkers of coconut-tree logs, reinforced with barrels of sand, and covered the structures with earth and quick-growing tropical grasses. These rugged bunkers could be destroyed by mortars or bombs only if they suffered a direct hit. Worse, they blended into the thick brush and were almost impossible to identify at distances over ten yards. The defenders also cleverly placed the several artillery batteries available.

The Japanese also took great care to clear fields of fire for their machine guns. Thus, the Allies usually first discovered Japanese positions by literally stumbling into fierce fire at extremely close range. In battle Japanese patrols fanned out of their prepared positions and occupied an even larger number of smaller ones, changing the battle line constantly. Consequently, Allied infantry, during most of the battle, never knew exactly where the front was.

Allied intelligence seriously underestimated Japanese strength and expected quick victory. Because the terrain prevented tactical flexibility the first major assault, beginning on November 19-20, was completely predictable. Elements of the AIF Sixth and Seventh Divisions attacked toward Sanananda Point and Gona. On the eastern side of the Girua swamp, most of the American 32nd Division assaulted Buna itself. The swamps split the American attack into one directed at the coconut plantation along the coast, and a second against the "triangle" in front of Buna Mission. With little coordination possible between the Allied fronts, the attacks bogged down almost immediately.

The first three weeks of the Allied assault were miserable, with gains measured in yards. Drained by the heat and humidity, debilitated by malaria and dysentery, and bewildered by Japanese defenses, American units in particular were soon in trouble. In many places near the front, Japanese and Allied positions were less than 50 yards apart for days on end, the nerve-wracking stress leading to a large number of "battle fatigue" casualties.

Despite the suffering, the Allies continued the assaults. Slowly the battle settled into a rhythm. Instead of a concentrated attack, the siege of Buna became a war of patrols and squad operations. Patrols would inch forward and locate Japanese strongpoints, calling in the limited artillery available. Sometimes the terrain, which shielded Japanese defenses, allowed an Allied unit to launch a close assault and destroy a Japanese bunker with hand grenades.

The slugfest reached its apogee on the Soputa-Sanananda Trail. After being attacked by the AIF for a week with no success, an American company managed to wedge itself onto the trail behind the first Japanese perimeter, withstanding furious counterattacks. The Japanese responded by creating another roadblock behind the Americans. The Australians created their own behind the Japanese until, by mid-December, the position resembled a strange necklace of interlocking links. For the time, however, each Japanese unit continued fighting, and the main Sanananda line remained intact.

Ultimately the AIF led the way to victory. Australians captured Gona on December 9. Disregarding the American belief that it was not possible to bring armored vehicles to the front, AIF engineers managed to deploy some Bren Gun Carriers (a type of half-track) and 12 M-3 Stuart tanks supported by an infantry battalion. After an initial reverse, an Allied tank-infantry attack on December 15 broke the Japanese position at Cape Endaiadere. Days later, the remaining tanks and AIF infantry spearheaded an Allied attack that broke over Simemi Creek and the airstrip. The Japanese began to lose cohesion.

Simultaneously, the American force in front of Buna Mission earned its major victory in what was an agonizing campaign. On December 5, a battalion of the 32nd Division managed to move down Entrance Creek and seize a beach position. After reinforcement, American infantry captured Buna Village on December 14. On December 25 the AIF and 32nd attacked toward Buna mission and took it on January 2, 1943 in relentless and vicious hand-to-hand combat. In over six weeks of fighting, the 32nd Division, with crucial assistance from the AIF, succeeded in moving three miles.

Although not appreciated by Allied intelligence, the Japanese were on the ropes. Almost every factor that made Buna a miserable campaign for the Allied soldiers had an even stronger impact on the Japanese. By mid-December food was running out and disease ravaged the Imperial forces. The Japanese, however, had no Dobodura to evacuate the ill and replenish supplies. By the end of the month the garrison faced starvation.

The last act, and the most grisly, was played out at Sanananda. After taking Buna Mission, the Allies deployed their forces toward the Soputa-Sanananda Trail. In late December, a fresh regiment of the American 41st Division arrived and the AIF tanks moved into action. The Japanese were now in a hopeless position. Surrender was not allowed under the Japanese military ethos, and thus the last portion of the campaign degenerated into a massacre.

The final attack began on January 9 and concluded on January 22. Throughout this period, the Japanese defense descended into desperation. One of the last positions taken on the coast was a Japanese field hospital that was defended to the last by medics and patients. A strong Japanese perimeter on the Sanananda Trail, which had survived weeks of sustained assault, simply collapsed under an American attack on January 21. Some Japanese tried escape, some committed suicide, others simply left their shelters shooting blindly. At the end of that day, the Americans buried 550 Japanese troops, probably more enemy killed than during the first month of operations. In return, one American died. The siege of the Buna beachhead was over.

The butcher's bill was high. The Japanese lost over 12,000 men killed in Papua, of whom approximately 8,000 perished in the Buna area. The Australians lost 2,200 men killed; 35,000 were wounded and 15,600 treated for disease in Papua. The 14,000 Americans at Buna, mostly from the 32nd Division, added 930 killed, 2,000 wounded, and 8,700 disease victims to the list. Including serious disease Allied units had loss rates of nearly 90 percent. In effect the American 32nd and Australian Seventh Divisions were shattered and required months of reorganization before ready for further action. After the battle, a shaken MacArthur was to swear, "No more Bunas."

Find, Fix, and Destroy
The Ia Drang Valley, Vietnam, 1965

ERIC BERGERUD

Between November 14 and November 17,1965, men of the U.S. Army confronted counterparts from the People's Army of North Vietnam (PAVN) in a fierce battle in the Ia Drang Valley in South Vietnam's Central Highlands. Although relatively small in scale, this bloody encounter highlighted many of the military and geographic elements that would shape the entire Vietnam War.

The encounter in the Ia Drang was propelled by the most important geopolitical factor of the overall conflict. Because Hanoi and its clients in the Vietcong either shared a manpower/resource base with the South Vietnamese government or could draw resources from politically secure sanctuaries (above all, North Vietnam itself), there was no single point inside South Vietnam that Communist forces had to defend.

This fact had crucial consequences. If Americans were unable to force a "decisive battle" on PAVN or the Vietcong, and thus gain political victory, the only military recourse was to fight a war of pure attrition.

The structure of the opposing forces amplified the quandary facing Washington. Being a rich country with a democratic political culture, the U.S. had a military that was extremely conscious of casualties. Therefore it emphasized firepower in all forms. Tempered by World War II and prepared to confront the Warsaw Pact during the Cold War, the U.S. Army deployed to Vietnam was trained to expend "bullets, not bodies."

Map of Southeast Asia, 1965

This map of Southeast Asia, published a mere month after the conflict in the Ia Drang Valley, is from the collection of Bill Beck, a machine gunner who fought at Ia Drang. Dense jungle vegetation in the valley area all but limited movement to infantry and helicopters.

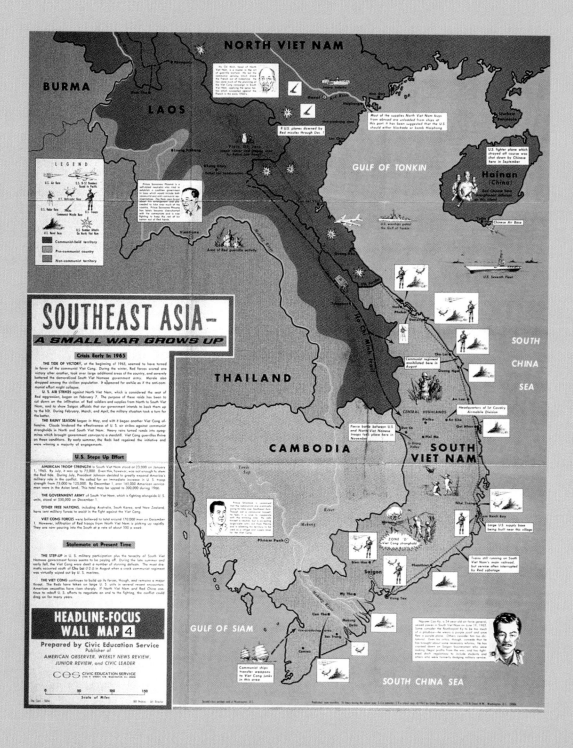

The victory over France formed PAVN. Without America's resources Hanoi put its assets into the development of a good light-infantry army armed with excellent small and medium armaments. Training in small-unit tactics was of a high order. Although PAVN lacked the "punch" that only sophisticated fire-power could provide, it did not need a large logistic support apparatus and could thus put a higher percentage of men "in the grass."

South Vietnam was a large country, and American commanders recognized they had to be able to move much more quickly than had the roadbound French forces. The answer, U.S. leaders hoped, lay in mass use of helicopters, and the apogee of "the airmobile concept" came with the creation of the First Cavalry Division (Airmobile) in June 1965.

The Americans badly needed mobility in Vietnam. Somewhat over half of South Vietnam was made up of rugged, forested terrain. Generically Americans referred to this area as the Central Highlands. The Highlands covered the central and eastern portion of South Vietnam, extending well into Cambodia, Laos, and North Vietnam. Compared with the coastal areas or the Mekong Delta, the Highlands were sparsely populated. There were a few small cities, the most important being Pleiku. The Highlands also possessed several points of entry for the famous Ho Chi Minh Trail, which connected North Vietnam with the battlefields in the south.

Specifically, the terrain near Pleiku included small mountains, ridge lines, triple-canopy jungle, and forests punctuated by natural or man-made clearings. Tall and dense "elephant grass" was present throughout. The few roads that existed were crude and perilous to use. The Pleiku area illustrated one of the central characteristics of war in heavy forest or jungle. Movement by road and water was slow and dangerous. Cross-country movement by mechanized units was slow or impossible. However, like most of the Highlands, the ground near Pleiku was crisscrossed by trails and paths, allowing very rapid movement by foot. The geographic equation was a good one for Hanoi. The dense cover could shield PAVN units from American reconnaissance and air strike. PAVN infantry, however, could still move quickly. It was this problem that the Americans hoped they could solve with helicopters.

Consequently in October 1965 General Westmoreland deployed the First

Cavalry Division to An Khe just east of Pleiku. Maj. Gen. Harold Kinnard, commander of the Cav, ordered the division's Third Brigade, under Col. Thomas Brown to "seek and destroy" PAVN units west of Pleiku. Specifically the target was a finger of the Ia Drang Valley which protruded to the north and northeast of a cluster of small mountains called the Chu Pong Massif. Chu Pong served as a major PAVN supply and assembly point. All that was necessary for the Americans was to "find them, fix them, destroy them." The Ia Drang appeared to be the ideal place for such an attempt. In addition, despite some skirmishing, the two forces had never done battle with each other, and both sides were spoiling for a fight.

Although several units participated in the overall action, the job of landing at the foot of Chu Pong was given to Col. Harold Moore's First Battalion of the Seventh Regiment. Moore's strength of 431 men was considerably less than the 633 assigned. Considering the task, Moore had a very small force. Geography complicated the situation further. As the air was warm and thin in the Vietnamese Highlands, American officers decided that only five, instead of the standard eight, troopers could be carried into battle per helicopter. Moore's first lift, therefore, would be 80 men, and, with a half-hour turnaround, it would take several hours to deploy. Conversely, if trouble erupted, the initial American force would be small and vulnerable. To compensate, artillery and air units were assigned to support Moore's mission.

Moore received final orders to move on November 13, 1965. Not oblivious to the irony of commanding the same unit once led to destruction by Custer, Moore showed unusual foresight in preparing for the unexpected. He personally chose the landing zone (LZ), code-named X-Ray, and decided to arrive with the first Huey to allow himself the opportunity to abort the mission. Throughout the coming days, Moore showed excellent judgment and served his men well.

Moore and most of the 1/Seventh's Company B were the first to X-Ray, arriving 11:00 a.m. on November 14. Weather was clear and temperate. X-Ray itself was a small rectangular clearing roughly 100 by 80 yards in size. There were tall grass and clumps of wood throughout the area, but the roughest terrain was to the west and southwest as the land ascended to the Chu Pong

Massif. Elements of two PAVN regiments, perhaps 1,600 men, were in the imme-diate area. Surprised by Moore's arrival, PAVN commanders decided on an immediate attack. Fortunately for the Americans, there were no PAVN at X-Ray itself, and it took the Vietnamese over an hour to begin effective operations.

At approximately 12:30 Moore ordered the platoons of Company B to begin a search. Soon one of these platoons was cut off and enveloped some 250 yards north from the center of X-Ray. Enemy fire against all of Company B began to increase dramatically.

Within two hours of landing at X-Ray, Moore realized that his battalion was in danger of destruction. From the headquarters position in the middle of X-Ray, Moore deployed his men to cover the northwest, west, and southwest portion of the landing zone. Any attacks, Moore reasoned, would come gen-erally from the south and west where the Chu Pong loomed. This left X-Ray's northern and eastern flanks undefended. Moore guessed correctly. The first cri-sis at X-Ray began with a PAVN attack against the Americans defending the southwest sector. Fierce American artillery and air strikes slowed and then stopped the advance. While the fighting was under way, American helicopters managed to slip in and land Company D. Moore immediately deployed it to the northeast, giving X-Ray a real perimeter for the first time.

Inside the American position, the battle broke down into a series of indi-vidual firefights. Moore did what he could to keep communication open between companies, but at the platoon level, men relied on training and instinct and engaged in a series of small-scale firefights. In most cases, men on both sides fired at anything that might indicate the presence of an oppo-nent. The grass greatly obstructed visibility, which protected American defend-ers but also allowed a close approach by those in a PAVN assault. Groups of men literally stumbled into each other and hand-to-hand combat ensued, an event that is extremely rare in modern war. Thus, despite the fact that the battlefield in and around X-Ray was very small, to the men involved, the "big picture" barely existed as handfuls of soldiers struggled to hold on to their lit-tle piece of Vietnamese earth.

At the end of the first day, Moore made an unsuccessful attempt to relieve his isolated platoon. While doing so, enemy forces, taking advantage of the rough terrain, moved in so close to American troopers that supporting fire could not be safely used. This "hugging" tactic became a PAVN staple throughout the war when the terrain allowed its use. Turned back, Moore's men reorganized their positions, resupplied units, and readied for the morrow. At sunset they received Company B of the 2/7th as a valued reinforcement. Other American units nearby were ordered to come to Moore's aid the next day. That night the isolated American platoon, huddling inside a 25-yard perimeter, received sharp attacks and was saved by artillery and automatic cannon fire coming from a "Spooky" gunship.

During the night small PAVN units probed the American line at very close range. These probes were in preparation for a massed dawn assault (later in the war PAVN almost never launched massed assaults against American units during daylight). The second crisis at X-Ray ensued just before 7:00 a.m. when PAVN units assaulted from the southeast. Within half an hour over 1,000 PAVN infantrymen were attacking X-Ray from three directions.

Years later, machine-gunner Bill Beck recalled that "without the artillery and air support we would have been overrun—all of the men agreed with that. The planes and artillery also did most of the killing." Because PAVN infantry were able to approach closely for attack, American fire support came down almost on top of the perimeter. However, because they lacked their own heavy "punch" the North Vietnamese were never able to shatter the position.

Soon the momentum of the assault slackened. The Americans were able to land another company of the 2/Seventh for support, and by noon the bulk of another company marched in without opposition.

By 1:00 p.m. Moore had reached the remainder of Company B's isolated platoon. It is testimony to the dense terrain and power of PAVN's light-infantry weaponry that it took Moore's men, supported by "marching artillery" fire, nearly two hours to travel the 250 yards to save their comrades. After more light probes on the night of November 15, PAVN attacked X-Ray from north and south at dawn on November 16. The day previously, PAVN had come close to complete victory. Twenty-four hours, however, is a long time in war, and the last attack was a fiasco as North Vietnamese soldiers came into the open only to be cut to ribbons by M-16 rifles of the Cav's troopers.

The results of the first phase of the Ia Drang were grim. Moore's command lost 79 men killed and 121 men wounded—a very serious loss for two days' work. No doubt PAVN lost far more; the Americans claimed a minimum of 634 killed.

The battle, however, was far from over. In the concluding stages of the encounter at X-Ray two more U.S. battalions, the Second of the Fifth under Lt. Col. Robert Tully and Second of the Seventh under Lt. Col. Robert McDade had reinforced Moore. This enabled Moore's battered force to make its flight home late on November 16. The next day it was decided to evacuate X-Ray. There were B-52 strikes scheduled against Chu Pong, the first time this fearsome weapon was employed in a tactical role. More to the point, X-Ray had served its purpose. As a geographic point it had no meaning. The last job at hand, therefore, was to deploy the remaining Americans to places more secure for final departure. The retreat from X-Ray, however, almost culminated in catastrophe.

Early on November 17 Tully's battalion marched, accompanied by artillery support on the flanks, three miles toward LZ Columbus. Most of McDade's 2/Seventh, accompanied by a company of the 2/Fifth, followed close behind, continuing an extra mile to LZ Albany. McDade ordered his men to march in a column and without artillery, believing that its presence would only alert the enemy. These decisions almost cost McDade's battalion its life. If McDade believed that an American battalion could march in close order through enemy territory without detection he was most certainly incorrect.

Tragically for McDade's men a PAVN unit was already near Albany. The PAVN commander quickly organized his 500 men for an ambush. At noon the lead American company arrived at Albany and McDade halted the column to confer with his company commanders. As the commanders came forward, the men relaxed on what was, for Vietnam, a balmy day. While the American troopers rested, the enemy prepared.

The ambush exploded at 1:15 p.m. In the words of a company surgeon, "everything dissolved into confusion."

The three middle companies were quickly overrun. Men milled about in the tall grass. Many groups of American soldiers fired upon other Americans.

Friend and foe became so intermingled that American fire support could not be employed. Indeed, the tall grass that enabled PAVN soldiers to approach so close was responsible for hiding small clusters of American survivors through the rest of the day and through the night.

Although better deployed, the lead company was also fighting for its life. One American platoon was isolated and annihilated. The remaining platoons tried to establish a triangular perimeter based on three termite hills. American airpower moved in with a vengeance to protect the lead unit. Simultaneously, the rear company formed an effective perimeter and defended itself against the only attack launched its way. At dusk a reinforcing company arrived as the PAVN assault slackened. The next morning the survivors at Albany began the grim job of removing casualties.

McDade's company began its march with about 400 men. In less than a day it suffered 151 men killed and 121 wounded; it was one of the worst days for the U.S. Army of the entire war.

Ironically, both sides believed victory had been theirs in the Ia Drang. Westmoreland considered airmobile operations a success and ordered bigger and bigger "search and destroy" missions. Never did one of these operations bring a major American victory. One might say that Westmoreland remembered X-Ray and hoped to improve upon it. If so, PAVN remembered Albany. After 1965, on scores of occasions PAVN and Vietcong units attempted to isolate and destroy American units or firebases. Often there were anxious moments. Always American firepower prevailed in the end. Always Communist soldiers paid dearly in blood.

PASSES

Passes can be perilous places, the military equivalent of running the gauntlet—as the British found out in Afghanistan in the nineteenth century. On January 13, 1842, a lone rider approached the British garrison at Jellalabad. It was the British Army surgeon, William Brydon, the sole British soldier to survive from a column 4,500 strong that had broken out of besieged Kabul. In the freezing mountain defiles through which the column had to pass, tribal Afridis and Ghilzais were waiting for it. Expert marksmen, the Afghans were armed with *jezails*, highly accurate long-barreled rifles. From their perches on the slopes they picked off almost the entire British force. It was one of the great military disasters of Queen Victoria's long reign. The Mitla Pass on the Sinai Peninsula has had an especially active military history in modern times because, as the main gateway to and from the Sinai Peninsula, it is of crucial strategic importance. During the Egyptian-Israeli Sinai Campaign in 1956, it was the focus of some very dramatic action. On October 26, 1956, the Sinai was Egyptian territory, and 395 paratroopers of the Israeli crack 202 Parachute Brigade were dropped behind the Egyptian lines at the eastern entrance of the Pass. Their mission was to interdict Egyptian forces coming through the Pass from the west and, once reinforced, prevent Egyptians' leaving the Sinai from the east. Moving into the Pass, the Israelis were heavily enfiladed from Egyptians deployed in the caves that honeycombed each side. Only after brutal hand-to-hand fighting were the Egyptians finally evicted. Again, during the Six-Day War of 1967, the Israelis "funneled" the Egyptian armor and infantry that was retreating across the Sinai Peninsula toward the eastern entrance to Mitla, their gateway to freedom, where they were comprehensively destroyed. The two battles in this chapter, Thermopylae and Kasserine, are separated not only by over 2,400 years but also a chasm of a different kind. We remember the Greek defenders at Thermopylae for an act of supreme sacrifice and heroism. Kasserine, on the other hand, will be remembered as one of the less heroic defenses in the history of arms.

Thermopylae, Greece, 480 B.C., West Point map

Thermopylae, shown on the insert, literally means "hot gateway." The mountain pass is named for the natural hot springs that jet through the crevasses in its rocky floor. At the time of Leonidas's valiant defense, the pass was narrow—no more than 50 feet wide—but river deposits have since widened it, and the pass spans three miles along some areas.

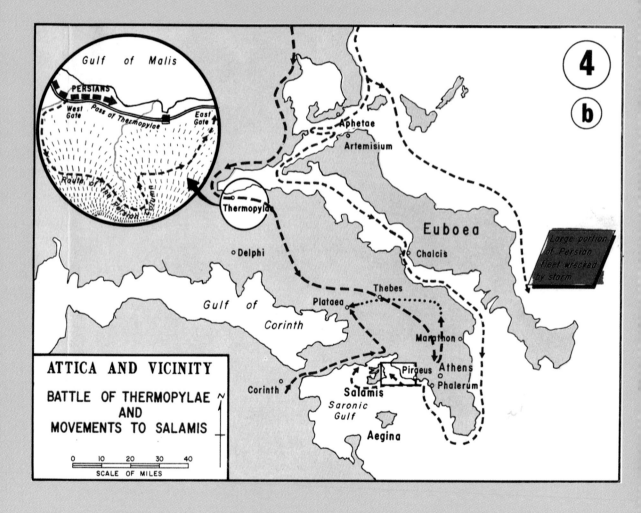

ATTICA AND VICINITY

BATTLE OF THERMOPYLAE
AND
MOVEMENTS TO SALAMIS

0   10   20   30   40
SCALE OF MILES

Leonidas' Last Stand
Thermopylae, Greece, 480 B.C.

MATTHEW BENNETT

It is a place where hot, sulfurous springs burst out of the rocks in a narrow defile between the mountains and the sea on the eastern coast of Greece. In geographical terms this is a pass and, what is more, a fortified pass, because three walls ("Gates") had been constructed to prevent movement through it. It was these that formed the West, Middle, and East Gates blocking a three-mile-long track, before the coastal plain widened out enough to provide an army with free movement again. The sea has retreated two miles or more over the past 2,500 years, making it difficult for a modern observer to imagine the ancient topography, but there can be no doubt that the "Hot Gates" were all but impassable if resolutely defended.

Indeed the whole outcome of the Persian invasion of Greece in 480-479 B.C. could be said to have depended upon geography and man's struggle to overcome its constraints. The valiant and futile attempt by the Greeks to hold the pass at Thermopylae was just one aspect of the campaign, although the best remembered. The Persians came by sea and land, and it was by sea and land that they were eventually defeated: in the Gulf of Salamis and in broken ground at Plataea a year later. Certainly, Xerxes, king of kings and ruler of the largest empire in the world, did not intend to be impeded by any physical obstacle. He had a canal cut across the Athos Peninsula to spare his fleet the sea journey around. This was to prevent the repetition of a naval disaster during an earlier invasion attempt in 492 B.C. , when most of the fleet had been lost in a storm. He also commanded not one, but two bridges of boats be built to span the Bosporus in order to march his vast army from Asia Minor dry-shod into Thrace.

The size of Xerxes' army has long been matter for debate. If we take the Greek historian Herodotus at his word, then the Persians, Medes, and their subjects numbered no fewer than 1,700,000 infantry, 80,000 cavalry, and 20,000 chariots and camels. Once on the European side, they were supposed to have been joined by 300,000 Thracian and northern Greek allies (although one commentator considers this equal to the entire manpower of the Balkans at this period!). One problem may be that the Greeks used the term "myriad" (10,000 men) to represent a great number. So, suspiciously, there were reputedly 10,000 Athenians at Marathon in 490 and 10,000 men in Xenophon's force when he marched to the sea from southern Asia Minor almost a century later. It may also be that the Greeks misrepresented the Persian *chiliarchs* (commanders of 1,000) as leading ten times that number. Reducing Herodotus's totals by a factor of ten does make them more reasonable, but still a logistical nightmare.

Why did Xerxes need to call on such a vast host? One reason was that as an imperial expedition, over 30 subject nations were expected to send a contingent. The Persian Empire was far from stable. The Ionian Greek cities of eastern Asia Minor had revolted in 499-495 B.C. (and in seeking support from their "homeland" had brought down the wrath of the Persians in Greece); and Egypt rebelled against over-heavy taxation in 486-484 B.C. One way of ensuring obedience was for Xerxes to take troops, effectively as hostages, overseas. Not that all his followers were unwilling, despite Greek propaganda that they had to be driven into battle with whips, unlike their own citizens, who served out of free will. The core of the invading army was the Persian Immortals, again "10,000" strong, and so called because casualties were immediately replaced by previously chosen men. The Medes were also well equipped and well motivated, as were the Sakae, both particularly strong in archers. Yet when it came to the almost naked, barely armed Ethiopians whom Herodotus describes, their usefulness in battle (if not in raiding and skirmishing) must be doubted. Against them stood the heavily armed Greek hoplites (named after their large, round, bronze shield, the hoplon), drilled to fight in the close-order phalanx, troops who had proved their superiority in hand-to-hand combat ten years earlier at Marathon.

In the intervening decade the Greeks had time to prepare for the coming storm. Yet although they shared a common language and culture they were politically very divided, belonging as they did to competing city-states. Indeed, some were sworn enemies. So, for example, in the Peloponnese the city of Argos opposed Sparta, which predisposed the Argives to accept Persian rule if their enemy, the Spartans, fought against it. Also, it should not be forgotten that Macedonia and northern Greece already lay under Persian domination, and in central Greece, Thessaly and Boeotia, where the important city of Thebes lay, were at the very least equivocal about submitting. Again, it was simply a matter of geography. The Peloponnesians might feel relatively secure, with Corinth guarding the isthmus into their lands. Athens relied upon its fleets to provide some protection, although it was vulnerable to land attack. Beyond that to the north, there was only the possibility of holding the passes against an invading force.

Themistocles of Athens tried to bring the Greeks together in a Hellenic League to counter the Persian threat. He had to overcome many mutual suspicions, not least of the Spartans, his city's greatest rivals. It is greatly to his credit that he managed to create an alliance, and to persuade the Spartans and their Peloponnesian allies to provide an army to counter the invaders, even though they would be the last to be threatened. There seems to have been an attempt to hold the pass at Tempe, near Mount Olympus, by sending a land and sea force there in late June. But this was soon withdrawn, as being too exposed and easily outflanked.

So it was that Leonidas, one of Sparta's two kings, led a force of some 7,000 hoplites to Thermopylae instead. According to Herodotus, this was composed of 300 Spartans, 500 men each from Tegea and Mantinea, 400 from Corinth, 200 from Philius, 120 from Orchmenus, 80 from Mycenae, and 1,000 "from other cities," all from the Peloponnese. They were joined by 700 Thespians and 400 Thebans (probably those within the city who opposed the Persians) from Boeotia. Finally, the Phokians and Lokrians, in whose territory the Gates stood, provided about 1,000 men each, the Malians from the north side of the gulf, perhaps 1,000 more. These last contingents, coming from less wealthy, less urbanized areas of Greece, should not be considered fully equipped close-order troops.

This was clearly a quite inadequate force with which to oppose the Persian horde, but it was supported at sea by an Athenian force of some 200 triremes, which performed very well against the invading fleet. This still left the Greeks facing heavy odds of three to one; but they managed to defeat the largely Phoenician vessels twice, in the Gulf of Artimesion, before retiring south, leaving Leonidas and his men to their fate.

It was probably in mid-August that Xerxes's host arrived in front of the Gates. We need not believe that he had more than 60,000 to 70,000 men with him (including the best warriors of the empire, the Immortals among them), but this was still ten times that of the defenders. Xerxes did not launch an immediate attack, possibly because he and his commanders preferred to assess the situation first, but also because it would have taken several days for the rear of the marching column to catch up with the leading troops.

There is also the famous story from Herodotus of a Persian scout riding up to the Middle Gate, which the Greek forces were defending, being left completely undisturbed. He witnessed what was to him an extraordinary sight: the Spartans, stripped naked to join in gymnastic exercises, or tending each other's long hair in the traditional manner. When he reported this to Xerxes, the Great King turned for advice from his tame expert: Demaratos, a former Spartan king who had been forced in exile a number of years earlier and had sought refuge at the Persian court. He explained that the hair-dressing was the Spartan custom when faced with a do-or-die situation, adding that if the Persians could defeat the representatives of the "first kingdom and city in Greece" no others would dare to resist any longer.

Median troops launched the first attacks on the Middle Gate walls. Yet the narrowness of the position negated their superiority in numbers. Together with the hoplites' protection from arrows and their undoubted fighting qualities in close combat, this meant that the attackers were repulsed with heavy loss. A follow-up attack by the Persian Immortals fared no better. For not only did the hoplites possess better offensive equipment in their longer spears, and better defensive protection from their shields, but they also feigned flight on occasion to draw in attackers. They then re-formed their ranks and over-whelmed those who had been incautious enough to pursue. Although the glory went to the Spartans, it should not be forgotten that all the contingents took their turn, fighting in reliefs.

All, that is, except for the Phokians, who had been detached by Leonidas to cover the possibility of a flanking attack through the mountains inland of the pass. This further suggests that they were lightly equipped and used to fighting in such broken terrain. Now it might seem strange that the Persians had not attempted an outflanking maneuver, but they were in foreign territory. Herodotus tells us that they found a turncoat, a certain Ephialites the Malian, who revealed to the Persians the existence of a goat track, three miles inland, on the slopes of Mount Kallidromos. Once he became aware of this, Xerxes ordered his Immortals to make a night march under Ephialites' direction, to turn the position. There was a full moon, which made this tricky operation somewhat easier. The Phokians, whose task it was to protect this route, failed in their duty. Taken by surprise and seemingly overwhelmed by Persian arrows, they withdrew up the mountain slopes to a defensive position, leaving the route clear. The Immortals merely ignored them and pressed on.

When Leonidas received word that the pass had been betrayed, he instructed his allies to escape, keeping with him only the Thespians and the Thebans. He may have had some intimation of the likely outcome of the campaign from the start, because being of mature years himself, he had ordered that he should be accompanied only by Spartiates who had living male progeny. So, in the case of their death, the family line would continue. It was now for death that the Spartans prepared themselves. After fighting hard against renewed attacks from the front, when the Immortals began to appear in their rear, the surviving Greeks withdrew onto a nearby hillock. Herodotus's final anecdote is of a Spartan, who upon being told that the enemy's arrows would blot out the sun, said he thought that this was good news, for "we shall have our fight in the shade!"

The final death blow was not long in coming. A combined assault overwhelmed the last defenders, who, their spears shattered, had to fight with stones and bare hands. And there they fell, the brotherhood of the defiant.

Kasserine Pass, Tunisia, 1943, Military Operations map

Kasserine, a pass in the Western Dorsale mountains of Tunisia, can be found in the upper-right corner of this map, which was used by the First Infantry Division of the U.S. Army. The arrows drawn on it point north to Maktar and Sbeitla, towns that were also sites of military activity in Tunisia. Sbeitla was seized by German Col. Gen. Hans-Jurgen von Arnim on February 17 but was reclaimed by the Allies on February 24, the same day they regained control of Kasserine.

The Blooding
Kasserine Pass, Tunisia, 1943

BRYAN PERRETT

Inland of the coastal plain, the terrain of central Tunisia is dominated by two ranges of hills, known as the Eastern and Western Dorsales. These meet in the north but diverge steadily as they reach southward so that in plan they resemble an inverted Y. The hills themselves are neither particularly high nor steep, although they offer excellent defensive positions. It follows, therefore, that for any army wishing to advance east or west through the Dorsales, possession of the passes is of critical importance. In the Eastern Dorsale there are passes at Pichon, Fondouk, Faid, and Maknassy, while in the Western Dorsale the most important passes are situated at Maktar, Sbiba, Kasserine, and Feriana. In winter heavy rainfall can quickly raise the level of watercourses, send flash floods down wadis, and turn off-road going into a quagmire. Settled agriculture was possible in many areas, but between these lay large stretches of desert or semi-desert that can be whipped into blinding sandstorms by high winds.

Following the November 1942 landings in French North Africa, British and American attempts to secure the ports of Tunis and Bizerta by quick, direct assault had failed, partly because the buildup of German and Italian forces had been so rapid, partly because Allied air cover was inadequate, and partly because of sodden weather. Since then, Gen. Dwight D. Eisenhower, Commander in Chief of Allied forces in this theater, had decreed that the line of the Eastern Dorsale should be held pending the arrival of reinforcements that would enable him to bring the campaign to a successful conclusion.

The northern end of the line was held by Lt. Gen. Kenneth Anderson's British First Army, consisting of V Corps under Lt. Gen. C.W. Allfrey; in the center was the Free French XIX Corps, commanded by Gen. L.M. Koeltz; and in the south, guarding the Allies' right flank, was the U.S. II Corps under Maj. Gen. Lloyd R. Fredendall. As the battle developed, First Army's authority would be extended to the whole front.

Comparatively few of the British, and none of the Americans, had experience fighting the Germans. The ease with which they had overcome the brief resistance of the few French units that had opposed their landings had engendered a dangerous overconfidence in both. Nor did either possess the type of tank with which they would have preferred to fight an armored battle. Although modern Sherman tanks had begun to reach British and American units in January 1943, the British 26th Armoured Brigade (part of Sixth Armoured Division) remained largely equipped with an incompatible mixture of Valentines and Crusaders. Of these the former, designed for infantry support, was slow and heavily armored, whereas the latter was fast but thin skinned; both were hopelessly outgunned by their German opponents. Likewise, the U.S. First Armored Division still possessed large numbers of Stuart light tanks and obsolete Lee mediums. The French, having decided to join the Allies, had virtually no tanks of their own, were equipped solely for colonial warfare, and would have to be extensively re-armed.

A further factor affecting the course of the battle would be the personality of General Fredendall. Eisenhower had had serious reservations about his appointment, and these proved to be fully justified. Fredendall disliked his British allies, was contemptuous of the French, and was possessed of an unfortunate personality. Finding it impossible to delegate, he interfered in the internal conduct of units down to company level, often ignoring the chain of command and issuing orders directly to commanders over the heads of their immediate superiors. The resulting confusion was aggravated by the curious manner of staccato veiled speech in which his orders were given, echoing contemporary gangster and Western movies. In this, tanks were referred to as "the big elephants," infantry as "the walking boys," and place names by their initial letter. Naturally, this did not fool the enemy's radio intercept operators for one minute. Fredendall, in fact, was in no position to exercise immediate command, for although his corps' thinly held front extended for approximately 100 miles, he lived in a splendid subterranean headquarters, excavated for him by his corps engineer regiment, no less than 60 miles behind the front. As if all this was not bad enough, he hated Maj. Gen. Orlando Ward, the quietly efficient commander of the reinforced First Armored Division, which was the only major formation that II Corps had in the line.

On the enemy side of the hill, the Axis forces shipped into Tunisia, including the Tenth Panzer Division and a force of Tiger tanks—then the most powerful in the world—had been designated the Fifth Panzer Army, under the command of Col. Gen. Hans-Jurgen von Arnim, a former Prussian Guard officer who had commanded armored formations on the Eastern Front. In January 1943, Field Marshal Erwin Rommel's Afrika Korps, having been defeated at El Alamein in Egypt, completed its long retreat and began entering southern Tunisia. Its leading element, the 21st Panzer Division, was promptly refitted and placed under von Arnim's command.

In general, the results of scrappy fighting in the Eastern Dorsale during January and early February had favored the Axis in that they had secured virtual control of several passes, notably at Faid. Although Montgomery's British Eighth Army was known to be closing up to the Libyan/Tunisian frontier, it was decided to strike first against the Allied First Army and destroy its offensive capacity. Rommel, tired, ill, bitter, and conscious that his defeat at El Alamein had lost him much prestige, wanted to break through the U.S. II Corps, then head through Kasserine Pass in the Western Dorsale and on into Algeria to Constantine and the important supply port of Bone. Such a move, he argued, would sever the Allies' communications and force them to withdraw many miles across the Algerian frontier. More cautious by nature, von Arnim simply wanted a spoiling attack that would penetrate some miles into II Corps' rear areas and neutralize it for a while. It was this view that prevailed at Comando Supremo in Rome. Rommel's and von Arnim's commands were to function separately but cooperate within this overall context. When the last of Rommel's rear guard passed into Tunisia on February 13 the total Axis tank strength rose to 280.

During the early hours of February 14 the Tenth Panzer Division burst out of the Faid Pass and advanced on Sidi bou Zid. Here, the defenders, drawn from First Armored Division's Combat Command A (CCA) and the 168th Regimental Combat Team, were grouped on three hills, Djebel Lessouda, Djebel Ksaira, and Djebel Garet Hadid. The hills were quickly isolated, but those holding them, under constant ground and air attack, fought back. CCA's armored element, containing some 40 tanks and a dozen tank destroyers, counterattacked with the support of two artillery battalions but was shot to pieces. At about noon, the 21st Panzer Division also began closing in on the village from the south, having approached along the track from Maknassy. The fate of Sidi bou Zid was sealed. II Corps had already lost 44 tanks, 59 half-tracks, and 22 guns.

The American infantry holding the three hills continued fighting in the hope that they would be relieved. On February 15, First Armored Division's Combat Command C, reinforced with a Sherman battalion from Combat Command B, counterattacked along the Sbeitla-Sidi bou Zid road. It ran into a well-concealed antitank gun screen and was then itself counterattacked on both flanks, losing 46 tanks and many other vehicles, and was forced to fall back on Sbeitla. That night the trapped infantrymen broke out and attempted to make their way to the American lines in small groups. A surprising number got through, although for many more the rest of the war would be spent in prison camps.

The advice of General Anderson, commanding First Army, was that II Corps and its French neighbors, should simply "roll with the punch." This was based on the correct appreciation that Axis reserves, particularly of fuel, were limited, but it was only a short-term solution, as events farther south were beginning to influence the strategic situation. With permission, Fredendall had abandoned Gafsa, through which Rommel's Afrika Korps Assault Group, including the Italian Centauro Armored Division, was pushing rapidly northeastward against negligible opposition. Fredendall was forced to rely on outdated knowledge because he was remote from events on the ground, and consequently the orders he issued were meaningless. He was unsettled by Rommel's approach and, worried that his troops would be trapped in Sbeitla in the same way they had been at Sidi bou Zid, he ordered his engineers to blow up the town's ammunition and supply dumps. In fact, the First Armored Division had conducted a successful defense, but the exploding dumps suggested to many that the enemy was now behind them. There followed a disorderly withdrawal from the town in which officers were forced to draw their pistols to quell signs of dangerous panic among their inexperienced troops.

On February 17 von Arnim took possession of Sbeitla and dispatched Tenth Panzer Division north to the Pichon/ Fondouk passes in the hope of trapping French and American forces there. This proved to be a waste of fuel, as they had already retired to the Western Dorsale. Simultaneously, Rommel passed through Thelepte, reaching Kasserine village shortly before noon on February 18.

Both sides now paused briefly to take stock and reorganize. For his part, von Arnim was satisfied with what had been achieved, but in Rome, Comando Supremo had become increasingly drawn to Rommel's concept of a deep thrust into the Allied supply lines in Algeria. The Tenth and 21st Panzer Divisions were transferred to Rommel's command and he was ordered to strike for Le Kef through Sbiba and the Kasserine Pass. The aristocratic von Arnim, who regarded Rommel as a parvenu, declined to relinquish his Tigers on the grounds that they were undergoing repair.

Meanwhile, Gen. Sir Harold Alexander had arrived at Allied Forces HQ to take up the position of Eisenhower's chief of staff. His opinion was that the front had rolled with the punch sufficiently and, suspecting that Rommel intended thrusting deep into Algeria, gave orders that the Western Dorsale was to be held, whatever the cost, simultaneously approving the movement of reinforcements that Anderson had dispatched from the north into the threatened areas.

Fredendall, having moved the rallied First Armored Division back to Tebessa, dispatched units to defend Kasserine Pass. Here, the 39th Combat Engineer Regiment laid 3,000 miles in the three-mile gap between Djebel Semmama to the north of the road and Djebel Chambi to its south, then prepared to fight as infantry. They were joined by I/26th Infantry, two American field batteries, a battery of French horse-drawn 75mm guns dating from World War I, and a tank-destroyer battalion, the whole being placed under the command of Col. Alexander N. Stark and known collectively as Stark Force.

Elsewhere, troops assembling at Sbiba included the First Guards Brigade, the American 18th Regimental Combat Team, three infantry battalions from the U.S. 34th Division, Second Bn The Hampshire Regiment, three American field artillery battalions, parts of two British antitank regiments, some French detachments, and the 16th/Fifth Lancers, newly equipped with Shermans, belonging to 26th Armoured Brigade. Those reaching Thala, 15 miles north of Kasserine Pass, were the two remaining armored regiments of Brig. C.A.L. Dunphie's 26th Armoured Brigade (17th/21st Lancers and The Lothian and Border Horse), Tenth Bn The Rifle Brigade, 2/5th Bn The Leicestershire Regiment, three field artillery batteries, an antitank battery, and a heavy mortar battery. In immediate command of the front to the north and northwest of Kasserine Pass was Brig. C.G.G. Nicholson, the Sixth Armoured Division's deputy divisional commander. The scene was now set for the final and decisive phase of the battle.

On the evening of February 18 the Afrika Korps Assault Group began probing the defenses of Kasserine Pass. The following day it began to mount attacks on Djebel Semmama, coupled with infiltration through the dispersed and outnumbered units of Stark Force. The Americans fought back, inflicting some loss, but by the morning of February 20 it was apparent that the Pass was about to fall. That afternoon, units of Tenth Panzer Division, returned from the abortive foray to Pichon/Fondouk, joined the assault and the defense collapsed. The escape of some of its survivors was covered by a small all-arms battlegroup, known as Gore Force, that Dunphie had sent down from Thala in anticipation of the event. All of the battlegroup's tanks were knocked out during its fighting withdrawal.

While the fight for Kasserine Pass was in progress, Rommel had directed 21st Panzer Division to break through at Sbiba. However, on February 19 the division ran into Allied positions south of the town, fronted by an extensive minefield covered by artillery fire, and, unable to make headway, it remained there for the rest of the battle.

All the Axis hopes were now centered on exploiting the capture of Kasserine Pass. On February 21 the Tenth Panzer Division advanced along the road to Thala, opposed by 26th Armoured Brigade, which took advantage of a series of parallel ridges to fight hull down with its undergunned Valentines and Crusaders. Having imposed hours of frustrating delay on his opponents at the cost of 15 tanks, Brigadier Dunphie withdrew through the lines of the Leicesters at dusk, covered by a smokescreen. Hardly had his regiments gone into leaguer to replenish than a Valentine approached the Leicesters, its crew sitting smoking on the turret. Believing that it was a straggler from the day's fighting, the inexperienced infantrymen, who had only just reached the theater of war from England, let it through. It had, in fact, been captured by the enemy earlier in the campaign and was now serving as a Trojan horse, for in its wake came a column of German tanks, self-propelled guns and machine-gun teams. The ensuing battle, fought by the light of blazing vehicles, was very much a soldier's fight in which the Leicesters were brought to the verge of destruction and antitank guns were knocked out. Returning from their leaguer, the 17th/21st Lancers and the Lothians tore into the fray while field gunners used their guns in the antitank role. By 10:00 p.m. the intruders had been beaten off, leaving nine burning tanks behind them, but of Dunphie's brigade only 30 tanks remained.

Both sides recognized that the battle had reached a point of balance. Satisfied that Sbiba was in no danger, Brigadier Nicholson ordered one of 16th/5th Lancers' Sherman squadrons and the Second Hampshires to move across to Thala, from which he decreed that there would be no withdrawal. The truth, however, was he had very little with which to meet a renewed onset by Tenth Panzer Division the following day unless a miracle happened to tilt the scales in his favor. The miracle appeared that very night in form of Brig. Gen. Le Roy Irwin, who had led the U.S. Ninth Division's artillery in a four-day drive from Tlemcen, Morocco, a distance of 800 miles. The British and American artillery was quickly integrated and a combined fire plan for the morrow orchestrated.

At first light on February 22 Dunphie sent a weak squadron of the Lothians to recapture a feature lost by the Leicesters the previous night. Most of the tanks were lost, but the impression given to Rommel was that the British had tanks to spare. Furthermore, as his troops came under a heavier fire from the concentrated British and American artillery than they had yet experienced, he reached the conclusion that the Allies were able to bring reinforcements into the line at a rate he could not match. Likewise, the poor flying weather of the previous two days cleared during the morning of the 22nd, enabling the Allied air forces to mount numerous sorties in support of their ground troops.

He was disappointed not only by the failure of the previous night's attack, but also by that of the Afrika Korps Assault Group, which he had dispatched from Kasserine Pass in the direction of Tebessa. On February 21 the latter had lost its way and in the region of Djebel Hamra come up against the tanks of Brig. Gen. Paul Robinett's Combat Command B of First Armored Division then, when it turned west, its progress was halted a mixed Anglo/American/French force, supported by artillery, dug in on high ground.

At this stage of the battle Rommel possessed sufficient fuel for approximately 180 miles' running and five days' rations, but only sufficient ammunition in hand for one day's fighting and little in reserve. He was also constantly having to look over his shoulder in the knowledge that his old enemies, Montgomery's Eighth Army, were closing up to the Mareth Line, ironically, built by the French to keep the Italians out of southern Tunisia and now defended by Germans and Italians against the British. During a conference with Field Marshal Albert Kesselring, the German commander-in-chief South, and von Arnim, Rommel's view that the offensive had run its course was accepted. While von Arnim mounted diversionary attacks, his troops began their withdrawal that night, and by morning they had gone. By the evening of February 24, Kasserine Pass was once more in Allied hands, as, shortly after, were Sbeitla and Sidi bou Zid.

The series of engagements known collectively as the Battle of Kasserine Pass had cost U.S. II Corps 2,816 men killed and wounded and 2,459 captured, plus much equipment destroyed or lost; the British suffered comparatively few personnel casualties but also lost equipment. Recorded German losses include 989 personnel casualties, 20 tanks and five more armored vehicles, 20 guns, five antitank guns, and 60 transport vehicles; Italian losses are not recorded but were smaller. This balance sheet does not reflect the fact that it was the Allied defense that held and the Axis offensive that failed.

The painful lessons of Kasserine Pass were quickly learned by the U.S. Army and absorbed into its tactical and command methods. Fredendall was replaced by the capable and energetic Maj. Gen. George S. Patton, Jr., as commander of II Corps and sent home; he never commanded troops on active service again. The war in North Africa had three months to run and would end with an Axis surrender comparable to Stalingrad.

BAYS AND HARBORS

Battlegrounds: Geography and the History of Warfare is, as the title suggests, primarily about "ground"—terra firma. And so, high-seas battles do not fall within its remit. However, there has always been an intimate link between sea and land warfare. The three battles in this chapter—Salamis, the Nile, and Mobile Bay—represent the connection where land and water meet. Through most of our history, warships have been tactically and strategically dependent on the land. As Matthew Bennett points out in his account of the Battle of Salamis in 480 B.C., the oar-driven warships of the time needed to make landfall each night in order to water and feed their crews. Land was never far away at any time because the demands of high-seas sailing were too perilous for such slender, low-slung craft. The trireme was designed for coastal waters, for ramming and boarding, and for landing troops ashore. Throughout the succeeding centuries, certainly up until the last 75 years, ships have been dependent on land not only for provisioning, but also for refueling: for example, coaling stations dotted around the world were essential supports for both mercantile and military fleets. In fact, one could argue that sea warfare has always been a matter of the land. The ownership of vast tracts of the Atlantic or Pacific is not in itself important (people cannot settle in the ocean or grow crops). The oceans are strategically important to deny the enemy provisions by sinking its supply ships, interdicting its forces, or neutralizing its ability to support land campaigns. For example, the Pacific naval battles of World War II were not about ownership of X number of square miles of ocean, but rather who would ultimately have ownership of the surrounding landmasses as a result of those naval battles. One harbor not included in the three battles covered in this chapter (because it has been so extensively written about elsewhere) needs a special word—Pearl Harbor. The geographic location of the U.S. Pacific Fleet on December 7, 1941, was a crucial factor in its destruction. Confined in a harbor, unprepared for attack, unable to flee or evade, it was destroyed not by an opposing fleet on the open ocean as at Jutland in World War I, but by a new technology—planes launched from ships. At Pearl Harbor all the elements came into play: air, water, and earth—and the terrible fire that followed.

Salamis, Greece, 480 B.C., West Point map
The narrow waters of the Salamis channel posed difficulties for the large ships of the Persian fleet, while the lighter vessels of the Greeks may have assisted in their victory.

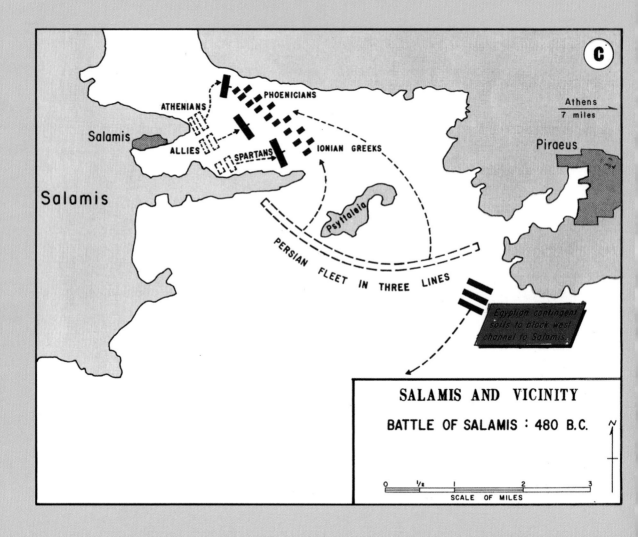

SALAMIS AND VICINITY

BATTLE OF SALAMIS : 480 B.C.

Ambush in the Straits
Salamis, Greece, 480 B.C.

MATTHEW BENNETT

The naval battle of Salamis played a crucial part in defeating the Persian invasion of Greece in 480-479 B.C.. The Persian King Xerxes ruled over what was largely a land empire, but he also controlled the eastern littoral of the Aegean and Mediterranean Seas. His determination to subdue the Greeks necessitated a naval expedition in support of his vast land army, which crossed the Hellespont by two pontoon bridges. Our main source for the expedition is the Greek historian Herodotus, writing a generation later. He was born in Halicarnassus (modern Bodrum in Turkey), on the western coast of Asia Minor, site of the later Mausoleum. It was, and is, a maritime city, so it was natural that Herodotus should have keen interest in and knowledge of the opposing fleets.

Herodotus claims that the Persians were able to muster 1,200 vessels from their maritime subjects. The greatest contributors, with 300, were the Phoenician cities of the Syrian coast, chiefly Sidon and Tyre, considered the most skillful sailors of their day. The Egyptians provided another 200, with 150 from Cyprus and 100 from Cilicia (on the southern coast of Asia Minor). The largely Greek nations of western Asia Minor and the Aegean Islands contributed over 350 more, with another 100 from the Hellespont region. About half were used in the construction of the bridge of boats, which left some 600 ships to accompany the army along the coast of Greece. The Persian fleet suffered a check in the Gulf of Artemesion, offshore from where the Spartans fought their doomed encounter at Thermopylae. Once this blocking force had been crushed, the Persian army flooded into Attica, bringing fire and sword to the region. The Athenians, prominent in the confederation opposing the Persians, were unable to defend their city, so they evacuated their population to the city of Troezen in the Megarid, but also to the island of Salamis, which lay in the Saronic Gulf, opposite Athens's harbor of Piraeus.

The combined Greek fleet lay along the eastern shore of Salamis. According to Herodotus, at Artemesion it comprised 207 ships, of which the Athenians contributed the largest contingent of 127, followed by the Corinthians with 40, the Megarians 20, and the Chalcedians (actually Athenian colonists) another 20. (At Salamis itself, there seem to have been an additional 100 vessels, mostly provided by Athens, bringing the total up to around 307.) Of the other smaller contingents, the Lacedaemonians brought only ten ships, but it was their Spartan commander, Eurybiades, who demanded the post of admiral. Given that Athens had provided half the fleet, and that, apart from the Corinthians the Peloponnesians were not exactly noted for naval warfare, this might seem a strange arrangement. It stemmed from the Spartans' jealousy of any challenge to their position as leaders of the anti-Persian coalition. So Themistocles, the Athenian commander, was prepared to go along with it in order to keep the alliance together.

Not all the voices at council wished to oppose the invaders in the Straits of Salamis. The Peloponnesians had already begun the construction of a wall five miles long across the Isthmus of Corinth, to hinder any attack by the Persian army. It took all of Themistocles's rhetoric to keep those contingents, about one third of the fleet, from returning to their homelands. His strategy, as it turned out, was to lure the larger Persian fleet into a narrow channel where its superior numbers could be neutralized by the constricted geography. It was also in Athens' interest to score a signal victory against the invaders if the city were to retain its influence in the League against the Persians. Herodotus represents the Corinthian commander, Adeimantus, criticizing Themistocles as one whose counsel should be ignored, because he was a "man without a city" after Athens had fallen to the Persians. Themistocles's reply was that he could withdraw the Athenian vessels from the fleet, persuading Eurybiades that he could not risk an encounter with such reduced numbers. Meanwhile, the Persian fleet, also augmented by another 100 vessels mainly from newly subjected Greek cities, was gathering on the shores opposite Salamis.

At this point it is worth considering the type of vessels used in naval warfare in this period. They are usually called triremes (although the word is Roman and in Greek they were called *trieres*) because they were constructed with three banks of oars. They also used large square sails, for nontactical movement, but in battle they depended upon up to 200 rowers for impetus, and were maneuvered by a linked pair of steering oars in the stern. Long, slender vessels (120 to 140 feet long by 18 to 20 feet beam) with a shallow freeboard (4 to 6 feet) and little decking except in prow and stern, their tactics depended upon ramming. A bronze-headed ram attached to the prow was driven into an enemy ship, allowing the small contingent of marines (ten hoplites and four archers) to board and seize an enemy. A lucky blow might sink an opponent outright, but in general the fighting resembled that on land, decided by hand-to-hand combat. The rowers were all freemen (not slaves as during the wars between Christians and Turks in the 16th and 17th centuries A.D.). Providing almost 200 ships, Athens must have had nearly every member of its male population at sea, with around 40,000 manning its fleet.

Despite the decisive outcome of the battle, it is difficult to be certain which side possessed the better ships or sailors. Certainly the Phoenicians had a high reputation for their seamanship. Their vessels, and others in the Persian fleet, also had raised decks to accommodate a much larger contingent of marines, perhaps as many as 40 men on each ship. They were Persians, Medes, and Sakae, the flower Xerxes' army, who had the dual role of keeping the allied contingents loyal as well as seeking to overwhelm the Greeks in boarding activities. At one point Herodotus describes the Greek ships as "heavier" than their enemies, but what he means by this is not clear. The conventional view is that the Greeks possessed lighter, more maneuverable vessels and this played a major part in their victory.

Naval tactics at the time depended upon two types of maneuver. Fleets were deployed in line, seeking to outflank their opponents. This enabled the overlapping vessels to turn inward, ramming the unprotected sides of the enemy (*periplus*). The other tactic was to seek to break through the enemy line, and then turn upon the exposed sterns or flanks of their ships (*diekplus*). A great deal depended upon the skill of the opposing helmsmen and the quality of their rowing crews. As a rule of thumb, though, it was to be expected that greater numbers would win the day.

So the Greeks, outnumbered by almost two to one, had to find a way of balancing the odds. Herodotus has a story that Themistocles sent a secret messenger to Xerxes, claiming that the Greeks were about to take flight, and urging an immediate attack. Whatever the reason, the king ordered his fleet forward into very narrow waters indeed. Nowadays, the Salamis channel is about three-quarters of a mile wide, measuring at its narrowest point between Perama on the mainland and the island of Aghios Georghios. But it is fairly clear that the sea has risen by about six feet (a full fathom) in the past 2,500 years. This means that the channel may have been no more than 800 yards wide. In addition, a group of small islands known then as the Pharmakousae (of which Aghios Georghios is the largest) would further have impeded movement. Just south of the eastern end of the straits lies the island of Lipsokoutali. This is probably ancient Psytaleia, where Xerxes landed troops to seal off the exit.

The general assumption nowadays is that the battle was fought with the opposing lines of ships deployed north-south, making it impossibly cramped for the Persians' 700-odd vessels. The problem with this is that Herodotus actually describes the invader's fleet as stretched out along the southern shore of Attica. According to this deployment, the Phoenicians were formed up opposite the Athenians on the western flank, leading to the Bay of Eleusis, while on the eastern flank toward Piraeus, the Ionian Greek subjects of the Persians opposed the Lacedaemonians. Herodotus does not specify the positions of any other formations, nor does he attempt to describe the course of the battle. Rather he presents it through a series of anecdotes, one of them involving the bravery of Queen Artemesia of Halicarnassus, clearly just a piece of propaganda for his home city.

One important point that both Herodotus and the playwright Aeschylus (whose *Persians* was performed only eight years after Salamis) make is that the

Persian fleet deployed by night, a hazardous enterprise indeed. Galley fleets, with their huge companies of rowers, needed to be beached each night in order to water the crew. They also tended to keep to the coastline when moving for reasons of navigation and lack of seaworthiness far from shore. The movement of a large fleet in a cramped channel further restricted by many islands must have been difficult to manage. But if we are to believe our sources, then it was what the Persian admiral Ariabignes (Xerxes' brother) and his captains achieved. By dawn they were in position, beneath the slopes of Mount Agaleus where the Great King had set up his headquarters in order to view what he confidently expected to be the crushing of the Greek fleet.

The Greek ships were probably drawn up within the shelter of two bays: Paloukia to the west, and Ambelaki (where the ancient city of Salamis stood). Herodotus talks of the Greeks backing water with their vessels, although what this implies is unclear. It may have helped the Athenians to take up position to the northwest of the channel, thus bottling up the Phoenicians, or it may have been a way of better aligning their ships. It is clear that the Greeks fought in good order, and their enemies in confusion. Also, Ariabignes was killed, possibly in the initial clash, leaving the Persians without direction. It also seems that, as the Phoenicians were driven back, the Greeks' western contingent emerged from Ambelaki Bay—where they had remained undetected—to take them in the flank and rear.

Later sources speak of the Greeks losing only 40 ships and the Persians 200. Certainly the invaders' fleet was devastated and rapidly withdrew to the Hellespont, so ending the threat of a combined assault on the Peloponnese. Geography had played a crucial part in defeating Xerxes. Had he not committed his ships to the Straits of Salamis he could have kept a fleet in being for the following year's campaign, grievously restricting the Greeks' strategic options. We do not need to believe all the stories of Themistocles's cunning to understand the significance of the sea fight. Over 60,000 Greeks, most of them rowers straining every sinew, fought for their liberty on battleground that suited them and not their opponents. Although the Persian Army remained in Greece until the following year, when it was also crushingly defeated at Plataea, it was the naval battle at Salamis that had built the platform for Greek victory.

The Battle of the Nile, Egypt, 1798

Printed and distributed in the U.K. in 1799, a year after the Battle of the Nile, this map portrays "an exact representation of the English and French fleets, under the command of Rear Admiral Horatio Nelson and Admiral Brueys, off the mouth of the Nile on the first of August, 1798."

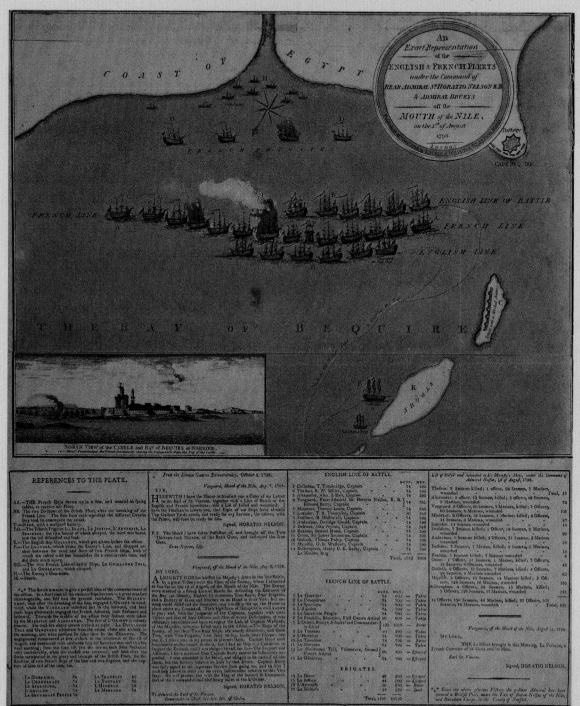

Nelson at the Battle of the Nile
Egypt, 1798

PHILIP HAYTHORNTHWAITE

In the early morning of the July 2, 1798, Gen. Napoleon Bonaparte stepped onto the shore of Egypt at the head of his army. Following his recent series of victories in Italy, the young Bonaparte (he was 28) had been entrusted by the ruling French Directory with command of an expedition intended to establish a French base in the Middle East, which could pose a direct threat to British interests in India. Bonaparte was already one of the most brilliant generals of the age, but ultimately the success of his expedition was not to depend upon his military skills, but upon a naval battle fought shortly after his disembarkation in Egypt.

Bonaparte's army had been carried across the Mediterranean in a fleet of some 400 transport vessels, with a French naval escort under the command of Adm. François-Paul Brueys d'Aigalliers. The British had received information that France was planning a large operation from their Mediterranean bases, and sent a naval squadron into the Mediterranean to investigate. Its commander was Rear Adm. Horatio Nelson who, at the age of 39, had established himself as one of the most gifted and daring naval officers of his day. Having lost the sight of an eye in action in 1794, Nelson had recently returned to duty following the loss of his right arm at Tenerife. His fleet comprised 15 vessels: his flagship HMS *Vanguard* and 12 ships-of-the-line, each mounting 74 guns, the weaker HMS *Leander* of 50 guns, and the 18-gun sloop HMS

Mutine. With fine ships and excellent captains, Nelson commanded a formidable force, but his lack of frigates, the fast-moving "eyes of the fleet," made his task of locating the French extremely difficult.

Nelson guessed that Egypt might be the French target, but when he called at the friendly port of Naples on June 17, the British ambassador there, Sir William Hamilton, was unable to provide any intelligence, so Nelson sailed directly for Egypt. In any event, the paths of the fleet crossed on the night of June 22 without either realizing it. Consequently, Nelson arrived at Alexandria before the French, on June 29, found only a few Turkish ships in the harbor, and sailed north again to continue his search. On July 19 he took in supplies and water at Syracuse in Sicily, then sailed back toward Alexandria. He arrived there on the morning of August 1 to find only the merchant ships and a few light warships in the harbor; but shortly after noon HMS *Zealous* signaled that a short distance away lay a fleet of warships, anchored in line of battle.

Tactics, ships, the proficiency of their crews, and leadership all had an influence in the outcome of the naval battles under sail; but a vital factor in deciding the action fought off the Egyptian coast was the location in which Brueys had anchored his fleet. Since the French landing in Egypt, Bonaparte had secured his position on land by a victory over the Mamelukes at the Battle of the Pyramids (July 21, 1798), but the position of the French fleet was less secure. Brueys had decided against keeping it at Alexandria, believing it was hazardous to enter the port, and apparently also declined to take it to Corfu. Instead, he found what appeared to be a safe anchorage a short distance eastward along the coast, in the bay of Aboukir at the mouth of the Nile, where he anchored on July 7. Evidently Brueys consulted his senior subordinates about the tactics to be employed in the event of a British attack. Most concurred that the best option was to meet it at anchor rather than at sea, considering the strength of the Aboukir position.

Indeed, Brueys's position appeared relatively easy to defend. The western end of the semicircular bay, where the fleet anchored, was overlooked by a fort at Aboukir Point, rocks and shoals lay off the coast to inhibit the maneuvers of an attacker, and an artillery battery was established on the nearby Aboukir Island. Brueys's fleet included 13 ships-of-the-line, which he anchored in a slightly convex arc, facing west and just beyond the four-fathom line. The center of the line was occupied by Brueys's flagship, the mighty 120-gun *L'Orient*, with the 80-gunners *Franklin* and *Tonnant* ahead and astern respectively. Five 74-gunners were in line ahead of *Franklin*, and four 74s and the 80-gun *Guillaume Tell* astern of *Tonnant*. Inside the line Brueys anchored his four frigates, while his bomb vessels and other small craft were in shallower water. Lulled by what appeared to be the security offered by his position Brueys made two serious errors that were to prove fatal (in his case literally): His ships were anchored with considerable gaps between the stern of one and the bow of another, and the line was positioned rather too far out in the bay than necessary to avoid the shoals.

In addition to these weaknesses, the French ships were not fully crewed, parties having been sent ashore to obtain water and provisions, and not all were able to rejoin the fleet before the battle. At 2:00 p.m. on August 1 the French 74-gunner *Heureuse* signaled the appearance of the British fleet, but it appeared not to be in order of battle, convincing Brueys that no action would occur that day. Nelson's plan, however, was to attack immediately and overwhelm the French van before the ships at the rear could intervene. He was so determined that he mounted the attack without delay, even though he had only 11 ships to hand (two were reconnoitering some distance from the fleet, and HMS *Culloden* was towing a prize).

As the British fleet formed its line of battle, Brueys realized that battle was imminent. Despite the comparative lateness of the hour, he attempted to use his lighter vessels to decoy the British onto the shoals, but without success (although HMS *Culloden* did run aground near Aboukir Island, and took no part in the battle). Fire from the French battery on the island proved entirely ineffectual.

In the lead was HMS *Goliath*, whose captain, Thomas Foley, noticed that the French stood sufficiently far from the shore for the British to pass on the inside of their position, and thus attack them down the landward side, on which the French guns were almost certainly not prepared to fire, because Brueys had convinced himself that he could be attacked only from the seaward side. Furthermore, it became obvious that the gaps between the French ships were such that the British could sail between them, raking their sterns with a murderous fire. Thus the French could be attacked from both sides at once, whereas only the starboard gun crews had been fully prepared for action. Foley's initiative gave the British a devastating advantage.

HMS *Goliath* passed around the bow of the *Guerrier* at the head of the French line, fired at her larboard (land-facing) side and then slipped by before engaging the second French ship in the line, *Conquérant*. HMS *Zealous* followed and anchored alongside *Guerrier*, both British ships pouring in their broadsides against the unprepared flanks of the French vessels. *Guerrier's* fore-mast was brought down within moments of the start of the action. The battle had begun at about 6:15 p.m., and by the time the first two British ships were fully engaged the sun was already sinking.

The next three ships in the British line—*Orion, Audacious,* and *Theseus*—either followed the same course or cut through the French line, to attack their unprepared side. Lying shoreward of the fighting, the French frigate *Sérieuse* opened fire on HMS *Orion* as she sailed down the French line, but the contest was very unequal, *Orion's* broadsides shattering the frigate. *Sérieuse* drifted, sinking, on to the coastal shoals. The next British ship in line, Nelson's own *Vanguard*, with HMS *Minotaur* following, engaged the French on the starboard (seaward) side, so that some of the French ships were battered from both sides at once. Succeeding British ships either cut the French line or engaged to starboard. By the time *Vanguard* came into action the light was fading, and shortly after 7:00 p.m., Nelson ordered the British ships to hoist lights to identify them from the enemy.

Although partially unprepared for so audacious an attack, the French fought back resolutely, but their van was annihilated. Dismasted and disabled, *Conquérant* was apparently the first to strike her colors. *Guerrier* was also reduced to impotence but refused to surrender until the captain of HMS *Zealous* sent a message begging the French commander to spare further bloodshed. As the ships at the head of the French line were knocked out of action, increasing pressure was placed on the next in line. In the center, Brueys's great flagship *L'Orient* dismasted the weaker HMS *Bellerophon* which, having fought for about an hour, had to drift away, disabled.

Both commanders were wounded. Nelson received a gash on the head which temporarily blinded his one good eye and forced him to leave his deck for treatment. At about 7:30 p.m. a ball took off Brueys's left leg. He refused to be taken below and died on his own deck. About 90 minutes later flames were seen to spread and at about 10:00 p.m. *L'Orient* blew up, showering the nearby ships with burning debris. So stunning was the sight that fighting temporarily ceased. The crippled *Franklin* recommenced the battle but was soon forced to surrender. By midnight only the *Tonnant* was still resisting, and she drifted shoreward, dismasted. The remaining French ships, which had hardly been in action at all, moved downwind toward the eastern end of the bay.

With less ferocity the battle resumed as dawn broke. Two ships from the rear of the French line, *Heureuse* and *Mercure*, had cut their cables and grounded on the shoals. They surrendered, and one of the French frigates, *Artémise*, blew up after striking her colors. Only two French ships-of-the-line, *Généreux* and *Guillaume Tell*, and the remaining two frigates, made good their escapes, the British too damaged to stop them. Of the others, the helpless *Tonnant* surrendered on the second day after the battle (August 3), and *Timoléon* was burned after running ashore. Although some of Nelson's ships were damaged, none was lost, and the total British casualties numbered 218 killed and 677 wounded. Eleven out of 13 of the French ships-of-the-line were sunk or captured, and two out of the four frigates.

Few naval victories were ever so comprehensive. In the dispatch that announced his victory, Nelson wrote, "Almighty God has blessed His Majesty's Arms in the late Battle, by a great victory over the Fleet of the Enemy," but in a letter remarked, "Victory is certainly not a name strong enough for such a scene as I have passed." Napoleon, on the other hand, was beside himself with frustration and rage. His secretary, Louis-Antoine Bourrienne, described how Napoleon was "overwhelmed with anguish" at the knowledge that "we are now cut off from all communication with France, and all hope of returning thither...he had lost all chance of preserving his conquest." Bourrienne recalled how at times Napoleon would declare, "Unfortunate Brueys, what have you done?" and much later he stated, "Had I been master of the sea, I should have been master of the East, and the thing was so practicable that it failed only through the stupidity or bad conduct of some seamen." This condemnation of Brueys and his brave sailors was harsh. More responsibility lay with Nelson's audacity in attacking in the manner he did and the fact that, as he remarked in his dispatch, "nothing could withstand the Squadron your Lordship did me the Honor to place under my Command." He had looked at what seemed an impossible geographic position and, with his characteristic aggression and imagination, pulled off one of the great victories in naval history.

"Damn the Torpedoes"
Admiral Farragut at Mobile Bay, Alabama, 1864

GARY GALLAGHER

The closing of Confederate ports ranked high among Union military objectives during the Civil War. Although the Confederacy built an impressive array of wartime industries, its economy could not produce everything necessary to fight a modern mid-19th-century war. Vessels carrying arms, ordnance, clothing, and other war-related European goods evaded blockading ships to deliver cargoes at ports along the extensive southern coastline. Mobile, Alabama, stood among the most important of those ports, joining Wilmington, North Carolina; Charleston, South Carolina; and New Orleans as the four most popular destinations for blockade-runners. By the summer of 1864, Mobile was the Confederacy's last major open port on the Gulf of Mexico. More than 200 blockade-runners had tried to enter Mobile, at least 80 percent of which had been successful. A number of Federal military leaders had argued for taking the city, most notably Gen. Ulysses S. Grant and Adm. David Glasgow Farragut, but various factors had prevented a full-scale campaign. Farragut had mounted the most impressive effort on February 16-29, 1864, bombarding Fort Powell, which guarded the western approach to Mobile Bay. The ineffectiveness of the bombardment prompted one Union naval officer to complain, "We are hammering away at the fort here, which minds us about as much as if we did not fire...."

The Confederates had devoted substantial effort to protecting Mobile,

Mobile Bay, Alabama, 1864, U.S. Survey map

This 1864 map of Mobile Bay shows forts, towns, and roads in the vicinity. Admiral Farragut's victory at this key Confederate port cut off a major supply route for Confederate blockade-runners and was the first of a string of Union victories that secured the outcome of the Civil War.

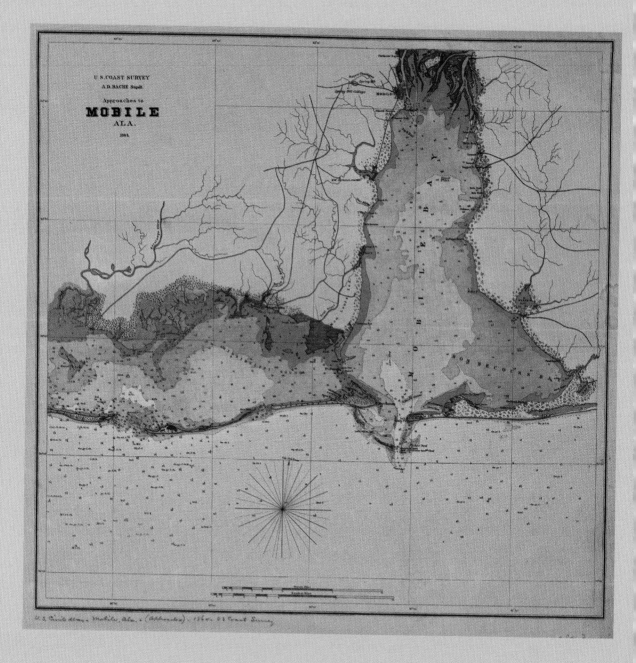

which sat at the northwest corner of Mobile Bay. Nearly 40 miles deep from north to south, the bay was 6 miles wide at its top and 15 at its bottom. Mobile Point, which stretched across the bottom of the bay from the east, and Dauphin Island, three miles to the west, formed a barrier between the bay and the Gulf of Mexico. The principal channel flowed into the bay near the western tip of Mobile Point; a secondary, shallower channel, entered the bay at Grant's Pass, just north of Dauphin Island. Three forts guarded access to the bay. Fort Morgan, the largest of the three, occupied the western tip of Mobile Point and commanded the main channel. Fort Gaines faced Fort Morgan from the eastern shore of Dauphin Island, and Fort Powell, an uncompleted work that had withstood Farragut's bombardment in February 1864, stood watch over Grant's Pass. The Confederates also had sunk piles between Fort Gaines and the main channel and placed a series of mines (called torpedoes during the Civil War) just west of the channel opposite Fort Morgan.

The Confederates supplemented their fortifications with a small flotilla in Mobile Bay itself. Commanded by Adm. Franklin Buchanan, the flotilla included three gunboats and the powerful ironclad, the *Tennessee*, covered with four to six inches of iron plating and mounting six heavy rifled cannon. Although underpowered and guided by vulnerable steering chains, the *Tennessee* posed a significant threat to wooden Union ships. By the end of May 1864, Farragut had received considerable information about the *Tennessee* and had examined it from a distance, pronouncing it "a formidable-looking thing." Knowledge about the *Tennessee* reinforced his earlier judgment that any Union fleet operating against Mobile Bay would require ironclads to engage "the enemy on an equal footing."

At the end of July 1864, Farragut made final preparations for a squadron of 14 wooden ships and four ironclad monitors to close Mobile as a Confederate port. He proposed to sail through the main channel into the bay, where his ships would engage Buchanan's flotilla. The Union ironclads would focus on the *Tennessee*. A Federal infantry force of 1,500 would cooperate with the operation, landing on Dauphin Island and taking Fort Gaines. Once Gaines had fallen and Buchanan's flotilla had been vanquished, Farragut's squadron and the Federal infantry would attack Forts Powell and Morgan. The plan did not contemplate the capture of Mobile itself, an operation that would require far more infantry than would be available for Farragut's initial offensive.

The rising sun on August 5 revealed a long line of Federal ships steaming toward the main channel. Farragut had paired his 14 wooden ships, lashing them together with the stronger ones nearer Fort Morgan, and deployed his four monitors between the wooden ships and the fort. Confederate gunners inside the fort quickly manned their pieces and sent a heavy fire into the Federal formation. Buchanan's flotilla also moved into position to engage Farragut's approaching ships. "Gradually, the fleet came into close quarters with Fort Morgan," recalled a Federal signal officer, "and the firing on each side became terrific." A torpedo rather than cannon fire precipitated the first crisis for Farragut. As the lead monitor, *Tecumseh*, maneuvered to confront the *Tennessee*, a massive explosion ripped through its hull. Within minutes, the ship sank with the loss of its captain, Tunis A.M. Craven, and 90 other members of its 114-man crew. The captain of the leading wooden vessel, the screw sloop *Brooklyn*, immediately ordered his pilot to stop, and the entire line of Federal vessels came to a halt within easy range of the guns at Fort Morgan.

Farragut reacted swiftly to the perilous situation. He first ordered the *Brooklyn* to "go on," but when its commander failed to respond, he decided to take the lead himself. Lashed to the rigging to get a better view of the action, Farragut ordered his flagship, the screw sloop *Hartford*, to move from its position immediately behind the *Brooklyn* to the front of the line. Well aware of the *Tecumseh*'s demise, he allegedly shouted "Damn the torpedoes—full speed ahead!" The *Hartford*, lashed to the side-wheel gunboat *Metacomet*, steamed past Fort Morgan and into the bay, exchanging shots with the *Tennessee* and receiving an effective raking fire from the Confederate gunboat *Selma*. The remainder of Farragut's vessels trailed behind the *Hartford*, and the weight of Federal gunnery soon overwhelmed Buchanan's three gunboats—the *Selma* surrendered to the *Metacomet*, which had separated from the *Hartford*; the *Gaines* ran aground; and the *Morgan* escaped to the protection of Fort Morgan's guns. At the rear of the Federal line, the side-wheeler *Philippi*, not part of Farragut's attacking squadron, tried to enter the fray but ran onto the shoals near Fort Morgan. Confederate gunners poured fire into the helpless vessel, whose captain ordered the crew to abandon ship. Confederates soon boarded and burned the *Philippi*.

After disposing of Buchanan's wooden ships, Farragut's squadron steamed to a point four miles into the bay. Some of the vessels had begun to anchor when it became clear that the *Tennessee*, Buchanan's flagship, meant to continue the contest. The imposing ironclad, hampered by its lack of speed, had tried without success to ram both the *Hartford* and the *Brooklyn* as they moved into the bay. Now Buchanan, who knew that he faced overwhelming odds, sought to inflict as much damage as possible on his opponents. The *Tennessee*'s surgeon scarcely could imagine taking on the entire Union squadron. "Are you going into that fleet, Admiral?" he inquired. "I am, sir," replied Buchanan. "We'll never come out of there whole," muttered the surgeon, turning away from his superior.

The next hour witnessed one of the grand naval dramas in American history. Farragut ordered his captains to try to ram the *Tennessee*, and soon the Federal ships surrounded their prey. One by one several vessels drove toward the slow-moving ironclad, attempting to ram it at the same time their guns fired point-blank. The monitor *Monongahela* struck first, its prow hitting with such force that it jolted the much heavier *Tennessee* sharply off course. Other jarring collisions followed in rapid succession, and all the while Union projectiles slammed into the *Tennessee*. Casualties mounted on board the Confederate ship, the interior filled with acrid smoke, and the temperature inside the casemate rose to well over 100 degrees. The 63-year-old Buchanan suffered a disabling wound to his leg, and shortly thereafter a Federal shot severed one of the *Tennessee*'s steering chains. Some of the gun ports also had jammed, making it difficult for the Confederates to return fire. Comdr. James D. Johnston, who had assumed command after Buchanan's wounding, determined that "the ship was now nothing more than a target for the heavy guns of the enemy." At about 10:00 a.m., he struck the Confederate colors and raised a white handkerchief. Thus ended what Adm. Farragut, who had logged a half-century in the U.S. Navy, termed "one of the fiercest naval contests on record." Casualties seemed relatively light considering the fury of the fighting. Buchanan lost 12 dead and 20 wounded, and Federal fire killed 1 and wounded 3 of Fort

Morgan's garrison. Farragut's loss totaled 143 killed (91 of them drowned on the *Tecumseh*) and 170 wounded.

The destruction of Buchanan's flotilla gave Farragut control of the bay, which freed the Federals to concentrate on the three Confederate forts. Subjected to a savage bombardment from Farragut's ships, the garrison abandoned Fort Powell on the night of August 6. Fort Gaines, defended by nearly 850 men and 26 cannon, held out longer. Fifteen hundred Federals had landed on the western shore of Dauphin Island on August 3 and, reinforced to a strength of 3,000 with artillery support, had laid siege to the fort from the west while Federal ironclads plastered it from the bay. The fort capitulated on August 3. It required far more effort for the Federals to take Fort Morgan. Beginning on August 9, Farragut's ships and cooperating army units applied relentless pressure. On August 21, Morgan's commander, Brig. Gen. Richard L. Page, reported that the enemy's fire that day "disabled all the heavy guns save two...and cut up the fort to such an extent as to make the whole work a mere mass of debris." Two days later, Page surrendered the fort's 600-man garrison and 46 guns.

Farragut had accomplished his goal of closing Mobile as a point through which blockade runners could help supply the Confederacy, but he lacked the necessary infantry support to capture the city itself, which remained in Confederate hands until the spring of 1865. Nevertheless, his victory helped inspirit a northern populace cast down by the absence of clear-cut victories in either Virginia or Georgia during the late spring and summer campaigning in 1864. The victory at Mobile Bay on August 5 began a string of successes that continued through William Tecumseh Sherman's capture of Atlanta in early September and Philip H. Sheridan's triumphs in the Shenandoah Valley in September and October. As a group, these military events ensured Abraham Lincoln's reelection in November 1864 and the continued prosecution of the war toward Union victory.

PENINSULAS

In military terms, a peninsula can either be a fortress or a prison. Surrounded by sea on all its borders except the gateway connection to the mainland, a peninsula can be a formidable defensive position. But, like all fortresses, it needs to be supplied. If that supply route is cut off, then the peninsula defender is in exactly the same position as a besieged castle—and doomed to the same ultimate fate. As Ian Knight shows in his account of Yorktown during the War of Independence, such was the fate of the British garrison. Once the British fleet had been neutralized and could no longer support them, the garrison was finished. So too on the Bataan Peninsula in the Philippines during the early days of World War II. Once Gen. Douglas MacArthur had elected to hole up there, his American and Filipino forces suffered the fate of the besieged: defeated by starvation, disease, and thirst. Ironically, it would be MacArthur, a decade or so later, who won his peninsula war on Korea by kicking in the back door with a brilliant flanking amphibious assault at Inchon. Other peninsula battles had different outcomes just as, to use the fortress analogy, did castle sieges—the attackers were not always guaranteed success. Peter A. Huchthausen's account of the Allied assault on the Gallipoli Peninsula in Turkey in 1917 describes one of the great Allied disasters in that whole disastrous war. Here the "perimeter" wall of the "fortress" held firm against the battering of the invaders, partly due to the ineptitude of the attacking commanders, good luck, and resolute defense. The Peninsular War of the Napoleonic period was also a salutary lesson to the attacker. Napoleon had invaded a largely undefended Portugal in 1807, but in the seven years of bitter warfare that followed, the Iberian peninsula sucked the French invaders into a "total" war, where civilians as well as conventional military forces hammered them with a ferocity born of intense hatred. By the end of the Peninsular War France was to incur something close to 240,000 casualties and be forced to withdraw—a pattern not unlike America's involvement in its own peninsula-like war in Vietnam.

Yorktown, Virginia, 1791

This French map of the Chesapeake Bay area was drawn, by order of French generals, on site at the Battle of Yorktown. The geography of the region's waterways made an escape for British Lt. Gen. Lord Cornwallis a near impossibility and helped ensure an allied victory.

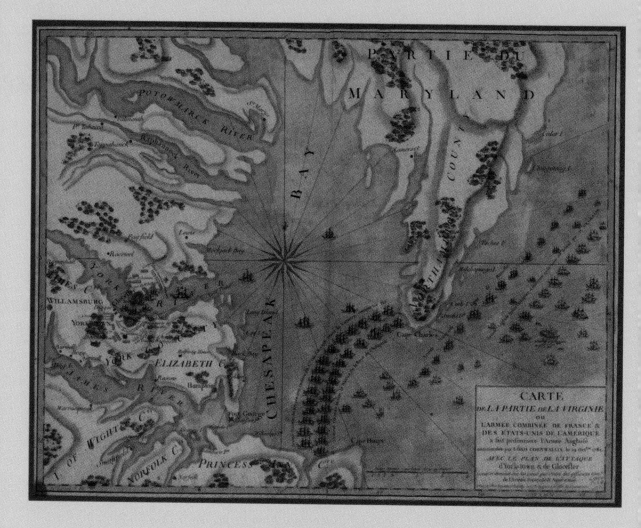

"The World Turned Upside Down"
Yorktown, Virginia, 1781

IAN KNIGHT

In May 1780, British troops under the command of Lt. Gen. Sir Henry Clinton captured Charleston in South Carolina, raising the prospect of a resurgence of British arms in North America. The importance of the victory went far beyond the capture of over 5,000 American troops—the largest American surrender of the war—for it revived in the British a hope that some had begun to doubt since the Saratoga campaign three years before—that it might, after all, be possible to suppress the American independence movement by military means alone. Yet Charleston's promise of victory was soon to prove a bitter illusion, for scarcely 18 months later, the British would find themselves on the receiving end of a siege, and with their defeat came the loss of the entire American colonies.

By 1781, both sides had become largely exhausted by nearly five years of conflict. In January of that year Washington was to declare: "We are at the end of our tether...now or never our deliverance must come." While the British had retained control of a number of important strategic centers, regular American troops of George Washington's Continental Army, supported by local militia, continued to dominate the countryside. Moreover, with the American success at Saratoga in 1777, both France and Spain had entered the war as American allies, and from that point, the character of the war changed for the British. It was no longer fought for possession of America alone, but was part of a long-running global struggle against rival European empires that stretched British resources beyond their limit.

With Charleston in British hands, the senior British officer in North America, Gen. Clinton, returned to New York, whose safety was still a major British preoccupation. He left the job of mopping up in the Carolinas to his subordinate, Lt. Gen. Lord Cornwallis. There was only one problem: Clinton and Cornwallis heartily disliked one another, a rift that could only be exacerbated by the great distance that separated them. They were also divided in their approach to the war. Clinton believed that the best hope of retaining British control of America was to rely on Britain's role as a world power—to hold only a series of strong bases on the coast, which could be reinforced and supplied by sea, and which would serve as strong points from which to wear down American forces in the countryside. Cornwallis, however, was convinced that the British had to take the war into the rural areas, which remained the heartland of revolution.

These differences became apparent once Clinton had left the Carolinas. Despite a number of victories, by early 1781 Cornwallis was convinced that he could not hold the south, especially with the prospect of a debilitating summer ahead. He looked instead for a decisive target elsewhere—and found one in Virginia.

Virginia was not only a stronghold of American support for the war, but a fertile source of supplies whose strategic position afforded the British an opportunity to drive a wedge between American forces in the Carolinas and General Washington in the north. At the end of April, Cornwallis—acting directly against Clinton's wishes—advanced into Virginia, and for a month, it seemed as if he had made the right decision; the only regular American troops in the area, commanded by the Marquis de Lafayette, fell back before Cornwallis's advance, while British dragoons, led by the infamous Lt. Col. Banastre Tarleton, swept through the countryside, and on one occasion nearly captured Thomas Jefferson.

Clinton, however, was unhappy at Cornwallis's actions. Worried that Washington might attack New York, Clinton felt that Cornwallis was beyond his control in the Virginia countryside, and could neither send troops to assist Clinton nor, for that matter, be reinforced himself. In a rare moment of firmness, Clinton ordered Cornwallis to move to a point on the Virginia coastline that could secure his communications with the outside world.

It was at this stage that Virginia's geography first began to shape the events that culminated in the British defeat. Cornwallis moved away from the wooded hills on the interior and into the low-lying ground that bordered the estuaries of the James and York Rivers. Furthermore, Cornwallis's engineers declared that the possible sites for a coastal base on the south side of the mouth of the James were unsuitable because of poor anchorages and defensive limitations. Casting around for alternatives, Cornwallis decided upon Yorktown, which lay back across the James.

The town lay on the tip of a spur of the York Peninsula bounded on its northern side by the York River, on its south by the James River, with Chesapeake Bay, and beyond that the Atlantic Ocean, to its east. Cornwallis would have little room to move if he were attacked, but in truth he did not expect to be, for the approaches to Yorktown could easily be entrenched, and Cornwallis had no cause to doubt that the British would remain masters of the water. Indeed, Cornwallis seemed relaxed about the possibility of attack from Lafayette, and for several days after he occupied Yorktown on August 2 he made no attempt to entrench the base. There were also some natural geographic advantages to the town, as far as defense was concerned, Gloucester was less than a mile away across the York, and might, in extremis, prove a useful bolt-hole. Swamps to the east and west bracketed the town and would channel the allied attack up from the south, where Cornwallis built a string of redoubts, backed by an inner line of stockades and gun-mounted parapets.

But Cornwallis's fate was sealed not in his peninsula redoubt but far out in the Atlantic. In March 1781, a French flotilla including nearly 30 warships had sailed with orders to support French colonies in the Caribbean against British attack, and to assist the American rebellion. The commander, Adm. de Grasse, needed to weather the winter in the Caribbean, but was prepared to sail up the American coast as far as time allowed—which in any event would bring him to the Chesapeake Bay, if only for a brief period. To Washington and Rochambeau, however, his presence offered a golden opportunity to concentrate allied forces against Cornwallis.

The combined Franco-American plan was an audacious one. Instead of mounting the attack on New York that Clinton was anticipating, Washington's and Rochambeau's troops would strike south, across New Jersey, toward the head of the Elk River. From there they would be transported down the river into Chesapeake Bay, landing on the York Peninsula. With over 6,500 troops between them, they would enjoy an overwhelming numerical superiority when united with Lafayette, but the plan depended for its success upon crossing 400 miles without being intercepted by the British, and before Cornwallis recognized the danger. If the British still dominated the waterways, the allies would be dangerously exposed on the Elk, yet at the same time it would be almost impossible to coordinate movements with the French flotilla once it had left the Caribbean. If it succeeded, however, it might prove the masterstroke of the war.

And so it was. Making diversionary movements to fend off Clinton in New York, Washington and Rochambeau began their march south in mid-August. Meanwhile de Grasse, evading the British fleet in the Caribbean, sailed north, and arrived at the mouth of Chesapeake Bay at the end of the month. Here he landed 3,500 French troops, who marched to join Lafayette. Thus reinforced, Lafayette pressed on to the outskirts of Yorktown, intent on holding Cornwallis in place until Washington arrived.

Cornwallis's head was now in the noose, but he did not yet realize it. Commanding 7,000 men plus 800 Marines, he no longer enjoyed numerical superiority over Lafayette, who matched him in regulars and was supported by a large number of militia. Trapped by the rivers on either side of him, Cornwallis could break out by land only if he chose a direct confrontation with Lafayette—which he could no longer be certain of winning. Despite the reported presence of the French fleet at the mouth of the Chesapeake, however, Cornwallis remained confident that the waterways would remain his salvation—and in this he was reassured by Clinton, who, once he realized New York was safe, promised to send Cornwallis reinforcements by sea.

Yet at this critical moment British naval supremacy collapsed. On September 5 de Grasse put out from the Chesapeake and confronted a numerically inferior British fleet under the command of Admiral Graves. After an indecisive action that spluttered on for several days, Graves withdrew, leaving the French still in position: in all practical respects a French victory. British ships could not get into the Chesapeake Bay, or out; Cornwallis could not be reinforced nor could he escape. Washington's advance continued unhindered, and the noose had drawn tight.

Ten days later, Washington and Rochambeau reached Virginia, where they joined Lafayette outside Yorktown. The allied force now numbered 16,000: 9,000 Americans, of whom 3,500 were militia, and 7,000 French. They formed a semicircular line, with each flank resting on the York. The Americans took the place of honor on the right wing. No sooner had the allies taken up their position than Cornwallis quit his outer defenses, to the astonishment of the French and Americans. In Benjamin Franklin's words the British "had the goodness to quit a situation from whence it might have escaped, and place itself in another from whence an escape was impossible." Cornwallis's logic was that his outer defenses were too extended, and by concentrating his troops closer to the town could hold off the allies until Clinton came to his rescue. But Clinton's troops would never arrive; by the time they were embarked and ready to break the French blockade, Cornwallis's fate was sealed.

The allies opened up a tremendous barrage of shot and shell on October 9 (3,600 missiles on the first day alone). The very first shot, legend has it, was fired by Washington himself and landed smack on the laden dinner table of the British commissary gen., killing him outright! Despite some spirited forays, it was soon clear that Cornwallis could not break out on the landward side because, in his words, he did not feel justified in "putting the fate of the war on so desperate attempt." On October 16, scarcely two weeks after the siege had begun, he attempted to evacuate Yorktown by transporting his troops across the James to the British garrison at Gloucester. Although the British held a secure foothold there, it is debatable whether the attempt could ever have succeeded, for once across, Cornwallis's command would face a journey comparable to Washington's to reach the nearest relief. In any event, they were frustrated by the weather; a sudden storm swept up the James, destroying many boats and forcing Cornwallis to recall his men.

The allies now pressed ever closer to the town, constructing an intricate series of trenches, saps, and gabions in what was to be the last siege in history conducted in the formal manner laid out by the great French siege master Vauban a century earlier. As it happened, both terrain and climate suited the besiegers admirably; the sandy soil made for easy digging, and the dark and stormy nights concealed the work of the entrenchers. By this time, conditions within the besieged town were truly appalling. Men were starving and sick and under intense bombardment by the allies, who now held prominent positions encircling the town. Bodies, some dismembered by artillery fire, lay in the streets untended.

The following day, Cornwallis recognized the inevitable and sent to Washington for surrender terms. When the British garrison marched out of Yorktown they were not led by their general (conveniently "ill") but a subordinate, General O'Hara. He first attempted to present his sword to Rochambeau, who, out of deference to Washington, refused, and directed the hapless O'Hara to the American commander-in-chief. Washington, conscious of O'Hara's lesser rank, also refused, and sent O'Hara to Benjamin Lincoln, who accepted the surrender. For so momentous a battle, the casualties on both sides were relatively light: The British lost 156 killed, 326 wounded, and 1,500 sick; the allies lost 75 killed and 199 wounded.

Five days later Clinton and Admiral Howe's rescue fleet arrived at the mouth of the Chesapeake, only to turn around and sail forlornly back to New York. As Gen. Lafayette had remarked at the surrender of Yorktown, "The play, sir, is over."

The Battling Bastards
Bataan, Philippines, 1941-42

MICHAEL STEPHENSON

We're the battling bastards of Bataan:
No momma, no poppa, no Uncle Sam,
No aunts, no uncles, no nephews, no nieces,
No rifles, no guns or artillery pieces,
And nobody gives a damn.

The Philippine archipelago, the dense conglomeration of islands in the South China Sea, is cradled within the wide sweep of Burma to the northwest through Borneo, Java, and New Guinea to the south. The main island of the group is Luzon, with the bight of the Bay of Manila bifurcating the island. On the east of the Bay is the capital, Manila, while on the west is the Bataan Peninsula, like a great bag, into which the Filo-American forces were destined to drop. Down the center of the Bataan Peninsula runs a north-south cordillera of mountains covered in thick jungle. On each flank of the peninsula are two coastal roads; the eastern and main artery of the peninsula borders the Bay of Manila, while the western runs along the South China Sea.

The Philippines had been an American dependency since 1898, when the archipelago, along with Guam and Puerto Rico, had been purchased from Spain for $20 million following the conclusion of the Spanish-American War. With the catastrophe at Pearl Harbor on December 7, 1941, the Philippines

Bataan, Phillipines, 1942

Published in Gen. Douglas MacArthur's reports of operations in the Southwest Pacific, this
Japanese map depicts the 14th Army's plan of attack on Bataan on March 22, 1942. The long
coastline of the Bataan Peninsula proved too difficult for MacArthur's underfed and diseased
troops to defend, eventually leading to an American surrender.

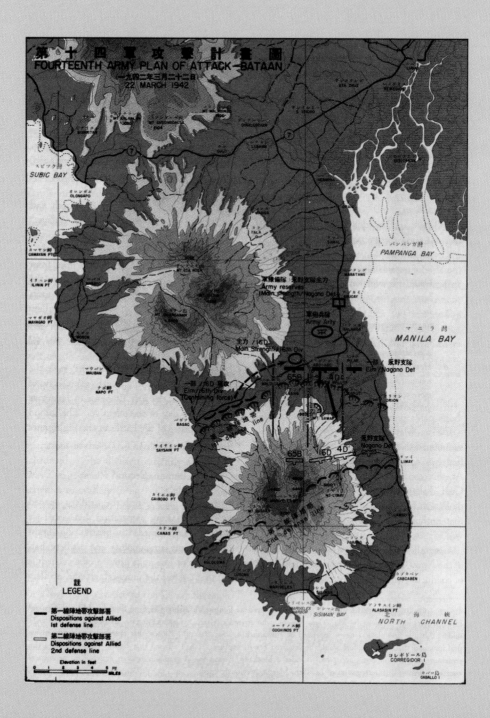

lay within the great scythe of Japanese conquest, and the day after Pearl, Japanese Betty bombers swept in to bomb Clark Field in northwestern Luzon, destroying most of the B-17s of the Far East Air Force.

Gen. Douglas McArthur, the commander in chief of American and Filipino forces in the islands, was caught in a dilemma largely of his own making. On taking up his post in July 1941 he had inherited a plan—War Plan Orange (WPO-3)—that stipulated a retreat into the Bataan Peninsula in the face of overwhelming Japanese attack. According to the plan, the peninsula was to be provisioned to support 100,000 troops for six months, turning it into a fortress that would deny the invader free use of the Bay of Manila.

But MacArthur did not like Plan Orange. It was, he thought, too defeatist and not aggressive enough for his robustly martial spirit. So, he replaced it with a do-or-die strategy: the enemy would be met and destroyed on the beaches. There would be no "withdrawal from beach positions," which were to be held "at all costs." As a consequence, the provisions that should have been transferred into Bataan under WPO-3 were left in Manila.

The main Japanese attack came at Lingayen Bay on the December 22, 1941. Lt. Gen. Masaharu Homma (who, in one of those ironies of history, had served with the British Army in France in 1918) and his 14th Army, about 40,000 strong, landed almost unopposed and started to fan out to the east and south down route 3. (Eight days earlier the New York Times had reported "Japanese forces wiped out in western Luzon," which had much cheered the folks stateside—proof that fabricating history is much easier than living it.) On December 24 another Japanese force landed on the eastern side of the island at Lamon Bay. MacArthur was now caught in a north-south pincer.

To a large extent MacArthur's aggressive stance had been based on his belief that his Filipino troops (in whom he took a proprietorial pride) would be sufficient to the day. However, as brave as they were individually, they were simply not well-trained, well-armed, or experienced enough to withstand the Japanese onslaught. A brief stand at the Agno River soon turned into a rout, and as MacArthur watched his men stream back from Lingayen, he completely discarded his initial strategy and invoked War Plan Orange. To Gen. George C. Marshall (his superior in Washington) MacArthur pointed to what he perceived as the "enormous tactical discrepancy" between the number of his force and the invading Japanese as one of the reasons to retreat into Bataan. He estimated the Japanese strength at 80,000 to 100,000 men and his own at 40,000. In fact, Homma's force was around 40,000, while MacArthur commanded 65,000 to 70,000. Under War Plan Orange there were meant to be rations to withstand a six-month siege. Now there were only enough for 30 days.

While Maj. Gen. Jonathan Wainwright (commanding the North Luzon Force) retreated into the peninsula from the north, Brig. Gen. Albert Jones (commanding the South Luzon Force) raced up Highway 3 from Manila to round the top of Manila Bay and drop down into the peninsula. It was a close-run thing, as the bridge at Calumpit was blown at 6:15 a.m. on December 31 just as the Filo-American troops made it across, closely pursued by the Japanese vanguard. That same day the Japanese invaded Manila, and on January 5 the last bridge into Bataan, at Layac, was blown. The drawbridge to Fortress Bataan had been raised. But not for long.

Both Washington and Tokyo had written off the Philippines, but for diametrically opposed reasons. Washington knew there would be little chance of resupplying Bataan despite Roosevelt's lofty declaration on December 30, "I give to the people of the Philippines my solemn pledge that their freedom will be redeemed and their independence established and protected. The entire resources in men and materials of the United States stand behind that pledge." Gen. Hideki Tojo, Japanese Prime Minister, felt the invasion was a done deal, and took the crack 48th Division away from Homma and sent it off to Java, leaving a weakened force of mainly older and badly equipped troops to finish off the retreating Filo-Americans.

MacArthur, now ensconced with his HQ on Corregidor, the small island off the southern tip of Bataan, gave Gen. Wainwright command of the western half of Bataan and Maj. Gen. George Parker command of the eastern side. They occupied a line across the peninsula—the Abucay Line—that was intersected down its center by a spine of mountains, of which the most prominent, Mount Natib, lay smack between Wainwright and Parker. Covered in deep jungle, Natib was undefended by the Americans because it was considered impassable. Surely no soldiers could traverse that matted mass of ravines and cliffs. But to the Japanese, who were experienced and skilled jungle warriors, it represented a five-mile-wide doorway to the vulnerable flanks of the Filo-American forces.

A peninsula has a very long coastal circumference to defend, and like the walls of a besieged castle, it is susceptible to breaching. Indeed, there were several Japanese outflanking amphibious landings on the southwestern coast of Bataan. But they were not in sufficient strength and were pinched out and completely destroyed by the defenders.

Lt. Gen. Akira Nara (who had been a classmate of President Coolidge's son at Amhurst College) commanded the Japanese 65th Division, which was pushing down the western highway. They battered the Abucay Line, wearing down the already demoralized and underfed defenders. Banzai attacks through the sugarcane fields of the coastal flats on the eastern side almost broke the Philippine Scouts of the 57th Regiment, but strong counterattacks with artillery and tank support restored the position. Meanwhile, on January 11, 1942 an intrepid Japanese officer, Col. Susumu Takechi, took his force off through the jungle of Mount Natib in a daring flanking movement that came within an ace of cutting off the eastern highway behind the retreating Americans. On January 21, over on the western front, Lt. Col. Nakanishi also managed to outflank Wainwright by pushing through the Natib gap.

By now MacArthur had two fronts on the point of collapse. The men were starving and exhausted. But even as late as January 15 he announced, "Help is on the way from the United States. Thousands of troops and hundreds of planes are being dispatched.... No further retreat is possible...our supplies are ample." All of which he knew to be untrue. On the January 23 he ordered the Abucay Line to be abandoned and a new defensive line held—the Pilar-Bagac highway, a cobblestone road that also ran across the peninsula east-west, behind which was a network of supply and communications trails. Harassed by strafing Japanese planes, exhausted, thirsty, starved, Americans and Filipinos jammed the western highway. On the western side Wainwright's men were also in full flight, scrambling down to the beaches to bypass Nakanishi's roadblock.

Again, the Americans managed to leave the front door of their defenses open when Gen. Jones, now in charge of the western half of the line, pulled the 31st and 33rd Infantry Regiments out of the center and moved them farther east, leaving a huge gap on either side of Trail 2, the major north-south supply route. At 3:00 p.m. January 26, the Japanese attacked down Trail 2 and it was only the foresight and determination of Brig. Gen. Clifford Bluemel (something of a martinet before the war, but just the man for the job when the chips were down) that the gap was plugged. If the Filo-Americans were in dire straits, the Japanese too were paying a very heavy price. Only three infantry battalions stretched across the entire line, and the Japanese were seriously concerned that MacArthur could turn the tables and crush the 14th Army. Gen. Maeda, Homma's chief of staff, suggested they simply blockade the peninsula and let starvation and disease do their work for them. But Homma knew that Tojo would never accept it (their relationship was one of undisguised mutual animosity). They must crush the defenders. On February 10 Roosevelt was still exhorting a "defense to the last man" while pressuring MacArthur to escape to Australia.

Typical of a besieged mentality, morale among the defenders rose and plummeted (fantastic rumors circulated: for example, Sergeant York, the First World War hero, was on his way with his own sniper force). The Japanese had been held, but dysentery, malaria, beri-beri, and malnutrition dissolved the collective resolve. "Dougout Doug" and those on Corregidor came in for special contempt.

On March 11 MacArthur ("I'm leaving over my repeated protests"), his family and a small entourage left for Australia. Gen. Wainwright became commander-in-chief of all the forces on the Philippines and moved his headquarters to Corregidor. Maj. Gen. Edward King was given command of all Filo-American troops on Bataan itself. Over 75 percent of his men were suffering from malaria, and of the 80,000, he could count on only 27,000 effectives. On April 2 they were attacked by 50,000 Japanese, including 15,000 fresh troops from the Fourth Division and Nagano Detachment. Following a ferocious Japanese artillery bombardment, Nara punched a three-mile hole in the front and within four days it had collapsed.

Wainwright realized that surrender was inevitable but MacArthur, now safely and comfortably settled in Australia, sent a cable: "I am utterly opposed under any circumstances or conditions to the ultimate capitulation of this command. If food fails, you will prepare and execute an attack upon the enemy." King, however, decided to rescue Wainwright from his impossible dilemma, and surrendered the men on Bataan on April 9 (the same day in 1865 that Lee had surrendered to Grant at Appomattox, and King remembered Lee's words: "I would rather die a thousand deaths").

It was the greatest capitulation in U.S. military history and the beginning of the infamous "Bataan death march." Of the 70,000 men who started the forced march back up the whole eastern length of the peninsula to the prison enclosure at Camp O'Donnell, 10,000 would die en route, of whom 2,330 were American. Starvation, dehydration, and disease took their inevitable toll on men already weakened by weeks of deprivation. The many atrocities committed by Japanese guards also thinned the ranks. At San Fernando the prisoners were crammed into railway freight cars for the final leg of their journey. Without water, ventilation, or sanitation, and broiled by a pitiless sun, many died in conditions of utmost squalor.

Corregidor was assaulted by amphibious forces on May 5 and, despite inflicting staggering casualties on the Japanese while they were still in their boats, Wainwright's garrison had no option but to surrender. Homma told Wainwright that unless he surrendered all of the Philippines (Mindanao and the Visayan Islands were still under American control) the Japanese would not honor the surrender, with potentially horrific implications for the men on Corregidor. It was a pistol to Wainwright's head, and he had to comply. MacArthur, however, repudiated Wainwright's surrender and instructed the garrisons on Mindanao to fight on: "Orders emanating from Gen. Wainwright have no validity. If possible separate your force into small elements and initiate guerrilla operations." Bravely, and to prevent further utterly futile bloodshed, Maj. Gen. William Sharp, the commander of Mindanao, disobeyed MacArthur and agreed to surrender.

The wheel of history turns—and it often turns the tables. MacArthur, of course, returned (duly recorded in one of the most famous "photo opportunities" in modern history) as he had predicted, and it was now the Japanese's turn to defend the Philippines. Interestingly, in December 1944 Gen. Tomoyuki Yamashita came to a very different solution to the geographic dilemma of defending Luzon than had MacArthur three years previously. He considered the Bataan Peninsula, quite correctly, as a cul-de-sac to be avoided and instead concentrated his forces in three mountain strongholds. Whereas the U.S. held on to Luzon for only four months in 1941-42, Yamashita held out for seven and a half months, right up to Japan's capitulation.

For Homma the end was ignominious. He was sacked soon after the Japanese victory (ironically, because Tojo thought him too lenient toward the Filipinos) and in 1946 was executed as a war criminal. MacArthur had taken his revenge.

The Geography of Hell

Warfare has largely been carried on within the confines and constraints of the natural landscape: its rivers, mountains, hills, beaches, deserts and jungles defining the nature of the fighting. But since ancient times war has also had the power to change the very topography itself and remake the landscape in its own image. The ditches and parapets of Iron Age Maiden Castle in Dorset, England, softened by the centuries but still quite distinct, are now part of the "natural" lie of the land. The earthen siege ramp built by the Romans at Masada in A.D. 73 is still visible and now subsumed into the configuration of the hill itself, as though it had always been there. The Great Wall of China, viewed from space, seems to be as natural a part of the Earth's geography as a river or mountain range. But modern warfare, as the three battles in this chapter demonstrate, unleashed a destructive potential of a magnitude unimaginable to earlier ages of war-makers. It could make a mockery of nature, and reconfigure the very geography of the battleground into a grotesque parody of its natural self. At 3:10 a.m. on June 7, 1917, one million pounds of explosives were detonated 60 feet below the surface of Messines Ridge, a German-held strong point in northern France. The explosion, which could be heard back in England, took off the entire top of the ridge. An infantry office remembered, "The waiting infantry felt the shocks and heard the rumble of an earthquake. It seemed as if the Messines Ridge got up and shook itself. All along its flank belched rows of mushroom-shaped masses of debris, flung high into the air." It was probably the greatest single man-made explosion in history to that date, but of course Hiroshima and Nagasaki lay 28 years in the future, sickening testaments to our complacent notion of "modern progress." Verdun, Passchendaele, and Stalingrad are each, in their similar and different ways, battles fought in a landscape utterly transfigured by destruction. In one of the abiding and moving ironies of history, so many of the soldiers slaughtered there themselves became part of the geography of those shattered battlegrounds—their bones still being unearthed like shards of pottery from an ancient civilization.

Passchendaele, Belgium, 1917

From *Military Operations: France and Belgium,* edited by Brig. Gen. Sir James Edmonds, 1948.
Uncharacteristic of Belgium's climate, many days of the summer and fall of 1917 saw torrential downpour, which turned the battleground into a quagmire of muddy chaos. This map of
the Second Battle of Passchendale is shaded to indicate areas that are "muddy" and those
that are "wet"—or submerged in water.

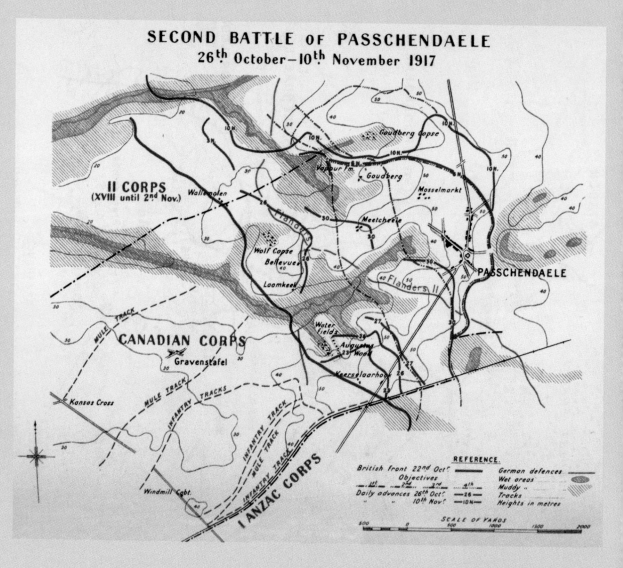

"The Abomination of Desolation"
Passchendaele, Belgium, 1917

STEPHEN BADSEY

In autumn 1917, for soldiers of the British Empire fighting in what was officially the Third Battle of Ypres, the insignificant Belgian village of Passchendaele became "Passion Dale," a landscape evoking Biblical images of death and desolation. At the start of the First World War German forces had occupied all of Belgium except for the northwestern corner near the coast, with the Allies holding the town of Ypres in a frontline salient. Two desperate battles in 1914 and 1915 left the German lines barely two miles from the town. In addition to its political importance, Ypres is less than 30 miles from the English Channel ports, and even closer to Bruges and the German naval bases in Belgium. In a war fought by massive heavy-artillery bombardments and gains measured in single miles, it was the one place on the Western Front where neither side could afford to give up any ground.

To most British soldiers Ypres was "Wipers" and the area was "France"; but Ypres with its great Cloth Hall and medieval ramparts is a Flanders town, an ancient center of cultivation and production lying on the Yser/Ypres-Comines Canal, which runs generally from southeast to northwest. Much of the Flanders plain is very low-lying, rich dark soil well farmed and manured for centuries, over impermeable clays mixed with sand and silt, with the water table very close to the surface. Ypres is only 65 feet above sea level, lying in a natural amphitheater formed by a continuous line of gentle ridges running from the southwest round to the northeast, 5 to 7 miles from the town. In 1917 the dominating height of

Kemmel Hill (521 feet) to the southwest of Ypres was behind British lines. Otherwise, the Germans held all the ridges around the Ypres salient, from Messines ridge to the south at just under 270 feet above sea level, dropping slightly onto the Gheluvelt plateau east of Ypres at 200 feet, and the Passchendaele-Staden ridge to the northeast at 150 feet. Gradients on these ridges were almost imperceptible, and the slightest elevation or variation in ground vital to artillery observation. Ypres is only 13 miles from Roulers, then the critical German rail junction, with Passchendaele village at 167 feet exactly halfway between them, well within long-range artillery fire and overlooking the Flanders plain in both directions.

Even before 1917, troops on all sides hated the frontline conditions in the Ypres salient, especially in bad weather. Even the place names, holdovers from 1914, were symbols of fear: "The chap who decided on the names of these places must have had a morbid mind. It's easy enough to get the wind up without the map making your flesh creep with such names as 'Hell-Fire', 'Hell Blast' and 'Shrapnel Corner.' The lunar-cratered landscape, with its tortured trees, flooded shell-holes and putrefying carcasses of horses...is enough without the implication that shrapnel may be expected to burst over you at any minute" (Lt. Huntly Gordon).

Because of the low water table and intense cultivation over the clay soil, water drainage was particularly important to the area. Apart from the canals, the farmlands between Ypres and Passchendaele were drained by numerous small culverts running into streams (the local name is a "beek") that flowed generally northwesterly toward the coast and so across the fronts of the opposing armies. There were also several artificial ponds or small lakes, of which the largest is near the village of Zillebeke, and areas of cultivated woodland, of which the most extensive on the Gheluvelt plateau was called Polygon Wood by the British. Previous fighting and shelling had already severely damaged this drainage system, as well as reducing farmsteads and villages to ruins and rubble, along with much of Ypres itself. The Flanders clay makes a particularly slimy, glutinous mud, and everywhere the larger shell holes filled up with mud and water, often overlapping each other. Pvt. Cyril Lee described what must have been a commonplace scene of horror: "I tried to assist a lad in this copse about 100 yards from our jumping-off trench. I called to him, 'Are you hit son? He said 'Yes I am....' There was no hope of getting to him as he was in the middle of this huge sea of mud, struggling. I saw a small sapling [and]...we tried to bend it over to this boy. The look on the lad's face, it was really pathetic....But I couldn't do a thing, had I bent a little more I should have gone in with him. Had anyone gone near this sea of mud we should have gone in with him as so many did."

Trenches also flooded just below the surface, and dugouts were impossible for both sides. Instead, defenses were built up with parapets aboveground, and ruins turned into strong points. By autumn 1917 the Germans had built a triple line of defenses stretching back over six miles across the ridges from their front lines, including small and exposed concrete bunkers called "pill boxes" by the British. Their carefully planned interlocking fields of fire would prove murderous for attacking infantry.

In some areas the ground allowed for deep tunnels for mine warfare, and as a preliminary to their main offensive the British dug mines under the Messines Ridge. "I do not know whether we shall change history tomorrow," said one British general, "but we shall certainly alter the geography." On June 7, 500 tons of explosives in 19 deep mines blew the top off Messines ridge in an artificial earthquake that was clearly audible in London, and British Empire troops seized the position.

For both sides on the Western Front, 1917 was the year of crisis. The United States had entered the war on the Allied side in April, but had yet to make an effective military contribution. Russia was collapsing into revolution; the French Army suffered major mutinies after the failure of its spring offensive; and unless the Belgian coast could be cleared, the British doubted their own ability to win the war at sea. On the other side, Germany experienced food riots and some mutinies, and also seemed close to collapse. The British commander on the Western Front, Field Marshal Sir Douglas Haig, after launching an offensive at Arras in April in support of the French, planned for his own major attack in Flanders. If all went well the first attacks would seize the Ypres ridges as the preliminary to much larger operations to liberate most of Belgium. But if the Germans stood and fought, Haig was confident that he could defeat them.

The Third Battle of Ypres (as Passchendaele was officially known) began with a British attack on July 31, in a summer that had already been unusually overcast and wet. Wartime meteorology was not an exact science, but the trend of previous years had been for dry late summers and autumns. The year 1917 was to be very different, with catastrophic results. The British Army's chief meteorologist was emphatic that the terrible rain was unusual: "...the weather in August 1917, in and around the battle area, was exceptionally bad. The rainfall directly affecting the first month of the offensive was more than double the average; it was over five times the amount for the same period in 1915 and 1916." All generals need a modicum of luck, but Haig's was all bad.

Even on the first day, heavy rain and overcast skies limited the effectiveness of artillery and aircraft, while the Germans fought hard for their positions and counterattacked each time to retake lost ground. Throughout August, the rain continued, torrential rain alternating with muggy stagnant weather that prevented the ground from drying out. The valleys of the streams became bogs, and the mud of the expanse of shell craters was a death trap for anyone who fell into them. Haig's own official dispatch reported that "the low-lying clayey soil, torn up by shells and sodden with rain, turned to a succession of vast muddy pools," through which movement was possible only on the few clearly defined tracks, to leave which "was to risk death by drowning." By the month's end, across the length of their front the British had gained less than two miles, despite French support.

In the second half of September the weather improved and the ground dried out slightly; there were even some hot, dry days. The British changed both their tactics and their objectives, concentrating on the higher ground of the Gheluvelt plateau rather than the swamps around Langemarck and St. Julien. A series of successful attacks methodically gained ground along the Menin road, capturing Polygon Wood. But fighting in these conditions was not just a matter of infantry and artillery: The British could not build or maintain the roads or the wooden platforms and planking to bring up the shells and guns, and their culminating attack at Broodseinde on October 4 just failed to break through the German line and force a major retreat.

October was again exceptionally bad weather, with only five days without rain and the autumn cold making its appearance: "It was mud, mud, everywhere: mud in the trenches, mud in front of the trenches. Every shell hole was a sea of filthy oozing mud. I suppose there is a limit to everything but the mud of Passchendaele—to see men keep on sinking into the slime, dying in the slime—I think it absolutely finished me off" (Bombardier J.W. Palmer). In these conditions, planned rates of advance of barely ten yards a minute became impossible for even the best troops. For both sides the mud became the most dangerous enemy, a vicious and ever-present predator that could kill a strong man in minutes. Maj. Nail Fraser of the Royal Field Artillery took refuge from intense machine-gun fire in a water-filled shell crater: "...we went to ground in the lip of a large crater filled with the usual reddish-colored slimy water. The Hun was shelling all around and a shell, luckily a dud, landed plumb in the water beside us, causing a great upheaval of slime. Then suddenly out of the depths arose a hideous helmet-clad head—a dead Hun with features contorted in a ghastly grin and one arm out-stretched, attempting as it were, to pull us into the mire also, and then slowly sank back into the loathsome depths from whence he came."

Haig recorded his men as being engulfed, struggling to advance in mud up to their waists, and of the light-rail system becoming useless for supply since the engines had "sunk up to the boilers in the mud." Mules and horses were swallowed whole by the morass. The only reasons now for continuing the battle were to demonstrate to Britain's allies that it was still in the war, and to finally get the troops out of the mud, giving them a line of high ground to hold through the next winter. The Germans were ordered to hold Passchendaele at all costs, but in a final attack begun on November 6, Canadian troops took the obliterated muddy smear on the map that was all that remained of the village.

So little reward for either side provoked a major argument about casualties, with open accusations of outright deceit. The Germans lost about 200,000 men killed, wounded, or captured, but the Allies paid a much heavier price: about 283,000. Haig believed that Germany was close to collapse and that just one more push would do the job—a conviction that was to prove tragically miscalculated.

Some years after the battle, a combatant looked back: "I suppose no name in history has ever had so dreadful a significance for so many human beings as Ypres....Every yard of the featureless slab of landscape held the menace of death. If you were not there the war films will have told you what it was like; if you were there the war films will make you laugh. For those few miles of ground north and south of the terrible road that runs from Ypres to Menin bear lasting witness to the indestructible tenacity of the human spirit...."

Verdun, France, 1916

This West Point teaching map shows Verdun, on the River Meuse, and other forts including Douaumont and Vaux to the east of Verdun. However, the military operations illustrated here do little to depict the landscape of the battleground—which became a virtual cemetery by the time this longest and bloodiest battle of World War I was over.

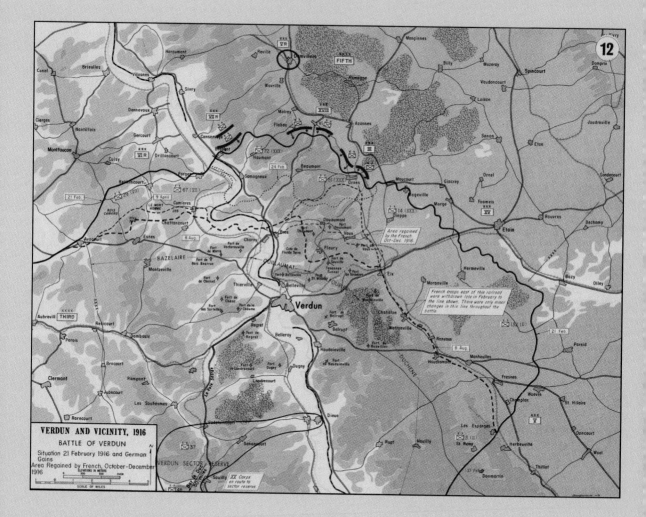

"They Shall Not Pass"
Verdun, France, 1916

STEPHEN BADSEY

The ancient town of Verdun lies in a steeply wooded valley through which the River Meuse flows almost from south to north. The overlooking hills on both sides of the river are heavy clay or marl over limestone, those to the east dominating the open plain of the Woevre plateau. In 1916 these hills were compared to an intermittently rocky coastline facing the sea, which in a past epoch is exactly what they were. Verdun is the only crossing-place over the Meuse for some distance for the direct route from Paris eastward to the River Moselle at Metz and so on to the Rhine, and is a site of great symbolic importance for France. In 1792 the fall of Verdun to Prussian troops had galvanized the new French Republic into its own successful defense, and in the Franco-Prussian War, Verdun had been the last important French fortress to surrender. The annexation of Alsace-Lorraine in 1871 had placed the town only a day's march from the new frontier, and the ring of forts surrounding the town was strengthened, with even larger forts built farther out on the hilltops. In 1916 the largest and strongest of these were Fort Douaumont, five miles northeast of Verdun, built on the summit of a 1,300-foot peak on the east bank, and Fort Vaux on a lesser peak two miles to the southeast. These forts, surrounded by dry moats, were great structures of concrete and steel built into the hilltops, only their roofs and gun casemates showing above the surface. Even the extensive forests were turned to a military purpose, with growths being cut down and plantations encouraged to provide fire-lanes, good observation, and traps for an advancing enemy.

At the start of the First World War in 1914, the speed with which new heavier German artillery overcame forts in Belgium convinced the French that the fortress system was obsolete; the Verdun forts were downgraded and most of their guns and garrisons removed. Verdun itself was not heavily attacked; rather the German trench lines solidified around it 8 to 10 miles to the north and east. The Verdun defenses stretched from beyond Hill 304 (304 represents meters high, or about 1,000 feet) to the northwest, through the ominously named Le Mort Homme (Dead Man's Hill), and across the Meuse before curving southeastward past Douaumont and Vaux. A deep German penetration over the Meuse 20 miles south of Verdun at St. Mihiel brought most routes into the town under long-range shellfire. Tunneling and underground warfare began underneath the heights, but otherwise Verdun was largely left alone. A quiet sector, with a single line of trenches and only the almost deserted forts as reserve positions, it was a low priority for the French for over a year, and complaints that its defenses were inadequate were ignored.

In December 1915 the German chief of the general staff, Gen. Erich von Falkenhayn, chose to make the main German effort of the next year against the French. Given the apparent impossibility of breaking through the Western Front, Falkenhayn chose a different approach: to attack a location the French had to keep for strategic and symbolic reasons, which was also perilously hard for them to defend. Falkenhayn chose Verdun, where the St. Mihiel salient made moving supplies and reinforcements difficult for the French, where the Meuse itself restricted communication between the hilltop positions, and where the heavy soil meant that the Germans could shelter their own troops in deep bunkers and even achieve surprise by digging underground tunnels close to the French positions rather than trenches in the open. If the French chose not to defend the east bank of the Meuse in the face of their attack, then the Germans might push through to capture Verdun, but that was not Falkenhayn's main objective. Instead, he intended the Verdun offensive to be the epitome of attrition: a protracted battle in which the French Army would be bled white trying to hold the heights on the east bank, and so weakened that it would not be able to continue the war.

On February 21, 1916, the Germans attacked from the north with 140,000 men, supported by an intense bombardment of more than a million shells from over 1,200 guns including heavy guns of 380mm and 420mm caliber, plus the first use of flamethrowers in warfare. Leading German assault troops broke out of their underground tunnels into the forests close to the French trench lines. Along a front of eight miles surprise was virtually complete, and on February 25 the Germans captured Fort Douaumont. Still planning for their own big attack together with the British on the Somme in July, the French decided to hold on at Verdun, including the east bank, in an improvised line of bunkers, tunnels, and shellholes in which both sides fought in bloody hand-to-hand combat. The previously despised forts became the only safe refuge on the battlefield.

On the day that Douaumont fell, Gen. Henri-Philippe Pétain was appointed to command the defense of Verdun, and later the entire sector. (The famous phrase "Ils ne passeront pas!"—"They shall not pass!"—which became the battle cry of the defenders, has been forever associated with Pétain, but may in fact have been coined by his subordinate, Gen. Robert Nivelle.) On a map the battlefield looked small, barely 24 miles across and 6 miles deep at its farthest extent. But in this little space, in the longest and bloodiest battle of the First World War, at least 330,000 Germans and 370,000 Frenchmen were killed or wounded, possibly many more. In the five months of the most intense fighting, both sides fired over 20 million artillery shells. The shelling shredded the trees, leaving only stumps, and turned the heavy ground into a nightmare landscape of craters, rubble, rock, and mud. Neither side could get enough ammunition, water, food, or replacements forward, and men lived a miserable existence through the frigid winter. As fighting over the same ground continued, the dead were used as parapets; corpses rotted into the soil and were blasted into the air again, so men were killed or injured by flying pieces of bone and flesh. After the war, fragments of up to 150,000 unidentified bodies were collected and interred in a massive ossuary and cemetery. Digging trenches, men believed that they were digging their own graves.

Because of the dreadful conditions and intensity of the fighting, most units spent only a limited time at Verdun. In the course of the battle 259 battalions out of just over 330 in the French Army were rotated through, leaving only when depleted and exhausted, a pattern of attritional slaughter as true for Germans as French. Verdun became "the mill on the Meuse," the grinding machine that wore down both armies. Replacements were shocked by what they saw on arrival. Lt. Georges Gaudy described watching his own regiment return from Fort Douaumont in May 1916: "First came the skeletons of companies occasionally led by a wounded officer, leaning on a stick. All marched, or rather advanced in small steps, zigzagging as if intoxicated....it was hard to tell the color of their faces from that of their tunics. Mud had covered everything, dried off, and then another layer applied....They said nothing. It seemed as if these mute faces were crying something terrible, the unbelievable horror of their martyrdom. Some Territorials who were standing near me became pensive. They had that air of sadness that comes over one when a funeral passes by, and I heard one say: 'It's no longer an army! These are corpses!'" (quoted in Alistair Horne, *The Price of Glory*).

Even Pétain noted the utter despondency of the troops, "crushed by horrifying memories." The one French lifeline into Verdun that was not under German shellfire was a light railroad and road running southwestward that became legendary as the Voie Sacrée (Sacred Way), and along which a constant line of trucks kept the town and its defenders supplied, at the height of the battle, at the rate of one vehicle every 14 seconds. Stone from local quarries kept the road in constant repair.

On March 6 the Germans extended their attacks to the west bank of the Meuse, again taking ground, but were held off by the French at Le Mort Homme. As the symbolic importance of Verdun increased with the losses, it became impossible for either side to break off the fighting or concede defeat. The French began to reduce their participation in the forthcoming attack on the Somme, which increasingly became more of a British battle. On June 7 the Germans captured Fort Vaux, using gas and liquid flame, but not without a vicious battle fought in the bowels of the fort itself: "Of all the horrors in the fighting at Verdun, it is difficult to imagine any more appalling than the struggle that took place day after day in the underground corridors of Fort Vaux. Here the battle went on in pitch darkness, relieved only by the flash of exploding grenades, in a shaft for the most part no more than three feet wide and five feet high, in which no grown man could stand upright. Machine-gun bullets ricocheting from wall to wall inflicting wounds as terrible as any dum-dum...Repeatedly men of both sides felt themselves asphyxiating in the air polluted by TNT fumes and cement dust stirred up by the explosions. Added to it was the ever-worsening stink of the dead, rapidly decomposing in the June heat, for whom there was no means of burial inside the fort" (Alistair Horne, *The Price of Glory*).

On June 23 the Germans pioneered another terrible new weapon, shells filled with phosgene gas, and their attack broke through to the last ridgeline, barely three miles from Verdun. But next day, the Allied bombardment started on the Somme as the preliminary to their attack on July 1, and on June 24 Falkenhayn ordered that no fresh divisions would be sent to Verdun. On July 11 the Germans went onto the defensive.

The end of the battle, in miserable autumn weather, was a mirror image of its opening. On October 24 Fort Douaumont was recaptured by the French, having been pounded with 120,000 shells by both sides but largely and incredibly still undamaged. Slowly the French pressed the Germans back away from the town, recapturing Fort Vaux on November 2. The battle officially ended in December after almost a year of fighting. Falkenhayn's strategy of attrition had rebounded on his own troops, causing almost as many German deaths as French. In August he was replaced, but his grim calculations had partly succeeded: In 1917 the French Army suffered widespread mutinies as troops refused to attack, only gradually recovering over the year. After 1916 the soldiers of France were "the men of Verdun," a title used with a pride and horror that they would never forget.

Nor would the landscape ever forget. Alistair Horne writing 50 years after the battle recorded the eeriness of that haunted terrain, trapped as though in an ancient nightmare: "The slopes of the Mort Homme are covered with a forest of young firs, planted in the 1930's when all other attempts at cultivation had failed. The wind whistles through the trees and the birds sing, and that is all. It is the nearest thing to a desert in Europe. Nobody seems ever to visit it. Even lovers eschew the unchallenged privacy of its glades. The ghosts abound....Everywhere in the spooky jungles the pathetic relics, the non-perishable debris of battle still lie; the helmets, the rusted water bottles, the broken rifles, the huge shell fragments—and still, the bones."

Stalingrad, Russia, 1942-43, from Office of Strategic Services (OSS)

Factories in the industrial city of Stalingrad became natural fortresses for the Soviet 62nd Army. This map, generated by the Office of Strategic Services, shows the different types of industries and businesses. By the end of the war most buildings had been destroyed, leaving only fragments of walls that were indistinguishable from one another.

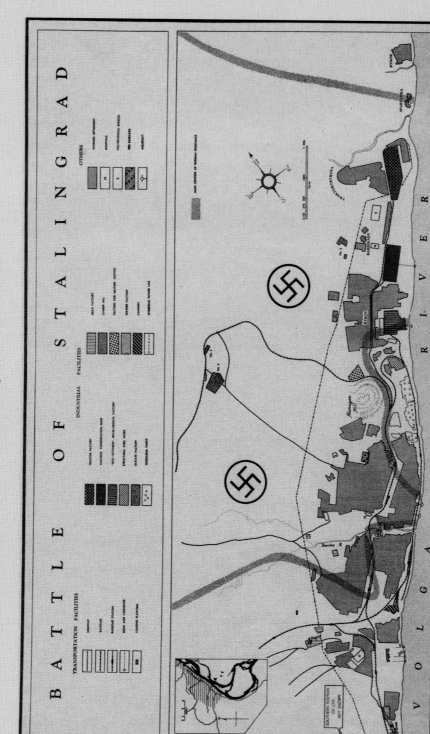

City of the Dead
Stalingrad, Russia, 1942–43

WILL FOWLER

Stalingrad had been rebuilt as a "model" industrial town in the 1920s and 1930s and renamed (it was originally Tsaritsyn) after the Soviet leader, Joseph Stalin. It now included parkland and solid public buildings and stretched along the west bank of the Volga in two distinct districts. To the north were workers' apartments and the Dzerhezinsky Tractor, Barrikady, and Krasny Oktyabr factories, each with its own schools, parks, housing development, and stores. The Lazur chemical plant was in the center of a circular railway layout and was to be nicknamed "the tennis racket" by German air crews. The capture of Stalingrad would give the Germans control of the Volga, access to Astrakhan, and the supply of petroleum from the south.

The north and south of the city were divided, and dominated, by the Mamayev Kurgan, a 335-foot-high ancient Tatar burial mound that was a popular prewar haunt for courting couples. To the south lay the city center, including the Univermag department store, Gorky theater, and Red Square. Beyond them were the massive concrete grain silos that would become a fortress during the fighting. Across the River Volga, on its eastern side, a new development, Krasnaya Sloboda, was connected by ferries that delivered workers to landing stages along the western shore in the southern sector. The river was fed by a number of small tributary streams around Stalingrad that had cut deep into the steppe soil and formed balkas or gullies of which the Tsaritsa and Krutoy in the southern district would prove invaluable access points for Soviet soldiers landing from ferries.

The 52-year-old German Gen. Friedrich Paulus commanding the Sixth Army began to attack the outer defenses of the city on August 19,1942, and on the 22nd the XIV Panzer Corps broke through the Soviet 62nd Army positions around the city's periphery. The outlying terrain was ideal for tank warfare, with little cover and good visibility, but in the factories and sewers of Stalingrad this advantage would be neutralized, and the advances of hundreds of miles enjoyed by the Germans earlier in that summer of invasion would be reduced to streets, individual buildings, even single rooms.

On August 24 Stalin ordered that the city should be held at all costs, and the man chosen was the tough and ruthless Gen. Vasili Chuikov. In overall command of the troops in the whole theater was the master tactician, Gen. Georgi Zhukov. By September 14 German attacks had forced the Soviet 62nd Army back into the industrial areas on the west bank of the Volga, but Paulus's Sixth Army was understrength and it was able to attack only on narrow frontages that reduced progress. A week later the German attackers and Soviet defenders had almost reached stalemate in the rubble. Like two exhausted boxers they staggered on, neither able to deliver a knockout blow.

By November 18, the 62nd Army had only held toeholds on the west bank of the Volga but they included the huge Dzerhezinsky Tractor, Barrikady, and Krasny Oktyabr factories: an area 12 miles at its deepest and 5 miles at its narrowest. The factories were, however, natural fortresses where battles were fought at incredibly short ranges down to hand-to-hand fighting in which the men of the 62nd Army used their short-handled entrenching tools like battle-axes. Dust and smoke made the air almost unbreathable and the supply of water as important as ammunition. The sewers provided a route to bring reinforcements forward, and at one stage Chuikov had an HQ built on a platform that straddled the vile liquids that flowed through the brick tunnel down to the Volga.

The smashed city created its own lethal geography: "Factory walls, assembly lines, the whole superstructure collapses under the storm of bombs, but the enemy simply reappears and utilizes these newly created ruins to fortify his defensive positions," noted General Strecker. A Luftwaffe pilot wrote home: "I cannot understand how men can survive such a hell, yet the Russians sit tight in the ruins, and holes and cellars, and a chaos of steel skeletons which used to be factories." Sniping was a particularly effective Red Army tactic among the ruins, and a "sniper cult" developed, complete with national "stars" like Vasily Zaitsev (the subject of the highly Hollywoodized movie *Enemy at the Gates*) credited with 149 kills. Many were experienced hunters, like Zaitsev, and were usually armed with the reliable bolt-action Mosin 1891/30 rifle mounted with a x4 PE telescopic sight. They often worked in pairs, one spotting, the other shooting, bringing a silent terror that demoralized the Germans.

The capture of the bitterly contested Mamayev Kurgan by the German 295th Infantry Division gave them a commanding view of the city and they were able to fire on the ferries, congested with fleeing civilians, wounded soldiers, and reinforcements. It was now virtually impossible for the remaining civilians (about 10,000) to escape, and they too were doomed to live troglodytic lives, freezing and starving among the rubble, sewers, and caves. Children, many of whom were orphans, were active and desperate foragers, often ruthlessly killed by German and Russian alike if they were caught stealing or aiding the enemy.

The German forces were now completely entangled in Stalingrad. Their northern flank on the River Don bend was held by the less well-equipped and trained Third Romanian Army and Italian Eighth Army, while the Fourth Romanian Army held the front to the south. Paulus and General von Weichs of Army Group B both warned the OKW (German High Command) that these flanks were now increasingly vulnerable. With the onset of winter the Sixth Army and Axis forces did not receive cold-weather clothing, and as temperatures plunged below freezing these crucial supplies remained in depots because ammunition and rations, themselves in short supply, had been given a higher priority.

As far back as September 1942 Stalin and STAVKA (Soviet High Command) had realized that the Sixth Army was now out on a vulnerable limb. Their plan for the counterattack at Stalingrad would be a double envelopment by attacks on the exposed German flanks. On November 11, in a cacophony of exploding shells and bombs, the Germans made one final effort at elimi-

nating the 62nd Army. Chuikov was urged to hang on as the trickle of reinforcements crossing the Volga went into action inspired or terrified by three
slogans:

"Every man a fortress!"

"There's no ground left behind the Volga!"

"Fight or die!"

For those who could not face the prospect of death in the city, Chuikov
had a simple solution, the firing squads of the NKVD secret police.

On November 19, 1942 Zhukov launched Operation Uranus, the carefully prepared enveloping attack. He had positioned the South West Front
(Army Group) under Gen. Nikolai Vatutin, consisting of the 63rd Army, First
Guards Army and 21st Army, a total of one million men, 13,500 guns, and 894
tanks, opposite the Romanian and Italian armies, and after a short but intense
bombardment the Soviet tanks and infantry attacked. The 21st Army initially
had a hard fight with the Romanians on the northern Don, but punched through
and swung south behind the German Sixth Army. On November 20 the Soviet
forces composing the Stalingrad Front attacked to the south of the city and by
the end of the day had penetrated up to 31 miles. Five days later the northern
and southern pincers met, and the Sixth Army was trapped in the Kessel, the
Cauldron.

On November 26 Hitler ordered Paulus not to attempt a breakout, as
Reichsmarschall Hermann Göring, with his characteristic bombast, had assured
the Führer that the Luftwaffe could supply the approximately 290,000 Axis
forces trapped in the Kessel. The Sixth Army staff estimated that it would need
750 tons of daily supplies. The daily average delivered by the Luftwaffe was
only 90 tons.

On November 27 Field Marshal von Manstein took command of the
newly formed Army Group Don and was ordered to break in to relieve the Sixth
Army. Operation "Winter Storm" rolled toward the city in an attempt to break
the Soviet stranglehold, only to be blocked short of its objective. By December 16 the Italian Eighth Army had been overrun and the key resupply airfield
at Tatsinskaya captured. The Germans in the Kessel were now literally starving to death.

German panzer units of Group Hoth got to within 18 miles of the Sixth Army and Manstein urged Paulus to break out, but Manstein himself was in danger of being outflanked and enveloped and Hitler sanctioned his withdrawal while still denying Paulus a chance to escape. For the German relief force it was like watching a drowning comrade slip from their outstretched hand.

Rokossovsky, commander of the Don Front army, offered Paulus surrender terms on January 8 but they were rejected. Two days later the Soviet offensive again rolled into action, squeezing the pocket from west to east. The 65th Army advanced six miles on the first day against determined German resistance and counterattacks, and only limited penetrations were achieved. By January 12 the western salient of the pocket had been overrun, and a day later Karpovka airfield in the south of the pocket was captured—there were now only six airfields. The daily Luftwaffe delivery rate had dropped to 40 tons. Gumrak airfield fell on January 22 and Paulus, signaling that rations and ammunition were now dangerously low, made an oblique plea for permission to surrender. In the snow-covered ruins of the city, the Soviet 21st Army linked up with the men of the 62nd Army, splitting the Germans into two pockets.

In the southern pocket Paulus moved his HQ to the basement of the Univermag department store. By now food was in such short supply that orders were issued that the 30,000 wounded in the pocket were not to receive rations. Many men had already died of starvation, disease, and the bitter cold. Those who had contracted dysentery soiled themselves rather than risk frostbite by dropping their pants.

On January 31 at 7:45 p.m. local time Paulus, gaunt from dysentery and exhaustion, surrendered after his HQ had been surrounded. He had recently been awarded a field marshal's baton because Hitler had stated that no German field marshal had ever surrendered and hoped that Paulus would commit suicide. Paulus's private response was, "I have no intention of shooting myself for this Bohemian corporal!"

For General Strecker and the remnants of the XI Corps in the northern pocket, a small area around the Dzerhezinsky Tractor factory, the situation was hopeless. Strecker signaled: "Troops are fighting without heavy weapons or supplies. Men collapsing from exhaustion. Freezing to death still holding weapons." On February 2 he too surrendered. The Russians were enraged by this further resistance, and many men who were wounded or had surrendered were shot or clubbed to death.

A few days later a British war correspondent described the geography of this piece of hell: "What the normal relief of the terrain had been no one could tell. You wound your way up and down, up and down; what was a natural slope, or what was the side of a dozen bomb craters that had merged into one, no one could say. Trenches ran through the factory yards, through the workshops themselves; at the bottom of the trenches there still lay frozen green Germans and frozen grey Russians, and frozen fragments of human shape....There was barbed wire here, and half-uncovered mines, and shell cases, and more rubble, and fragments of walls, and tortuous tangles of rusty steel girders. How anyone could have survived here is hard to imagine" (quoted in Anthony Beevor, *Stalingrad*).

The casualties for both sides had been horrific. During the whole battle for Stalingrad, German and Axis losses were in the region of 1.5 million. The Red Army is estimated to have lost 1.1 million, of whom 450,000 were killed. One hundred and eleven thousand German and Axis troops were captured in the Kessel. Death from disease, starvation, intense cold, indiscriminate execution, or simply being worked to death was the fate of most. Only about 5,000 lived to return to Germany in the 1950s. Paulus was one of the survivors, principally because he agreed to collaborate with his captors. As punishment for his defection, his wife, Coca, was imprisoned by the Nazis and died in 1947. Paulus was released in 1953 and spent the rest of his life in East Germany, writing endless papers justifying his actions at Stalingrad. Only in death (in 1957) did he return to his homeland, for burial at Baden-Baden, next to his beloved wife.

Acknowledgments

Compiling a book of multi-authored contributions can be as frustrating as dragooning recruits into some semblance of military discipline. Some turn up late, some have left their weapon behind, some turn up not at all. I, however, have been extraordinarily fortunate with my recruits. They all turned up on time, their equipment and training in impeccable order, and they were all ready to do battle. It has been a great pleasure and privilege to work with such a thoroughly professional cadre.

Others showed equal professionalism: from National Geographic, Senior Editor Lisa Lytton planted the seed for this book and saw it through to publication with skill and good humor; Kevin Mulroy, editor-in-chief, was instrumental in getting the project off the ground, while Margaret Johnson and Bey Wesley did invaluable work researching the maps.

Lionel Leventhal of Greenhill Books, doyen of military publishers, was characteristically generous with his advice, as was another distinguished military publisher, Charles Hewitt of Pen & Sword. Literary agent Alexander Hoyt, no mean military historian in his own right, was also a prime mover.

—Michael Stephenson, Editor

Colonel Joseph H. Alexander, USMC (Ret) is the author of *Utmost Savagery: The Three Days of Tarawa; Storm Landings: Epic Amphibious Battles in the Central Pacific; A Fellowship of Valor: The Battle History of the Marines,* and *Edson's Raiders: The 1st Marine Raider Battalion in World War II.* He has been the principal military adviser on many History Channel and A&E biographies and is Chief Historian, Exhibit Design Team, at the National Museum of the Marine Corps. He served two tours of duty in Vietnam.

Dr Stephen Badsey is a Senior Lecturer with Special Responsibilities in the Department of War Studies at the Royal Military Academy Sandhurst, Great Britain. He is a specialist in the role of the media in warfare and on the history of military ideas. He has authored, edited or contributed to over thirty books and articles, including *The Hutchinson Atlas of World War II Battle Plan; The Media and International Security; Normandy, 1944,* and *The Gulf War Assessed.* Dr Badsey is a Fellow of the Royal Historical Society.

Matthew Bennett is a Senior Lecturer at the Royal Military Academy Sandhurst with a special interest in pre-modern warfare. He has published numerous books and articles, including *The Cambridge Atlas of Medieval Warfare,* and *The Hutchinson Dictionary of Ancient and Medieval Warfare.* He is a Fellow of the Royal Historical Society and the Society of Antiquaries (London)

Eric Bergerud is Professor of History, Lincoln University, Oakland, California, and has published *Touched with Fire: The Land War in the South Pacific; Red Thunder, Tropic Lightning: The World of a Combat Division in Vietnam; Fire in the Sky: The Air War in the South Pacific,* and *Dynamics of Defeat: The Vietnam War in Hau Nghia Province.*

Ian Castle is a specialist in the warfare of the nineteenth century. His publications include *Aspern and Wagram 1809; Eggmühl 1809; Austerlitz 1805; Majuba 1881: Hill of Destiny,* and with Ian Knight *Zulu War 1879: Twilight of a Warrior Nation, The Zulu War: Then and Now, Fearful Hard Times: The Siege and Relief of Eshowe 1879; Rorke's Drift,* and *Isandlwana.*

Nigel Cave is the co-editor, with Professor Brian Bond, of *Haig: A Reappraisal Seventy Years On.* He was the founding author and is the General Editor of the *Battleground Europe* series, and is the author, among other titles in that series, of *Vimy Ridge.* He is currently working on *Le Cateau 1914.*

Robert Cowley is the founding editor of *MHQ: The Quarterly Journal of Military History.* He has edited three *MHQ* anthologies: *No End Save Victory* about World War II, *With My Face to the Enemy,* about the Civil War and, most recently, *The Great War.* He has also edited three volumes in the *What If?* series.

Will Fowler has written over fourteen books on mil-

itary subjects, including *Eastern Front: The Unpublished Photographs, 1941-1945; Atlas of the Eastern Front Battle; Commandos at Dieppe: Rehearsal for D-Day.* He is the Editor of *Jane's Amphibious Warfare Capabilities.* He served with the 7th Armoured Brigade (Desert Rats) during the 1990–91 Gulf War where he was awarded the Joint Service Commendation Medal by the US Central Command.

Gary Gallagher is the John L. Nau III Professor of the History of the Civil War at the University of Virginia. His many publications include *Lee and His Generals in War and Memory; The Myth of the Lost Cause* (with Alan T. Nolan); *First Day at Gettysburg* (ed.), and *The Confederate War.*

Philip Haythornthwaite is one of the world's leading authorities on the Napoleonic period and the author of many books, including *Weapons and Equipment of the Napoleonic Wars; Nelson's Navy* (with Mike Chappell); *The Napoleonic Source Book; Die Hard! Famous Napoleonic Battles; Corunna 1809; The Russian Army of the Napoleonic Period,* and *Wellington's Army: The Uniforms of the British Soldier 1812-1815.*

Captain Peter A. Huchthausen US Navy (Ret) served for more than twenty years as a Soviet naval submarine analyst and in anti-submarine warfare positions on the staffs of Naval Forces Europe, the US First and Third Fleets, and the Commander-in-Chief Pacific. For three years he was US Naval Attaché to the USSR during the years immediately preceding the fall of the Soviet Union. He is the author of, among other titles, *Echoes of the Mekong; Hostile Waters, K19: The Widowmaker,* and *October Fury.*

Ian Knight is widely regarded as an authority on British colonial campaigns and has written over thirty books on British campaigns in India, the Americas and, in particular, southern Africa. His previous titles include *Go To Your God Like A Soldier: The Victorian Soldier Fighting for Empire* and *Brave Men's Blood.*

Bryan Perrett served in the Royal Armoured Corp with the 17/21st Lancers, the Westminster Dragoons and the Royal Tank Regiment. He is a noted military historian who has written many popular works on a wide range of military subjects, including *The Battle Book: Crucial Conflicts in History; Impossible Victories: Ten Unlikely Battlefield Success; The Taste of Battle: Front Line Action 1914-1991; Iron Fist: Classic Armored Warfare,* and *Seize and Hold: Masterstrokes on the Battlefield.*

Agostino von Hassell was born into a distinguished military family. His great-grandfather was Admiral von Tirpitz, and his grandfather, Ulrich von Hassell, was executed for his role in the July 1944 plot to assassinate Hitler. He is the author of *Warriors: The United States Marine Corps; Strike Force: Marine Corps Special Operations,* and (with Herman J. Dillon) *West Point: The Bicentennial Book.*

CREDITS

BATTLEGROUNDS
GEOGRAPHY AND THE HISTORY OF WARFARE
Edited by Michael Stephenson

Published by the National Geographic Society

John M. Fahey, Jr., President and Chief Executive Officer
Gilbert M. Grosvenor, Chairman of the Board
Nina D. Hoffman, Executive Vice President

Prepared by the Book Division

Kevin Mulroy, Vice President and Editor-in-Chief
Charles Kogod, Illustrations Director
Marianne R. Koszorus, Design Director

Staff for this Book

Lisa Lytton, Project Editor
Judith Klein, Consulting Editor
Katy Hall, Editorial Assistant
Margaret Johnson, Illustrations Editor
Bey Wesley, Illustrations Researcher
Meredith Wilcox, Illustrations Assistant
Bill Marr, Cover Design
Lisa Lytton, Interior Design
Carl Mehler, Director of Maps
Gary Colbert, Production Director

Manufacturing and Quality Control

Christopher A. Liedel, Chief Financial Officer
Phillip L. Schlosser, Managing Director
Vincent P. Ryan, Manager

MAP CREDITS

AP/Wide World Photos: 28, 174; Courtesy of Bill Beck: 204; Collection et cliché Ecole nationale des ponts et chaussées (cote 1 SI 13-5): 58 (lower); International Mapping Associates: 14, 52, 114; Collections of the Library of Congress: 2-3, 22, 36, 44, 58 (upper), 72, 86, 94, 100, 134, 140, 160, 182, 242, 248, 264; Marine Corps Historical Center: 106, 152, 166; National Archives of Canada: 146; National Archives and Records Administration: 80, 126, 218, 276; NGS Book Division: 10; Royal Naval Museum: 234; U.S. Army Center of Military History: 64, 120, 196, 256; Department of History, United States Military Academy: 190, 212, 228, 270

One of the world's largest nonprofit scientific and educational organizations, the National Geographic Society was founded in 1888 "for the increase and diffusion of geographic knowledge." Fulfilling this mission, the Society educates and inspires millions every day through its magazines, books, television programs, videos, maps and atlases, research grants, the National Geographic Bee, teacher workshops, and innovative classroom materials. The Society is supported through membership dues, charitable gifts, and income from the sale of its educational products. This support is vital to National Geographic's mission to increase global understanding and promote conservation of our planet through exploration, research, and education.

For more information, please call 1-800-ngs line (647-5463) or write to the following address:

National Geographic Society
1145 17th Street N.W.
Washington, D.C. 20036-4688 U.S.A.

Visit the Society's Web site at www.nationalgeographic.com.

Library of Congress Cataloging-in-Publication Data

Stephenson, Michael.
    Battlegrounds: geography and history of warfare / edited by Michael Stephenson ; introduction by Robert Cowley.
       p. cm.
    Includes index.
    ISBN 0-7922-3374-3 (hc)
    1. Battlefields. 2. Battles. 3. Military geography. I. Stephenson, Michael, 1946–

D25.5.B28 2003
355.4'09--dc21

2003054069